Transcending the Self

Transcending the Self

An Object Relations Model of Psychoanalytic Therapy

Frank L. Summers

THE ANALYTIC PRESS

1999   Hillsdale, NJ   London

Published by The Analytic Press, Inc.
101 West Street, Hillsdale, NJ 07642

Set in Garamond 12/14 by Qualitext, Bloomfield, NJ

Library of Congress Cataloging-in-Publication Data

Summers, Frank L.
    Transcending the self : an object relations model of psychoanalytic therapy / Frank L. Summers.
      p. cm.
    Includes bibliographical references and index.
    ISBN 0-88163-231-7
    1. Object relations (Psychoanalysis). 2. Psychodynamic psychotherapy.   I. Title.
    RC489.O25S86   1999
    616.89'17—dc21   98-42974
                                              CIP

Printed in the United States of America
10 9 8 7 6 5 4 3 2 1

To Kristen, Nicole, and Todd

"I only wanted to live in accordance with the voices of my inner self. Why was that so very difficult?"

—Herman Hesse, *Damien*

"He who is not being born is busy dying."

—Bob Dylan

"What is done by chance may be done by art."

—Aristotle, *The Rhetoric*

Contents

Preface

This book is written for practicing clinicians who are looking for useful ideas in treating their patients. Although this volume presents yet another theoretical model to join the plethora of existing psychoanalytic viewpoints, its purpose is clinical. I am concerned that too many of the current debates in psychoanalysis target theoretical concepts with too little focus on how personality change occurs. I hope to have constructed a theoretical model with clinical application for many of the patients psychotherapists counsel on a daily basis. Although this volume engages some of the most hotly debated theoretical issues in contemporary psychoanalytic thought, the purpose of this discussion is to contribute to understanding the change process. I offer here a theoretical model that I hope will illuminate how psychoanalytic therapists can help patients move beyond their existing limitations—a theory, that is, of self-transcendence.

Despite the variety of current viewpoints, I have not found a current model that fits just the right combination of classical, contemporary, interpretive depth, and relationship focus that I believe is most useful for patients. I agree with many contemporary critics of classical and ego psychology that these traditional analytic paradigms are too narrow and reductionistic to have optimal clinical value, but I am also concerned that some of the proposed alternatives have moved too far from the depth psychology that has always been the strength of psychoanalytic therapy.

It is my conviction that an object relations model, broadly conceived and carefully elaborated, embraces the strengths of both extremes and provides the most useful guide for psychoanalytic therapists. In my reading of the analytic literature, I have found important elements of such a broad model in the work of a variety of theorists, such as Winnicott, Kohut, Fairbairn, Guntrip, Bollas, and Benjamin. The proposed model incorporates components of the work of each of these theorists but is not to be found in any of them; the findings of much developmental research from a variety of viewpoints corroborate these theoretical ideas. I believe I have constructed a theory that carries out the implicit theoretical and clinical ideas embedded in much current psychoanalytic theory and is substantiated by the experimental evidence on infancy and childhood.

In 1994, I published a text, *Object Relations Theories and Psychopathology,* that showed the unique clinical contribution of each of the major object relations theories. In the final chapter of that book, I brought together my own integration that utilized elements of each theory to outline a broad object relations model. In this book, I have elaborated the theoretical and clinical ideas implied in that outline to develop in greater detail a model that, I believe, can be put into practice by psychoanalytic therapists.

In the introductory chapter, I use a clinical case to situate my model between two broad psychoanalytic paradigms, ego psychology and relational psychoanalysis. The next two chapters present the empirical and theoretical basis of the model. Chapter 4 begins the discussion of clinical implications by presenting a concept of therapeutic action derived from the theoretical model. The following three chapters show how the model applies to different categories of patients, traditionally conceptualized as borderline, narcissistic, and neurotic; and a brief concluding chapter moves the discussion once again to a more abstract level by reflection on the craft of conducting psychoanalytic therapy.

Acknowledgments

My deepest gratitude to Dr. Paul Stepansky for the extraordinary effort he put into editing and improving the manuscript. His suggestions for both content and writing enhanced immeasurably the quality of the manuscript. I also wish to thank Renee Summers, Dr. Peter Shabad, and Dr. Alana Baum, all of whom generously gave their time to read some of the chapters and stimulated my thinking with their comments. I also owe a special debt to my students over the years in a variety of seminars, case conferences, classes, and study groups whose eager and enthusiastic discussion of issues has inspired me.

Chapter 1

One Case, Three Views

This study is a clinical application of an object relations concept of psychoanalytic therapy. Because the emphasis throughout is on the clinical process, it is fitting to begin the investigation with a case study. My analysis of Dexter provides a clinical basis for introducing this object relations approach by comparing it to two other broad psychoanalytic paradigms, the ego-psychological and the relational. Via this comparison, I hope to show the differences among these three approaches and, ultimately, through the course of this volume, to demonstrate the utility of the object relations framework for the conduct of psychoanalytic therapy.

Dexter entered analysis to resolve two major problems: chronic, destructive verbal battles with his wife and, most important, a chronic history of struggling in his work and underachievement. A third issue that bothered him, although he did not regard it as central, was a recent tendency to have extreme emotional reactions to seemingly trivial events. For example, a coworker recently brought him coffee, and he found himself tearing up as he thanked her.

The middle of five children with two older sisters and two younger brothers, Dexter grew up in a middle-class suburb. His mother was a homemaker, and his father held a position Dexter described as "the lowest level of management." His mother often discussed with him her dissatisfaction with the father's income and lack of education. He entered treatment feeling that he loved and respected both parents, but he had especially fond memories of his mother, including taking walks with her while she devalued various neighbors and friends (they would laugh together at her sarcastic remarks).

In high school, Dexter began to play sports, but he was injured and never returned to them. Until that time, his social circle consisted of other athletes, but, after discontinuing, he felt he did not belong with them and felt more socially isolated. Inexplicably, his academic performance also declined markedly at this point. In college, he developed a pattern of going to school part-time and dropping out frequently until his graduation, which required 10 years. During this period, Dexter was married. At the beginning of the analysis, he continued in the same job he had secured after graduation and was about to begin a part-time program for an advanced degree. His wife had ceased working since the birth of their child about one year before.

Despite his stable employment, Dexter felt that his career was languishing because he had not made any vertical moves and was not fulfilling his potential. He was prone to making careless, forgetful errors, and he was afraid this pattern was hurting his professional growth and ambition and could even jeopardize his job security. Also, although there had been tension throughout the marriage, in recent years and especially since the birth of the child, the couple had been engaged in increasingly explosive verbal battles, typically stimulated by Dexter's feeling that his wife had been verbally abusive to him. At times, these disputes reached the point that Dexter was fearful he would strike her. On one occasion, he had to drive off the expressway, park the car, and get out because they had become so enraged at each other that he feared for both their safety.

The analysis began with many memories of Dexter's relationship with his mother, especially discussions alone with her. It became clear that he felt he had a special relationship with her and that she looked to him as the child with the most academic potential. Believing that his mother was beautiful and smart with unfulfilled intellectual ambition, Dexter recalled her frustration and disappointment with his father because of the father's limited education, lack of success, and limited income. Dexter believed that his mother was dissatisfied with her lot, and, early in the analysis, he realized that he had unconsciously felt the burden of his mother's unfulfilled ambitions. In recognizing that he had been feeling chosen by her to become successful intellectually and financially (as his father had not), Dexter also became aware of his feeling that he could not please her. He became conscious of a new view of his mother—a view he called the "ice princess." Unlike his conscious feeling for his mother, this image was of a beautiful, cold, implacable, rigid, and unsatisfiable woman whom he could not please. This realization brought to light his unconscious anger toward his mother for her narcissistic exploitation of him.

Once he became aware of his negative feelings toward his mother, he felt a sense of burdensome guilt. His feeling that she believed in him and his intellectual potential—and her recent death—made the awareness of negative feelings especially guilt invoking. Nonetheless, he could repress neither the anger at her for what he now felt was her exploitation of him nor the negative image that coexisted with the positive.

The realization regarding his mother tended to produce material about his relationship with his father. When he discussed his mother's dissatisfaction with her husband, he had two reactions to his father. The more conscious response was his empathy for his father, who worked hard to support a wife and five children, only to be the object of his wife's dissatisfaction. However, his heretofore unconscious feeling was anger at his father for not being more successful and ambitious, a perception that evoked a burdensome sense of guilt. Underneath his conscious feeling of empathy for his father's situation were his desire to outdo him and his anger at his father for not being more successful. As he became aware of the latter, he realized he was identified unconsciously with his father, a feeling that he was limited intellectually and should not be educationally or financially successful. He was also angry at his father for not confronting his mother. As Dexter became aware that his father's limitations angered him, he realized that he equated his desire to be successful with his wish to outdo his father. His intense longing to be successful where his father was not was another source of guilt. If he succeeded, he would surpass his father and simultaneously do for his mother what his father could not. In his experience, pleasing his mother put him in direct conflict with his father, and he felt the burdensome guilt of injuring him.

All of this was eventually seen in the transference. He believed that I needed him to be a successful analytic patient, but he also idealized me as a representation of all he wished he were: intellectually, educationally, and financially successful without struggle or conflict. This idealization was decidedly ambivalent: He found himself in frequent, intense, competitive battles with me in which he tended to feel he came out on the "short end." Continually comparing his intelligence, education, training, and profession with mine, he felt, for example, that whereas he had struggled to achieve a modest education, I had easily completed an advanced degree program. However, in other arenas he claimed "victory": Believing that I had no children, he felt that, being a father, he was "ahead."

The intensity of the aggressive competitiveness with me was clearly shown in a dream in which he was riding a tricycle as fast as possible in a race with a figure who was physically similar to me; the analyst-figure unfairly had a better vehicle and was pulling ahead, so Dexter pushed the analyst-figure off the road and over a cliff. This dream provoked Dexter's angry and competitive feelings toward both his father and me. Dexter's negative transference had components from both parental relationships. Not only was he reenacting his desire to surpass his father and its attendant anxiety, but also he was becoming aware of his perception of the analyst as an implacably demanding figure whom he desired deeply to satisfy. The analyst had become the ice princess, and his anger at this image was growing.

Dexter's perception of analytic rigidity and his anger at it became a focal point of the transference. Convinced that nothing he did was good enough for the analyst, Dexter felt that I believed he was neither smart nor articulate enough and that he was not doing the analytic work properly. He was so burdened by these fantasized expectations that, during one session, he slumped deeply into the couch, put his hands over his eyes, and pleaded loudly, "Please leave me alone!" This reaction carried an emotional intensity so powerful that he was shocked into realizing that the burden and criticism he experienced were within him and had led to his perception of the analyst as impossible to please.

During the time he felt burdened by my expectations, Dexter enacted his anger at the analyst-mother ice princess by "forgetting" to do the analytic work. He began to pause rather than free-associate and avoided material in a more sustained way than he had before. He immediately associated these experiences to his careless errors at work and his frequent lapses in concentration; whereas before he had thought his erratic and self-defeating work pattern was solely a repetition of his competitive conflicts with his father, he now saw that it had more to do with his mother's perceived implacable expectations. His anger at the ice princess being so intense, he sought to defeat her. This anger had two primary components.

1. He believed that no matter how successful he became, the ice princess would never be satisfied. He was enraged at the sense of inadequacy he inevitably felt in conjunction with her expectations and, out of frustration, frequently withdrew into a state of dysfunction. In the analysis, this dynamic manifested itself in the feeling that he was not doing the analytic work properly, would never meet my expectations, and in the subsequent despair that his analysis could never be successful.

2. If he were to become successful, the ice princess would benefit and rob him of any credit. To be successful was to do her bidding and therefore implied submission to her exploitation of him. Similarly, if the analysis were to succeed, I would receive all the credit, and Dexter's role would be submission to my exploitive need for self-enhancement. To defend himself against such exploitation, Dexter attempted to defeat the analyst by "careless errors" in the analytic work.

For the first time, Dexter became aware of the anxiety of retaliation. At this point, he had a dream of a snake ready to bite his head off, to which he associated memories of his father's responses to his academic success. When Dexter was a high school sophomore, his father could no longer help him with his mathematics homework, which seemed to upset the father. Dexter's mother remarked that he had reached a level of education beyond his father's achievements. He could now trace the precipitous fall in his academic record to this event. His mathematics grades quickly tumbled, and his other grades soon followed. His academic performance never recovered. He realized now that he was afraid he had hurt his father and that he would be in danger of incurring his father's wrath if he had continued academic success. There was little evidence of the father's anger but many indications of his withdrawal in response to Dexter's achievements—a reaction that evoked anxiety in Dexter. For the first time, Dexter saw the depth of his retaliatory anxiety for success.

He was now able to reinterpret his quitting sports in high school—an event he had previously attributed to his injury. Even though the injury ended his sophomore season, he could have played the next year. The reason for his withdrawal from sports now became apparent. He had been a starter on the freshman and sophomore teams, but the next year he would have been on the varsity team, and there was a senior ahead of him. Unable to tolerate being "second-string," Dexter used the injury to avoid this experience. Despite his guilt over success, he regarded any experience of less than complete success as humiliating. This reaction reflected his unresolved ambivalence toward his father. Less than top performance, which he expected to have in football, was mortifying because he equated it with the shame of "losing" to a man who was devalued by his mother. Further, a less-than-perfect status threatened to confirm and make conscious the unconscious identification with his father that had already made him feel like a failure. Thus, he could tolerate neither success nor failure. His life reflected this ambivalence: He took steps toward success but continually stumbled and injured himself on the way. He wished the analysis to succeed, but he sabotaged the analytic work in an effort to ensure its failure.

At this point, he recalled two frightening, previously repressed adult memories. In the first, he was scuba diving and went down too far, neglecting the amount of oxygen in his tank. He began to feel giddy but was saved by a fellow scuba diver who went down to get him. In the second memory, he was working on a freight elevator when he accidentally raised it and was hanging by his fingers until he was again rescued. He now understood that these occurrences were not accidental, as he had thought, but part of his pattern of injuring and defeating himself, rooted in his excessive guilt over surpassing his father.

Dexter's success anxiety had roots in his representation of both parents: his mother as the implacable, exploitive ice princess who desired his success for her self-aggrandizement and at whom he was enraged and unable to please and his father as the threatened competitor who would withdraw and retaliate if his achievements were equaled or surpassed. In the transference, he alternated between these positions, and each led to hostility and its enactment in the analysis. However, both parental transference images had two sides. As much as Dexter felt that I sought to exploit him by making him successful, his idealization of me was a way of exploiting me by enhancing his self-esteem via connection with an idealized figure. This awareness led to a new consciousness of the gratification in his mother's selection of him as the child having the most potential. As angry as he was about her expectations, he felt gratified by the feeling of "specialness," from which he obtained considerable narcissistic pleasure. It was no different in analysis: Dexter's perception that I needed his success to bolster my self-esteem gave him to feel that he was a specially favored patient, a feeling that provided a great deal of narcissistic gratification.

The same two-sided relationship applied to the competitive father transference. Not only did he wish to outdo me, he assumed I was equally competitive with him and sought to win "victories" in our interactions. He construed many of my interpretations as efforts to "one-up" him and "put him in his place." Although he was usually himself as the child (with the analyst the father), in this case the analyst was the patient, and the patient was the threatened father, fearful of being outdone. Both transference constellations were understood as reenactments of the most critical object relationships in Dexter's personality makeup. The first included the exploiter–exploited poles with the patient enacting either side; the second consisted of "competitor" and "threatened, competed with," with the patient on either side of this pattern as well. The transference constellations revealed the object relationships Dexter tended to enact in all meaningful interpersonal relationships.

Even after Dexter saw clearly the origins of the critical aspects of the transference in his relationships with both parents, he did not alter these perceptions. He experienced a split between what he knew to be his reenactments of early relationships and his stubborn experience of the analyst in accordance with those early relationships. This resilience in his experience of the analyst constituted the most stubborn barrier to the resolution of his neurosis.

Dexter could see that his attempts to please me and his perception of me as "unpleaseable" and exploitive hid his longing for a close, intimate bond in which the analyst and patient would "really know" each other, which he had believed had occurred between his mother and him. His evaluation of this experience now was that his feeling of specialness to her was not a genuinely close bond but a substitute for an emptiness he felt with her. He had defended against his longing for intimacy with her as he now did with the me: by feeling frustrated with and exploited by an unpleaseable object. As these feelings were interpreted as defenses, he was confronted with the possibility of an intimacy he had never before experienced. Now threatened with that possibility in his relationship with me, he felt disrupted and disorganized.

At this point, Dexter used the same maneuver with me as he had throughout the relationship: He returned to his view that he had a special relationship with me in which he was exploited. In this way, he maintained his anger and remained stuck in the same self-defeating pattern that he had with his mother: He forgot to do the analytic work out of anger at exploitation while experiencing the narcissistic gratification of specialness. Breaking through the old pattern threatened to lead him to a new relationship with me as someone with whom he wished to achieve a closeness he had never before experienced. He resorted to the internalized object relationships of exploitation and specialness that had paralyzed his life and from which he was unable to extricate himself.

Three Perspectives

How are we to understand Dexter's symptoms and conflicts, and, most important, how are we to comprehend the analytic relationship in which patient and analyst find themselves? Is the analysis stuck, and, if so, what is the way out of the stalemate? These are the critical questions with which the analyst must grapple. Given the plethora of current psychoanalytic theories, there is a variety of viewpoints from which to answer these questions. The theoretical viewpoint set forth in this book is best highlighted not by enumerating a list of theoretical perspectives but by contrasting this viewpoint with the two broad psychoanalytic paradigms between which it falls. Let us look at how analysts from the ego-psychological and relational analytic paradigms would likely attempt to answer these questions and then proceed to address the same issues from an object relations point of view.

The Ego-Psychological Viewpoint

One cannot expect to propose a single formulation with which all ego psychologists would be expected to agree in all particulars. Nonetheless, broadly conceived, it is fair to say that contemporary ego psychology is a psychoanalytic paradigm that views human motivation as a compromise among the competing psychological pressures of drive, defense, anxiety, and guilt (e.g., Brenner, 1979; Wilson, 1995). Thinking in terms of compromise among these competing psychological forces and certain content themes (e.g., the Oedipus complex) is inevitably a centerpiece of any ego-psychological formulation, although its manifestation will vary with the styles of individual clinicians. What follows is a representation of thinking within the ego-psychological paradigm on the understanding and treatment of Dexter, recognizing that details would undoubtedly differ among analysts of this persuasion.

From the viewpoint of classical psychoanalytic theory, Dexter is struggling with conflicts over both libidinal wishes and aggressivity stimulated by the oedipal constellation. The special place he believed he had with his mother constituted an oedipal victory that excited his libidinal wishes, thus exacerbating his anxiety and increasing his burden of guilt. Furthermore, his aggression is inhibited due to the oedipal guilt generated by his wish to outdo his father and take his place with his mother. Although narcissistically gratified by this "victory" over his father, Dexter paid a dear price in the form of excessive anxiety leading to intensified defenses and burdensome guilt. Dexter's potentially successful life experience to some degree represents this oedipal victory, a fact that evokes anxiety and guilt to the point that he sabotages his chances for success in life in a desperate effort at self-punishment. The lengthy, painful ordeals of his academic struggles, the precipitous decline in his academic per-formance in high school, and his self-defeating errors at work are all dire efforts to avoid the successful life experience that would sym-bolize an oedipal victory. Additionally, they are a means of self-pun-ishment for his unacceptable oedipal strivings and aggressive wishes toward his father.

Nonetheless, less than total success is also intolerable to Dexter, a fact seen clearly in his quitting the football team rather than accept being second-string. Unconsciously, being second-string even for one year represents defeat and disappointment in the eyes of his mother. Although such a "defeat" might pacify his guilt, it also creates intolerable narcissistic injury because it promotes an unconscious identification with an inadequate father. Thus, anything less than perfect success symbolizes failing his mother as his father has done and triggers an unconscious identification with the father who was not good enough for his mother. His inability to tolerate anything less than perfect performance and the accompanying exquisite nar-cissistic sensitivity are rooted, from this viewpoint, in a deep anxiety generated by an unconscious identification with his father.

His ambitions are fueled greatly by the fear that his life is fated to follow in the older man's footsteps. Failure to be at the top symbolizes inability to meet his mother's expectations by achieving educational and intellectual superiority to his father and satisfying her as his father could not. As much as he rebelled against this role, he derived immeasurable gratification from it, and failure to achieve it represents intolerable disappointment to his mother. Because any experience short of absolute success symbolizes painful disappointment, top-level performance in all areas is required. In an effort to avoid confronting the possibility that he may fail to be the top man his mother wanted, Dexter developed an almost phobic avoidance of being "tested," whether in football or academics.

That his unconscious oedipal conflicts infiltrate both success and failure accounts for his lifelong pattern of struggling to achieve and then sabotaging his own efforts. If he resolves his unconscious conflicts around his desire to be the oedipal victor, he will no longer suffer from intense narcissistic vulnerability.

A primary outcome of the successful repression of his libidinal wishes requires that he defend against the intimate contact that threatens to stimulate these desires and break through the repression barrier. Marriage, by the nature of its demand for intimacy, threatens to awaken this unconscious conflict, resulting in an explosive marital relationship. From this viewpoint, a primary reason for Dexter's rage at his wife is the threat of the marital relationship to evoke the long-repressed oedipal desire and its associated affects of guilt, anxiety, aggression, and retaliatory fear. Marital tension and discord produce the distance required to defend against the intimate feelings that would threaten to evoke the excitement of his mother's seductiveness.

Because the intimacy of the marital relationship threatens to rouse Dexter's libidinal longings, it also stimulates his repressed aggression toward both parents. Anger at his mother for her demanding expectations of him and at his father for not being a more satisfactory object for her has now broken through the repression barrier that was in operation since the oedipal phase. Again, it may be presumed that the marriage, with its demands for intimacy, is responsible for this increased pressure on the defenses that eventually caused them to give way. His uncontrolled outbursts of rage toward his wife may be seen as displaced expressions of his unconscious rage at his mother for her seductiveness, exploitation, and implacable rigidity.

Additionally, by attempting to defeat the analyst-mother ice princess by sabotaging the analysis, he is protected from awareness of being sexually aroused by his mother in the oedipal phase. He punishes the analysis and himself in a desperate effort to "bribe" the superego so that he need not be aware of the excitement he felt in her "narcissistic exploitation" of him. Thus, his unconscious anger at his mother has two roots: his perception of her as making unfulfillable demands on him and the defensive function of protecting against being excited by her.

Additionally, it may be presumed that he projects his aggressive wishes onto his father, leading to fear of retaliation, which further exacerbates his anxiety of becoming successful. His dream of the snake ready to bite his head off and the association to his father's feeling of threat in response to his academic success are clear evidence of a deep anxiety that he will suffer paternal retaliation for his aggression. To gain relief from retaliatory anxiety, Dexter turns his aggression against himself, thus relieving his dual anxieties of injuring his father and of retaliation and, in the process, satisfying his superego strictures by punishing himself for the forbidden wish. In this way, retaliatory anxiety is a major source of his crippling inhibitions and inability to allow himself to succeed. From this perspective, his nearly catastrophic episodes are especially dangerous symptoms of his unconscious efforts to punish himself for his unacceptable aggression.

It needs to be emphasized that, from this viewpoint, Dexter's crippling perceptions of both parents are fantasies. For example, he fantasized his mother's desire for his success and her need for him to be special. Similarly, he seethes with aggressive fantasies toward both parents, which create the anxiety of retaliation. The fantasies per se being sufficiently disturbing to create the need for defenses, the ego psychologist does not presume that Dexter's perceptions reflect an actual relationship with his mother, but neither is the actual relationship the important factor. Dexter's relationships with women are impaired by the fantasy of his mother, which he then projects onto other female figures, such as his wife.

The current sticking point of the analysis is Dexter's resistance to awareness of these oedipal conflicts. As Dexter began to feel a greater degree of intimacy toward me, libidinal longings for his mother were stimulated and the anxiety of oedipal victory reawakened. He then intensified his defenses against the transference by (a) unconsciously sabotaging the analysis by forgetting to do the analytic work and (b) viewing me as exploitive, thus creating distance between himself and me. The enactment of sabotaging the analytic work and his perception of chronic competitive struggles with me indicate his displacement of unconscious libidinal and aggressive wishes onto me and the self-punishment of turning the aggression toward defeating his efforts at self-improvement. One sees abundant evidence of transference aggression in Dexter's competitiveness with me, a dynamic underscored in the dream of pushing the disguised figure of me off a cliff. Efforts to defeat potential analytic success constitute a punishment for the forbidden wishes to injure me. Thus, the carelessness in the analytic work is the transference of his aggressive, competitive struggles with his father. Because this aggression evokes guilt and self-punishment, the analytic process must be defeated. Every step of success is met with regression to avoid guilt and anxiety. Thus does the analytic process mirror Dexter's lifelong pattern of oscillation between movement toward success and self-sabotage. The current point of the analysis is another step of resistance that serves to avoid the unconscious conflicts evoked by positive life experiences.

The case of Dexter may be seen as illustrative of a neurotic compromise among drive-induced wishes (aggressive and libidinal), superego prohibition (guilt), the anxiety both of wishing to injure his father and of the retaliatory fear, and repression of both libidinal and aggressive wishes. The analytic task is to make conscious these unconscious elements of the conflict. As the analytic process threatened to make these unconscious forces conscious, Dexter resisted awareness of the oedipal wish by regressing to the maternal, narcissistic transference in which he felt both exploited and special. The elements of the maternal transference—fears of exploitation and the gratification of feeling special—are not primary issues but defensive retreats from the more anxiety-provoking oedipal wishes. Thus, all the elements of the conflict—the sexual and aggressive wishes, their repression, guilt, and anxiety—are present in the transference and defended against by the patient's resistance to doing the analytic work.

From this ego-psychological perspective, the purpose of making conscious the elements of the compromise formation is to make possible a new arrangement of psychological forces (Brenner, 1979). When the components of the conflict become conscious, the ego is able to achieve a greater degree of control over them. There is no perfect solution to Dexter's dilemma, as all mental functioning involves conflict and compromise, but the persistent interpretation of resistance will eventually bring all the relevant psychological forces to consciousness so that the defenses may lessen in intensity and the degree of ego control over the conflict may be enhanced. In this way, a new, more adaptive compromise can be achieved—one that allows a greater degree of instinctual gratification and therefore avoids a symptomatic outcome.

The Relational Viewpoint

From the viewpoint of relational psychoanalysis, the ego-psychological formulation relies on the reductionistic and "experience-distant" hypothesis of endogenous drives. Even if Dexter's problems could be attributed to conflicts with sexuality and aggression, these powerful affects gain expression, form, and meaning only in the interpersonal contexts in which they originated and are currently sustained. To ascribe conflicts over these troublesome affects to endogenous drives misses the relational context from which these feelings derive their meaning. Thus, from a relational perspective, the keys to Dexter's symptoms of self-defeat, chronic underachievement, and emotional explosiveness lie in his pattern of interpersonal relationships—perhaps originating in the past but now maintained and enacted in the present—rather than in the vicissitudes of the drives.

From a relational viewpoint, Dexter's self-sabotage and resistance to becoming successful are symptoms of his two primary relational patterns, competition and exploitation, each of which is related to a complex configuration with one parent. He fears that emotional closeness to another person risks exposing himself to the danger of engulfing demands and expectations he may not be able to meet. After attempting to navigate his relationship with his mother by avoiding situations of potential failure and achieving such success as he could be reasonably assured of, his later life configurations, most notably his academic record, have followed this pattern. Seeking to create relationships that would minimize the anxiety of failing without threatening continuity, he adopts the strategy of attempting to be successful but engaging in activities only if he can be the top man. From this viewpoint, quitting football to avoid being second-string must be seen as an interpersonal tactic designed to avoid the experience of failing to meet expectations. Ironically, this "avoidance-of-failure" strategy leads to considerable external failure. For example, to avert unsuccessful academic experience, he drops out of school repeatedly and avoids his coursework. His desultory educational career reflects his tightrope walk of avoiding work he fears he cannot perform with complete success but doing enough not to fail completely.

Dexter's other primary relational configuration, tied to his relationship with his father, is a pattern of failure designed to avoid threatening the other. As success evokes anxiety, Dexter believes that he cannot succeed where the other has not. Consequently, when he feels success is near, he sabotages himself to minimize anxiety in the relationship. He adopts the interpersonal strategy of defeating himself, the first instance of which was his relationship with his father. This pattern conflicts with his desire to be successful in order to outdo the other so that he can be the top man who meets expectations—a pattern connected to his maternal relationship. These two relational configurations are in conflict with each other. Success would please figures identified with his mother but threaten relationships more closely linked to his paternal pattern, and failure would have the opposite result. The strategy Dexter adopts to maintain both types of ties is an oscillating pattern of partial success, self-sabotage, and renewed efforts at success. His pattern of underachievement and self-sabotage results from conflicting relational configurations that he is trying desperately to negotiate, each of which threatens a needed relationship. From this viewpoint, his symptoms may be regarded as a compromise, but this compromise is not between competing intrapsychic forces (as in the ego-psychological formulation) but is between conflicting relational patterns. The commonality between the two approaches is the principle that the symptomatic pattern is an effort to minimize anxiety caused by conflict, but the source of the anxiety and the nature of the conflict are intrapsychic for ego psychology and relational for relational analysis.

From a relational perspective, the problem is not only that the relational configurations are in conflict but also that these patterns of relating are too narrow. Dexter has very few ways of forming relationships: His primary patterns are competition and fear of exploitation. Such limited modes of engaging others are a primary problem from the relational viewpoint due to the resulting constriction of interpersonal life. A major goal of the analysis is the broadening and expansion of Dexter's patterns of interaction. Consequently, treatment must address not only the conflict between these competing ways of relating but their virtual monopoly on his manner of engaging others.

From this relational perspective, the unit of analytic focus is the relational configuration between patient and analyst. The distinction between the relational emphasis on what is created between both parties to the analytic couple and the ego-psychological focus on the patient's intrapsychic life defines most succinctly the clinical difference between the two approaches. From the relational viewpoint, the focus of ego psychology is aimed too narrowly at the patient's contribution to the analytic relationship to the exclusion of the analyst's participation. According to relational theory, the analyst is no less a participant in the creation of the analytic relationship than the patient is, and a primary analytic task is to discern the analyst's role in the patient's patterns. From this viewpoint, rather than attempt to stay outside of Dexter's world of anxiety over exploitation and competitiveness, the analyst recognizes the inevitability of his or her participation in it.

The relational analyst would want to know what behavior of mine the patient is responding to when he fears being exploited. In what way did I need a successful analytic outcome from the patient? To some degree, all analysts feel a need for the patient to be successful in the analysis. Is the patient reacting to my need for him to be successful? Was there something that made me feel an especially high degree of pressure to achieve a successful outcome? Additionally, the patient's belief that he was engaged in a competitive battle with me must in some way be replicated in my experience with him. In what way was I competitive with the patient? In response to the patient's competitive search for ways he was outperforming me, did I feel a need to keep my own competitive "scorecard" of pluses and minuses? Even more poignantly, was Dexter's competitiveness a response to competition he experienced from me? The assumption of the relational approach is that I am in some way engaged in the competition, and the patient's unconscious effort to sabotage the analysis by careless errors is the outcome of mutual competition rather than a symptom of the patients's internal struggles.

From this perspective, Dexter's experience of my interpretations as criticism is only one side of a mutually critical relationship. His complaints about my exploitation and narcissistic use of him constitute a criticism of me. Most poignantly, from the viewpoint of relational analysis, a key question in his feeling criticized is whether I was in fact being critical of him in some way that he is sensing. Have we become engaged in a mutually critical relationship? From the viewpoint of relational analysis, it is inevitable that I would in some way experience myself as critical (e.g., very likely in response to Dexter's accusation of being criticized) and that participation in Dexter's self-devaluing relational pattern must be used to inquire how the analytic couple became engaged in this criticism and why they seem so locked into it.

If the analyst only participated in this world, no therapeutic movement would be possible. To effect change, the analyst struggles to achieve a new way of engaging the patient within their shared world. This new "voice" or position allows questioning of the patient's relational patterns. A key analytic intervention is to inquire with the patient why these particular forms of relating (in this case, exploitation and competition) are the only ways the analytic couple seems to engage. For example, the analyst will in some way join the competitive battle of "victories" and "defeats" but then must find a new stance toward this "scorecard keeping" within which the patient may be asked why this mode of relating is a primary and persistent part of their relationship. To use the metaphor contained in the dream, the analyst questions how patient and analyst became locked into a race in which winning is so important that the competitor must be pushed off a cliff in order to achieve victory.

The current sticking point in the analysis from this viewpoint is not Dexter's resistance but a problem of the analytic couple. It misses the point, from the relational perspective, to describe Dexter as returning to his old patterns in response to potential analytic breakthrough. A more apt description of the situation is that Dexter and I constructed a stalemated relationship from which neither of us can free ourselves. The assumption of this viewpoint is that there must be a block in me and in Dexter to the engagement of a new relationship. That Dexter reverted to anxiety over exploitation as soon as he began to feel a closeness with me is symptomatic of a problem with closeness in both participants. My task, from this perspective, is to address both my own and Dexter's anxiety regarding closeness in our relationship. So, while I inquire with Dexter as to how the relationship became more distant after seeming closeness, I should also be struggling with my own need to distance.

The goal of this approach to Dexter's chronic patterns is to broaden and enrich his relational configurations rather than abolish old patterns and replace them with new modes of engagement. Dexter and I must find new avenues of relating that go beyond the narrowness and rigidity of our current patterns. Important components of these new relational patterns would be to experience success in the analysis without feeling the relationship threatened by com-petitive envy on either side and to experience conflict without the threat of abandonment. If this process is successful, the analytic couple engages in ways of relating that are new for Dexter and enriching of his life experience.

For the relational analyst, the therapeutic action will lie primarily in the new relationship created by Dexter and me. Interpretations of what the analytic couple is doing together may be useful for the purpose of locating the analyst in the patient's relational configura-tions; however, analytic change comes about primarily through new ways of relating. If Dexter's modes of engaging others in relation-ships are appreciably enriched and expanded beyond the narrow confines within which he entered the analysis, the analytic goals are achieved.

The Object Relations Viewpoint

From the object relations perspective, the primary symptoms of self-defeat and chronic underachievement are rooted in the early object relationships with both parents. To minimize the anxiety with his mother, Dexter avoids "tests of his mettle" because failure to meet expectations threatens the very existence of the maternal relationship. Dexter feared that losing the special place with her that made him feel whole, alive, and having import in the world would rob his life of meaning and importance. The anxiety of losing the top spot in his mother's affections rendered impossible the confrontation with his limitations, a confrontation he believed would threaten this feeling of specialness. The relationship with his mother being unable to allow such limitations, he attempted to navigate a relationship with her that avoided all possibility of failure. In this way, the object relations view is similar to the relational perspective: Both see Dexter as seeking ways to maintain the maternal relationship.

The pressure Dexter felt to please his mother resulted in an exploiter–victim object relationship that he now uses as a guide for navigating the social world. The legacy of the maternal relationship is not simply an internalized representation of his mother projected onto significant others but an object relationship of exploitation–victimization, either side of which may be his role at a given phase. When a relationship begins to become intimate, he tends to experience the connection as exploitation, but he is also capable of using others in an exploitive manner. This object relationship of exploiter–victim is the source of one of his primary ways of relating—that is, a core component of his self structure. The relationships he forms on this basis, such as with his wife and analyst, are not ends in themselves but vehicles for the formation and maintenance of his self.

Enraged at his mother's exploitation of him for her narcissistic needs, he is unable to give direct expression to his anger for fear that he will lose the relationship. The need for her warm glow in response to his presence is such that he cannot risk any direct conflict with or anger toward her. Thus, self-defeat is not only a way to avoid being tested but also a protest against exploitation by maternal expectations he feels compelled to meet. This neurotic pattern emanates from the burial of his rage against his experience of being victimized by the prison of his mother's unsatisfiable demands, a disavowal that protects the specialness of the maternal relationship. Consequently, a major part of his self is concealed from himself and others, split off from contact with the interpersonal world. His feelings of unfairness and anger regarding his mother's demands gain expression only in self-defeat, a form of communication from the hidden self.

The chronic pattern of sabotage and avoidance of pursuing his consciously sought academic goals, along with his inconsistent work performance, is seen from this viewpoint as an indirect communication from the buried part of the self. His "failures" are his way of saying, "There is something very wrong inside, but I cannot say this directly. Can anyone out there hear me?" His pattern of underachievement and periodic outbursts of rage constitute a protest, the only way he is able to let the world know there is someone alive inside him who desires direct expression. Unable to pursue his own interests and give authentic expression to the anger at his compliance, he appears to be "going along" on the surface, but his self-sabotage is his way of telling himself and others that he is enraged at feeling locked into being top man so that his mother can have a hole in her life filled by his success.

Why must he give voice to this protest? Why does he not comply and leave his other feelings buried? To say that he is appealing for help in the only way he can begs the deeper question: What does he need help for? The answer defines a decisive difference between the object relations and relational models. From the object relations viewpoint, Dexter wants help so that he can realize potential aborted by the excessive restrictiveness of the maternal relationship. The combination of his special role with his mother and anxiety about maintaining it has obstructed his ability to use his aggression and explore conflicting feelings toward his mother. In consequence, he missed the opportunity to find out what his strengths and limitations are in major areas of his life: interpersonal, academic, professional, and athletic. Because his interpersonal relationships had to be kept at a shallow restrictive level, he lost the opportunity to explore intimacy and resolve conflicts within it. That is to say, the development of his self has been arrested, and frustration in his ability to realize potential ways of being and relating has gained symptomatic expression.

From an object relations perspective, early relationships are not ends in themselves but exist to serve a function: the development of the self. Dexter's lack of contentment is attributable to the fact that his relationships have blocked a large part of his potential as a person and professional, arresting his growth and development. Although most relationships are undoubtedly both limiting and growth facilitating to some degree, his relationships are excessively restricting of his potential, a process that resulted in a symptomatic appeal for help. Dexter's conflict is that he needs his mother, but the relationship he feels forced to shape with her conflicts with, rather than lies in concert with, his need to become who he is. His maternal relationship did not provide the space for Dexter to make mistakes, to find out what his talents and limits are, and to explore intimacy by having a genuine closeness based on his real qualities. His symptoms are the vehicle for communicating the pain produced by this inhibition of his self development.

The object relations view of pathology as arrested development defines a decisive difference between this paradigm and a relational perspective. From the latter viewpoint, developmental considerations are de-emphasized in favor of the current coconstructions between patient and analyst. The focus from this viewpoint, as we have seen, is the narrowness of Dexter's competitive and exploitive interactional patterns and the analyst's participation in their repetition, with the analytic focus being on their expansion and enrichment via the analyst's new ways of relating to the patient. By contrast, from the object relations perspective, Dexter's pathology is defined by his areas of developmental arrest—intimacy, aggression, and the pursuit of ambition—with the treatment focus being on the finding, uncovering, and developing of blocked potential.

To maintain the maternal relationship, Dexter had to fulfill his mother's need for him to be more successful than her disappointing husband. However, the very basis of this relationship as being the top man set him into conflict with his father. He wanted to prove to his mother that he could be successful where his father could not, but his father's withdrawal indicated that this "victory" threatened the paternal relationship. The anxiety of losing the latter connection led to guilt over his aggressive strivings, dictating a feeling of being undeserving of success. Furthermore, convinced that aggression threatened his father's availability, Dexter buried his aggression, thus becoming unable to utilize it for the development of potential ways of being. Construing his father's withdrawal as a competitive reaction, Dexter psychically registered the paternal relationship as a competitive dyad. Furthermore, to relieve the anxiety of being like the man his mother found wanting, Dexter strove for success, an ambition that reinforced the competitiveness of the paternal dyad.

The encoding of this object relationship issued in Dexter both competing with others and experiencing others as operating the same way with him. Dexter may assume the active role of competitor or the more passive role of being competed with, but in either case he tends to assume competition in relationships, especially with men. Victory cannot be achieved, and defeat, although it must be ensured, is simultaneously intolerable.

The result of this competitive object relationship has been a paralyzing ambivalence issuing in a tortuous and halting academic career and a desultory professional life constantly on the precipice of failure. The psychically encoded paternal dyad is an ambivalent competitiveness in which neither victory nor defeat is tolerable, a process that resulted in a crippling inability to utilize many capacities. In this way, it may be said that the maternal object relationship interfered with Dexter's ability to be intimate as well as successful, and the paternal relationship impaired the deployment of his aggression to realize ambitions. It bears emphasis that neither of these object relationships is to be viewed as a simple "recording" of the early interpersonal relationship; both are complex constructions based on actual relationships.

Dexter brings these primary modes of object relating into his significant relationships. Depending on his wife stimulates the anxiety of being exploited by her, but he cannot give her up. This repetition of the maternal relationship is an enactment of his exploiter–victim object relationship: He needs to comply with demands he regards as excessive and imprisoning, but he suffers a precious loss of self and a humiliating feeling of exploitation for so doing. Seeing his wife as an unpleaseable figure brings forth the rage he was unable to experience toward his mother. A major difference between the maternal relationship and his marriage is that in the latter he occasionally allows himself explosions of anger, an index of the relative safety he feels in that relationship. Thus, his ability to become overtly angry at his wife may be regarded as a positive sign, although the manner of its expression is indeed destructive.

In the transference, he is reenacting both modes of object relationship. He sees me both as the exploitive ice princess mother and as the father threatened by his success, with whom he must compete to gain approval from the mother. An oscillating pattern of productive analytic work and self-sabotage of the analytic process is the inevitable result of these ways of relating. His analytic "failures" defeat the implacable mother but appease the father, and analytic success gratifies the ice princess but threatens the father. A primary task of the analysis is to interpret these modes of relating as fundamental components of Dexter's self structure, but the goal of the analysis goes beyond the elimination of object relationships that impair self development to include their replacement with others that promote the realization of self potential.

Dexter is becoming aware of the crippling nature of his competitive and exploitive–victim ways of relating and understands their origins, but this awareness has not led to the desired analytic shifts because interpretation alone does not provide alternative patterns. This is the object relationship understanding of the presumed sticking point of the treatment: The analysis has reached the limits of what interpretation by itself can provide. Dexter's regression is not "resistance" but a desperate and expectable effort to maintain the forms of object relationships he knows.

Dexter's object relationship patterns were formed in response to the anxiety of potential loss of needed relationships rather than genuine experience. This anxiety-driven motivation required the burial of authentic experience and ultimately led to symptom formation. The problem embedded in Dexter's object relationships is not that differing patterns are in conflict but that they are divorced from his authentic experience. Thus, the object relations viewpoint, like relational analysis, emphasizes early relationship patterns and the need to navigate them in the formation of pathological patterns. Unlike the relational viewpoint, however, the object relations model does not seek simply a more enriching relationship but a new self structure based on a greater degree of authenticity and realization of self potential than existed in the pathological patterns.

From an object relations perspective, Dexter suffers primarily from two pathological object relational patterns—exploitation–victimization and competition—that define his core sense of self. The therapeutic task is to help him relinquish these patterns and replace them with others based on his authentic experience. As we shall see, to achieve this goal requires both understanding the current object relational formations and the provision of a relationship in which new object relationships can be constructed. In this way, the object relations model utilizes both the understanding stressed by the ego-psychological model and the new relationship emphasized by the relational approach. The process by which these tools are utilized to accomplish the goal of constructing a new self structure is the theme of this book.

Conclusion

This discussion of Dexter shows that the object relations model lies between the ego-psychological and relational perspectives both theoretically and clinically. From the theoretical viewpoint, the object relations model concurs with the relational critique that ego psychology relies on an assumption of endogenous drives that leads to an excessively narrow and reductionistic concept of human motivation and is too exclusively intrapsychic. However, from the object relations perspective, the relational model, by making relational patterns the target of analytic inquiry, loses the focus on self and psychological structure that is the very domain of psychoanalytic therapy. From this perspective, the relational model avoids the reductionism of the drive model at the cost of obscuring the goal of the psychoanalytic process.

An object relations perspective, unlike the ego psychology model, looks at Dexter's ways of relating as the royal road to analytic progress but, unlike the relational model, views these modes of engagement not as ends in themselves but as a means for understanding his self structure and its costs. Implying an inborn movement toward the creation of self, this object relations model is in agreement with the ego-psychological view that psychoanalysis cannot do without some sense of an inborn core motivation. However, the decisive difference between the ego-psychological model and the object relations view lies in the nature of this core sense of self. From the object relations viewpoint, the underlying human motivation is not biologically based drives but a need for self realization. Readers familiar with self psychology will see the similarity between this concept and Kohut's notion of a "nuclear program of the self" striving to achieve its ambitions and ideals, the primary difference being that self realization is a broader concept encompassing more aspects of the personality than ideals and ambitions. As we saw with Dexter, frustration in his ability to fulfill his potential in a variety of areas resulted in a symptomatic expression of his latent capacities longing to gain expression in the world.

In this model, the key distinction is between authentic expression of the self and inauthentic ways of relating in which interpersonal contact is achieved at the cost of potential avenues of self develop-ment. The object relations approach substitutes anxiety-driven inau-thentic modes of engagement for the ego-psychological concept of defense against drive-based wishes. Both theories conceptualize defenses as anxiety-driven protective strategies, but they differ in the content of what is protected.

The relational critique of both the ego-psychological and object relations views is that neither shows sufficient appreciation of the inherently interactive nature of the self. The relational viewpoint eschews the idea of a self that can be developed or arrested as being too close to the concept of a monadic self existing apart from a relational matrix. From the object relations viewpoint, psychoana-lytic therapy depends on the concept of a self striving to be realized. Although interaction is required for self realization, the analytic focus is on the articulation and development of the core potential self arrested by previous experience. Nonetheless, this core self is not a "homunculus" waiting to be brought forth fully formed, but potential ways of being and relating, the ultimate shape of which will be influenced by relationships. In this way, the object relations model emphasizes the concept of inherent movement toward self realization while recognizing the importance of relationships in the ultimate formation of self structure.

In the clinical arena, the issue is joined by the difference between the "one-person" and "two-person" models. From the ego-psycho-logical viewpoint, the clinical process consists of the analyst's obser-vations of the patient's unconscious conflicts. In this one-person model, the domain of inquiry lies entirely within the patient, and the analytic vantage point is outside these conflicts. By contrast, the relational model sees analyst and patient as inextricably imbedded in a relational matrix and clinical material as "cocreated." In this two-person psychology, the analyst has no position outside the relation-ship from which to "observe" the patient, and the therapeutic action is not insight but a new relationship. Again, the object relations model assumes a middle ground. The analyst is neither an external observer, as in the ego-psychological model, nor as implicated in the process as maintained by relational theory. To the degree that analytic treat-ment is successful, the buried potential of the patient becomes articulated in the analytic dialogue. The analyst's role includes both interpretation and the facilitation of a previously arrested develop-mental process. This emerging potential cannot be reduced to the interactions by which it becomes articulated. Although from a rela-tional perspective such a view relies too heavily on an endogenous concept of self, from the object relations view the relational notion of a completely social self runs the danger of a theoretical quagmire in which the very target of the analytic process becomes murky.

This model has defining implications for therapeutic action based on a paradigm of psychological structure, development, and pathol-ogy that falls between the social concept of relational analysis and the purely intrapsychic posture of ego psychology. The next task is to elucidate this model in order to lay the basis for the clinical theory. We now turn to the explication of this object relations model of psychoanalytic theory and the developmental process.

Chapter 2

Self and Object

In the discussion of Dexter, we have seen that the object relations model is situated between the intrapsychic drive–ego model and the interactional perspective of relational psychoanalysis. The contention of this book is that the proposed model features a concept of personality development, psychopathology, and clinical technique that includes contributions from both theories. The task now is to elucidate the theoretical and clinical premises of this model so that we may derive the clinical strategy for the conduct of psychoanalytic therapy. Because the key features of this model are best highlighted in contrast with those of the ego-psychological and relational views, alternative paradigms are examined to demonstrate the need for an object relations model that includes components of each.

The Ego Psychology Model

The original psychoanalytic theory of motivation viewed biologically based drives as the foundation for all human activity (Freud, 1915a).

The advent of ego psychology amended this theory to include some autonomous ego functioning but did not alter the principle that drives are the basis of the conflicts that forge the psychological organization (e.g., A. Freud, 1936; Fenichel, 1945). From this viewpoint, a drive-based unconscious fantasy, at the root of all such compromises, is the underlying motive of all psychological organization. Because this fantasy stimulates anxiety, it must be kept unconscious, and conflict between the fantasy and defenses against it results in the compromise formation that organizes the psyche. Contemporary ego psychology, sometimes called contemporary structural analysis, views the psyche as the product of compromises among the conflicting forces of drive, guilt, anxiety, and defense (Brenner, 1979; Bachant, Lynch, and Richards, 1995; Sugarman, 1995). According to this view, interpersonal relationships and productivity are both motivated by the need to manage tension states created by the drives and defenses against them.

This drive-based view of human motivation has come into disfavor by an increasing number of psychoanalytic clinicians for several reasons. First, the overwhelming evidence from infant, child, and ethological researchers is that early attachment to caretakers cannot be reduced to their role in tension reduction. The wealth of data supporting this contention has been discussed in considerable detail elsewhere (Bowlby, 1969; Lichtenberg, 1983; Stern, 1985) and need only be briefly summarized here. Ethological research has shown that young animals attach to older animals, of a different species if necessary, even if the latter have not met any biological needs. One of Harlow's most famous experiments demonstrated that young monkeys attached to a cloth mother-model that did not provide for any biological needs rather than to a wire mother-model that did (Harlow and Zimmerman, 1959). Human infant research has found that the neonate is preadapted to interaction with the mother within the first few days of life (Lichtenberg, 1983; Stern, 1985). Fairbairn (1944) observed, and subsequent research has confirmed, that infants are not born into an unrealistic pleasure-seeking state that requires taming by reality as assumed by the drive–defense model; rather, they are born with an array of competencies, including reality orientation, despite their initially primitive psychological organization (e.g., Demos, 1992, 1994). Preadapted for contact and relating, infant and mother almost immediately set up a pattern of interaction in which each expects certain behavior from the other and reacts negatively if this "conversation" is derailed (Stern, 1985; Beebe and Lachmann, 1992). This aversive reaction occurs whether or not the disrupted pattern is related to tension reduction. Moreover, such evidence as is available from older children indicates that they form attachments to figures who play no part in the meeting of their biological needs (Bowlby, 1969).

Beyond the controlled research data, considerable clinical evidence also points to a shift from a drive-based model of motivation to the recognition of autonomously motivated attachment. Many clinicians have been impressed with the intensity of the abused child's attachment to the abuser (e.g., Davies and Frawley, 1992). This clinical phenomenon became the impetus for Fairbairn's (1944) premise that libido is object seeking rather than pleasure seeking, the principle that became the basis of his revision of psychoanalytic metapsychology. Fairbairn, like many clinicians, could not account for the adhesive attachment of the abused child to his caretaker within the framework of the drive–defense model. Further, as Fairbairn and others have pointed out, the greater the abuse, the closer the victim tends to cling to the abuser. This pattern is precisely the opposite of what the tension-reduction model would predict.

Furthermore, if tension reduction is the goal of the psyche, as the drive–defense model presumes, the person who operates on the pleasure principle of immediate tension reduction should be happy. Clinicians who have treated such people know otherwise. Patients who continually seek pleasure tend to need tension discharge addictively and never seem satisfied. For example, sexually promiscuous patients tend to feel chronically dissatisfied as they desperately pursue a seemingly endless series of objects. It is for this reason that Kohut (1977) referred to states of pure pleasure seeking as "breakdown products." In Fairbairn's language, pure pleasure seeking occurs only in a "fractionated ego." Both Fairbairn and Kohut recognized that one finds hedonistically dominated life-styles only in chaotic, disorganized, desperate persons who are continuously seeking something they never seem to find. The clinical evidence is clear that the pleasure principle is a pathological condition rather than a state of contentment.

At this juncture in psychoanalytic history, a wide array of psycho-analytic clinicians has expressed dissatisfaction with the drive model as a framework for understanding their patients. Object relations theorists (especially in England), self psychologists, interpersonal theorists, and relational analysts, although differing in details, have all turned away from the classical drive model toward the concepts of self and other, or object, for guidance in their clinical strategies (e.g., Summers, 1994; for an especially good summary of the British Independent School, see Rayner, 1991). These varied theorists tend to see the drive model either as limited to a restricted number of patients or as inadequate for treating the conflicts and difficulties prevalent in all patients.

In brief, the research and clinical evidence demonstrate over-whelmingly that human motivation does not originate in tension reduction and, perhaps most important, that interpersonal relating cannot be reduced to instinctual gratification. People are autono-mously motivated to relate to others rather than forced to do so in order to achieve tension reduction. This theoretical shift raises the question of what is to replace drives as the basis for human motivation. The autonomous nature of the need for others has led some analysts to believe that the formation of relationships is the most fundamental human motivation. The inherently relational nature of the human condition is the basis for the contemporary psychoanalytic approach broadly labeled relational psychoanalysis. This clinical model is a currently popular reconceptualization of psychoanalysis—one that emphasizes the social nature of the psy-che in opposition to the intrapsychic focus of the ego-psychological model. Although often confused with object relations theories, this model, as seen in our discussion of Dexter, provides a counter-point, on the other side of the psychoanalytic spectrum, from which to grasp the object relations model.

The Relational Model

As we saw in chapter 1, the relational analyst replaces the drive concept with the view that all human activity is inextricably "embedded in a relational matrix" (e.g., Greenberg and Mitchell, 1983; Mitchell, 1988). Theorists of this persuasion exchange the biologism of classical theory for the inherent social nature of the human condition. Although differing in emphasis, relational theorists tend to view units of mind as relational configurations and theoretically change the unit of psychoanalytic investigation from the patient's psychological structure to the "interactional field." From this perspective, any analysis of the mind apart from its interactional patterns is regarded as a remnant of an outmoded "monadic" concept of mind.

Relational analysts are not content to view the mind as an enduring self structure formed from past interactions. Referring to such theories, Mitchell (1988) states, "They tend to retain a stress on the 'self' dimension of the relational matrix. Even though they derive self from interaction, once established, the self is often viewed as existing and operating more or less independently of interactions with others" (p. 9). In his view, concepts such as self-organization, ego functions, homeostatic regulation of affects, developmental needs, and a true or nuclear self possess remnants of the outmoded monadic theory of mind. Mitchell replaces the concept of an enduring self with multiple, overlapping, fluid selves in continual interactional flux.

Theorists of this school contend that relational viewpoint results in a technical shift from the intrapsychic model to a view of the analytic dyad as "codetermined" by the two participants (e.g., Burke, 1992; Mitchell, 1993; Aron, 1996). The analyst can never separate his influence on the patient from what he sees in the patient. Consequently, interpretations are not observations of an observer on an intrapsychic field but a form of interaction (Mitchell, 1991). As we saw in the discussion of the relational view of Dexter, the target of relational psychoanalysis is not the patient but the transactional dyad, the way the analytic couple interrelates.

In their shift from a one-person to a two-person model, relational theorists regard all free associations as reactions to the analyst, and transference is never simply the patient's experience of the analyst but always includes the analyst's participation in the patient's pattern of relating. These theorists conclude that the subjectivities of patient and analyst are inevitably and inextricably "commingled" (Aron, 1990, 1992, 1996). Nonetheless, Aron, a primary proponent of this view, warns against an exclusive interactional approach because making the analyst continually present can interfere with the "analytic space" and needs the patient may have, such as analytic regression. Adopting Winnicott's view that the analyst's interpretations are offerings for the patient "to reshape according to his own needs," Aron (1996, p. 86) warns against the danger of the analyst's subjectivity imposing itself on the process in such a way that the patient's needs become stifled.

Despite the current popularity of the relational perspective, there are several major problematic aspects of this paradigm. First, the commingling of the patient's analytic material with the analyst's participation eliminates the patient's enduring psychological organization from the analytic process. This is so because to regard the patient's psychological organization as a field for psychoanalytic inquiry is to presume the ability to differentiate this organization from the analyst's contribution, and it is just such a separation that relational theory opposes. However, once the patient's enduring psychological organization is removed from the analytic process, the target of analytic inquiry is severely restricted. Relational theorists such as Mitchell state explicitly that analysis must include both the interpersonal and the intrapsychic, but their statement contradicts their fundamental tenet that the unit of analysis is the relational configuration. Inclusion of the intrapsychic is a tacit acknowledgment that interaction is not the analytic unit. To say this another way: If the intrapsychic is a legitimate object of analytic inquiry, all analytic material is not coconstructed. Consequently, one must question the usefulness of a consistent application of relational theory.

However, there is good evidence that relational analysts do not practice in a manner consistent with their theory. For example, Aron (1996) contends that an exclusive inquiry into the analytic interaction can be unresponsive to important needs of the patient, such as the need to be alone or to regress. The implication of Aron's warning is that the analyst should always keep the patient's self and its growth in mind as the overriding aim of the process, with the patient–analyst interaction subserving this goal. If the analyst must be watchful that the imposition of his subjectivity can impede the patient's growth, the analytic unit is the patient's self, not the interaction. Aron treats the needs to regress and to be alone not as coconstructions of the analytic relationship but as needs of the patient. Furthermore, acknowledgment of such needs assumes the analyst's ability to distinguish between the patient's subjectivity and his own. Aron's recognition of patient needs apart from the analytic interaction contradicts the relationalist contentions that the unit of psychoanalytic investigation is the interaction and that the subjectivities of patient and analyst are inevitably commingled. Aron acknowledges in practice what relational analysis does not accept in theory: that the patient has needs that can be separated from the subjectivity of the analyst.

Even more poignant is a brief clinical vignette reported by Mitchell (1997). His patient, George, felt he was unable to decide how much time was reasonable to spend away from his wife and children, so he let his wife decide when he had the right to have an evening out. On those occasions, he tended to stay out longer than his wife liked and drink too much. Mitchell commented to George that George was turning power over to his wife in a way that, Mitchell imagined, might make him angry and resentful, and the defiant "abuse of his privilege" was understandable. The importance of this episode for our purpose is that the intervention is about George's psychological organization, not about the interactional field. This simple clinical example illustrates the fact that Mitchell, in practice, does not consistently carry through with the relational claim that the domain of psychoanalytic therapy is the interactional field and that the subjectivities of patient and analyst are indistinguishably commingled. It is not Mitchell's or Aron's clinical strategy that is at issue but the fact that neither adopts a clinical stance consistent with relational theory. This inconsistency is understandable given the severe restrictions that such a consistent application would place on the therapist. Psychoanalytic therapy simply depends on the analyst's ability to understand the patient's psychological organization as well as the interactional field—a fact acknowledged in practice by both Aron and Mitchell.

Second, the redefinition of mental units as ever-shifting relational configurations necessarily implies discontinuous "multiple selves" rather than self structure—a view that regards continuity as an illusion (Mitchell, 1993, p. 104). Such a conception cannot adequately differentiate pathological fragmentation from the healthy personality. Patients whose behavior is as discontinuous and situation-bound as Mitchell describes—such as Deutsch's (1942) "as-if" personalities—are severely pathological. Mitchell, aware of this possible objection to his view of multiple selves, regards such patients as having "too much discontinuity." Such an explanation is impossible in his model given that he regards continuity as an "illusion."

Dexter had two primary modes of relating: competition and victimization–exploitation. According to the relational view of multiple selves, he should have become a different "self" with the analyst. That his lifelong patterns dominated the analytic relationship despite a new relational environment indicates that the personality does not forge new relational configurations and a new self in response to each new interpersonal context. On the contrary, clinicians are continually struck by the resiliency of patterns despite our best efforts to create a different environment. Indeed, Mitchell (1997, pp. 39–53) emphasizes the prevalence of patients' continually fitting analytic material into frustratingly rigid, preset categories. Such persistent categorization of experience bespeaks continuity of experience rather than the discontinuous, shifting selves of relational theory.

Furthermore, having abandoned a concept of a continuous self, relational theory has difficulty accounting for autonomy and authenticity, both important goals of analysis. Relatedness without a continuous sense of self is environmental enslavement. Discontinuous selves formed in response to new interpersonal contexts cannot account for why we are not all slaves to environmental influence. Autonomy, in the sense of a relative degree of control over how the personality is influenced by biological and environmental pressures, is a goal of psychoanalysis from any perspective.

Blatt and Blass (1990, 1992) have marshalled an abundance of evidence from personality research and theory to support two primary motivational dimensions: self-definition and relatedness. They point out that these motives are mutually dependent: A differentiated sense of self depends on positive interpersonal experiences, and the development of increasingly mature interpersonal relationships is contingent on the solidification of identity. Blatt and Blass (1992) see life as a "complex dialectical process in which progress in each developmental line is essential for progress in the other" (p. 406). They view the major task of life as finding a balance between these two motivations such that both needs are fulfilled. From this viewpoint, relational analysis is an imbalanced theory that overemphasizes the need for relatedness at the expense of autonomy, a differentiated, defined sense of self.

Similar problems apply to the conceptualization of authenticity. As clinicians, we see people who frequently agree behaviorally with others' views that they secretly dispute, or who adjust their behavior to what they feel others expect, even if such behavior has no affective basis (Summers, 1996). Complaints of feeling "fake" and unfulfilled have become so common that authenticity has become the goal of many patients. The problem for relational theory is that authenticity implies motivation consonant with a deep, enduring sense of self. Relational psychoanalysis, by opposing such a concept of self, has not been able to find an adequate way to conceptualize authenticity consistent with its theory. Mitchell's (1991) attempt to provide a relational account of authenticity by shifting the language of the self from spatial to temporal metaphors is inadequate because all experience fits the temporality of the self. Behavior that disregards genuinely felt affects in favor of interpersonal pressures fits the temporality of the self as well as authentic experience.

The response of relational theorists to this type of critique is to assert that their model includes both one-and two-person components, and, therefore, that the critique offered here is not a criticism of relational analysis at all but a misunderstanding of the tension it maintains between both models. This response ignores the fact that relational theory attempts to shift the analytic unit to the interactional field and regard analytic material, including all free associations, as coconstructed. From such a theoretical perspective, there is no room for the patient's individual psyche.

Despite these weaknesses in relational theory, one should not lose sight of its contribution to psychoanalytic thinking. Perceiving the pitfalls of a purely intrapsychic model, relationalists recognize the importance of relationships and interaction both developmentally and clinically. Such a theoretical basis allows relational theorists to emphasize the fact that the analyst often does participate in the pathological configurations from which the patient and he are attempting to extricate themselves. The relational perspective sensitizes the therapist to aspects of his own behavior that may be influencing the patient's experience of the analytic relationship. This inclusion allows for a greater appreciation of the complexity of the analytic interaction and enriches the clinician's understanding of it.

The contributions of relational theory must be incorporated into a model that is theoretically consistent with the concepts of autonomy, authenticity, psychological structure, and the continuous self that lie at the very heart of the psychoanalytic process. To elucidate a model that consists of both types of elements, we must turn to analytic theorists of the relationship between self and object.

The Object Relations Model

Like relational theory, the object relations model adopts the view that the need for relatedness is not reducible to another motive, such as tension reduction. In contradistinction to relational theory, this model views the child as having inborn affective tendencies, in addition to the need for relatedness, that play a crucial role in personality formation. For example, Dexter strove to realize his aggression but found his father to be threatened. Dexter's aggressive striving is not born of interaction, and it cannot be reduced to a need for relatedness. His aggression is an inborn affective capacity that strives for realization and that requires an object for its growth and development. In this case, Dexter's need for a paternal relationship conflicted with the need to exercise his aggressive capacity. This view does not imply that aggression is a drive, but it is one of many inborn capacities that is either facilitated or impeded by the response of the caretaker.

These inborn tendencies allow the child to construe the caretaker's responses in his own way. From these attributions, the child develops ways of categorizing the world—patterns of expectation of the world and of his relationship to it. This pattern of expectation is the meaning the child creates from the engagement of his inborn affective tendencies with environmental responses. The encoded meaning the child takes from the situation includes both affect and object. For example, Dexter construed his father's discomfort with his academic success to mean that his ambition threatened the paternal tie. Ambition took on the meaning of object loss, and this encoded meaning became a significant part of Dexter's expectations and impeded his ambitious strivings. Dexter's connection between success and object loss is a good example of meaning creation: The child constructs meaning from the way he construes the environmental response.

Patterns formed from this encounter between self and object are object relationships. Thus, the created meanings are object relationships consisting of an affective connection between self and object (Kernberg, 1976). These object relationships provide self structure, the guides for ways of being and relating. The meaning of Dexter's aggressive strivings became encoded in his object relationship with his father. For Dexter, his ambition, the desire for success, meant that he threatened a needed other. From the paternal tie he encoded an object relationship in which the object is threatened by his ambitions, and this object relationship became an important component of his self structure.

Dexter struggled to realize his aggressive capacity, but, believing that his success threatened the relationship with his father, he sabotaged his strivings for success. We call this motive to realize the inborn capacities of the self the need for self realization, and it is this need that may operate in concert with or opposition to the need for relatedness. Recall that Dexter entered analysis to find solutions to his pattern of chronic underachievement and periodic outbursts of rage at his wife. Both issues were understood as symptoms of his rage at exploitation by his mother, whom he experienced as engulfing, and his father, whom he felt was threatened by his competitiveness. Neither parental object relationship facilitated his aggression and self-assertion for the achievement of ambitions. He failed in order to defeat the ice princess mother and to please his fragile father, and the aggression that could not be deployed to serve his ambitions became hostile, resulting in outbursts at his wife, who represented his unpleaseable mother. Dexter's rage may be seen as a symptom of the inability of both parental object relationships to make room for his aggression, resulting in the suppression of his ambition and the transformation of his aggression into hostility requiring defense. When his defenses failed, the rage at having to stifle himself led Dexter to hostile outbursts toward his wife. Dexter's sabotage of his potential success is symptomatic of the suppression of authentic strivings due to the inability of either parental object relationship to facilitate his aggressive potential.

Dexter's symptoms of self-defeat and outbursts of rage are not understandable without postulating a motive for the realization of aggressive capacity. If facilitated, inborn aggression can become the capacity for construction and ambition; if blocked, however, it will be indirectly expressed through self-destructive aims. Similarly, Dexter's desire for intimacy, arrested by his anxiety regarding his mother's exploitation, was expressed symptomatically in his outbursts of rage. Both the constructive use of his aggression and his desire for intimacy were authentically experienced desires blocked from direct expression.

Self realization is analogous to both physical and mental development. Just as the body requires and seeks exercise for its full development, and cognition seeks stimulation and challenge for the exercise and growth of cognitive functioning, the self strives for the realization of potential through the expression and development of affects. The unexercised body is unlikely to achieve full development of its inborn capacities, and the unstimulated mind is in danger of atrophy, but both body and mind have an inborn tendency toward development given proper attention and nurturing. Similarly, the self seeks realization, a goal achievable with optimal environmental responsiveness.

From an object relations viewpoint, the inborn movement toward self realization is a postulate imbedded in the very nature of psychoanalysis. All defense interpretation implies the uncovering of a more authentic expression than the defense. In our analysis of relational theory, we saw the problems inherent in any effort to formulate an analytic understanding without a concept of a self motivated to fulfill its potential. The buried potential of this self, experienced as authentic affects and strivings, is the goal of psychoanalytic understanding. This model of development and pathology is supported by major theoretical movements in psychoanalysis and the weight of the evidence from various lines of developmental research. To demonstrate the theoretical and empirical foundations of this object relations model, we consider both types of findings.

Theories of Self and Object

The concept of inborn movement toward self realization is founded on Winnicottian theory, especially as articulated through Bollas, and on Kohut's self psychology. Based on observations and understanding of infancy as well as psychoanalytic findings, these three theorists have made the most important theoretical contributions to the concept of inborn motivation of self realization. For this reason, a brief consideration of their contributions is in order.

Winnicott

In Winnicott's (1963b) view, the infant has an inborn disposition to grow in a particular direction—a maturational process that cannot be altered but that can be either facilitated or impinged upon. As evidence for this viewpoint, Winnicott pointed to the infant's "spontaneous gesture," the reaching, grasping, and natural curiosity that is not reducible to tension reduction or any other motive and that

requires no external stimulation. Winnicott equated the inborn maturational process with the true self, the potential to become the unique
self one most truly is. If the environment is facilitating, the infant or
child can live life from the "inside out"; that is, the growing child
learns that he can rely on his affects and states of excitement to guide
his path through life. Equally significant, because the child is able to
utilize his states of excitement (e.g., aggression and erotism) in
relating to others without undue anxiety, he is able to have full
satisfactory relationships with others that include healthy aggression,
affection, sexual fulfillment, and the ability to play. However, if this
process is impinged upon, the child must utilize defenses: To protect
"the kernel," he focuses on "the shell." The self then becomes split
between a false-self adaptation to the environment and the true self
of inborn potential that lies buried beneath the protective shell, thus
arresting the maturational process.

According to Winnicott (1963a), "the inherited potential of an infant
cannot become an infant unless linked to maternal care" (p. 43). In
Winnicott's view, the mother does not provide meaning to the child;
rather, the child's inborn potential is met by the mother's provisions,
and, out of this mix, the child must create a new experience that
facilitates growth. The "good-enough mother," according to Winnicott, adapts to the child well enough that he can continue the
maturational process. The infant has no single way of being; the
maternal responses must be good enough that the infant can respond
with genuinely experienced affect. When authentic experience and
environmental responsiveness meet, the child is able to make creative
use of the mother to form self structure.

Bollas

Bollas (1987), building on Winnicott's theory of the relationship
between the maturational process and facilitating environment,
points out that the mother is initially experienced not as an other but
as a process of transformation. In Bollas's view, the developing ego
capacities of the infant change his world, and he identifies these

transformations with the object because he depends on maternal availability for the development of his new capacities. The child's inborn potential meets the mother's rules of relating, and, out of this dialogue, the child forms a psychological life expressed as the grammar of his being, his character. Bollas emphasizes that the mother's earliest mode of communicating is her handling of the infant, a process the infant assimilates in rules of being and relating. These rules become the ego grammar of the infant's being, and these processes become the infant's and growing child's character, his personal idiom.

The primary motivator of the psyche, for Bollas (1989), is the need to become oneself, which he calls the "destiny drive." The mother must assist in the expression of the personal idiom by the provision of herself and other objects to serve as elaborators of inborn potential. He acknowledges that nobody can expect to fulfill all of one's inborn potential, but the degree to which the destiny drive is realized is the degree of health in the personality. The elaboration of our unique personal idiom in the world via the use of objects is the most fundamental human motive, and relationships subserve this larger human purpose.

According to Bollas, the very fiber of our being is composed of the dialectic between our potential and the rules for being and relating to which we have been exposed. If parents threaten or are threatened by the child's true self, the child's potential will be buried. Because this potential so immediately meets up with maternal care, its burial includes both the true self and the internalized set of rules for relating and being with which it is associated. All pathology is an expression of some block in the inborn need to elaborate the self.

Kohut

In Kohut's (1977) view, the earliest phase of infancy is prepsychological, but, because the environment responds to the child as though he possessed a self, one can justifiably speak of a self *in statu nascendi*. The infant is born with innate potential, but the early ministrations of the maternal environment, constituting the first selfobject experience, initiate the process that results in the birth of the self. The necessary selectivity of this responsiveness channels the child's innate givens into a "nuclear self," and the realization of its "nuclear program" rests with the self–selfobject relationship. Because the self is formed by the absorption of parental objects into its very fabric, once the selfobject functions have been internalized, they can no longer be differentiated from the self. "Transmuting internalization" blends what was a distinguishable object into the self.

In Kohut's view, if selfobjects are appropriately responsive, the self will be strong, vital, and harmonious, and life will be meaningful and fulfilling. However, if selfobjects fail, self development is arrested, resulting in a weakened, vulnerable self. In this situation, natural affection and assertion become distorted into untamed drive manifestations, such as lust and hostility, symptoms of a breakdown in the functioning of the self. "Drivenness" reflects the distortions of a weakened self, Kohut reasons, rather than a "natural state" that has been uncovered by defensive breakdown.

A self-psychological formulation of Dexter's dynamics would emphasize the failure of selfobject responsiveness to promote his healthy ambitions and self-assertive strivings, a view that fits well with the formulation advanced here that Dexter's early object relationships did not sustain his aggressive efforts to achieve goals.

Despite significant shifts in self-psychological theory since Kohut, the principle that the self is formed from inborn needs and the internalization of parental functions is consistent in self psychology from Kohut's work to its current-day proponents. Fosshage (1992) pointed out that the concepts of the nuclear self and the self–selfobject relationship make self psychology a theory of innate potential as shaped by early relationships. Such a view is in concert with the Winnicottian tradition, most notably as elaborated by Bollas, that development is a product of the maturational process of innate potential and environmental facilitation. Winnicott's "environmental mother," who meets the needs of the maturational process, is barely distinguishable from the self psychologist's selfobject functions. Kohut's nuclear self describes the same phenomenon as Winnicott's concept of the true self that has an inborn maturational unfolding but that requires facilitation by an object to realize its potential.

The major conceptual difference between Winnicott's view of object relations and self psychology lies in the way the object becomes part of the self. Transmuting internalization implies a passive "taking in" that includes no conceptualization of the child's creative use of the object. The meaning of the experience appears to be defined by the object; transmuting internalization is a concept of received, rather than created, meaning. Winnicott's concepts of the transitional object and object usage and Bollas's expansion of them are concepts of the child's creation of meaning out of the givens of self and object. The Winnicottian conceptualization fits the object relations model advocated here due to its emphasis on the creative relationship between self and object. The passive language of Kohutian thought cannot account for why we are not all replicas of parental responses. The model of creative production from the child's innate potential and parental responsiveness explains why there is no clear, easy predictability from the parental environment to the child's later behavior despite the powerful importance of parental responsiveness.

Winnicott, Bollas, and Kohut, with slightly different emphases, have made important theoretical contributions to the model of self development composed of a creative combination of inborn potential and environmental response. This model, being developmental, is not based solely on the speculations of analysts using clinical data. We now have an abundance of evidence from developmental research that supports the primary postulates of this type of psychoanalytic thinking. We now turn to a consideration of these data on infant and child development to substantiate the empirical basis of this model of development.

Developmental Research

There is now an abundance of evidence (which did not exist when Winnicott was writing) that indicates that the infant is not only

inherently active but also born with an impressive array of competencies that tend toward development (Demos, 1992, 1994). Close
observation of neonates shows that, from the first days of life, they
spend at least some time in quiet, alert states and playful exploration,
the duration of which increases to about six hours by one year of age.
Neonates actively seek stimuli within the first few days, actively
tracking visual phenomena, even interrupting feeding to do so
(White, 1963; Stern, 1985). Tomkins (1962, 1963) has shown that
the infant is born with a full range of human emotions: interest,
enjoyment, surprise, distress, anger, fear, disgust, and shame. In
addition, the neonate has the ability to recognize stimulus patterns,
invariance in patterns, contingencies between action and the environment, the difference between internal and external, perceptual
differences, and light–dark contrasts (Demos, 1992, 1994). One
example of the capabilities of the neonate comes from an experiment
by DeCasper and Carstens (1981), who found that infants learned to
increase their sucking pauses in order to turn on a recording of a
female voice. When the contingency was removed, the infants
showed visible signs of upset. This single experiment demonstrates
that newborns can detect contingencies, show emotion (as evidenced
by interest in the stimulus), plan (as shown by their ability to repeat
the event), have the capacity for both voluntary motor control and
memory, and possess the ability to coordinate all these activities. In
brief, infants are not passive; they can and do actively influence what
happens to them.

The capacity to organize various capabilities to bring about a
desired goal exists from birth, although the ability to execute is
restricted by physical limitations (Demos, 1992). The infant will
learn to do voluntarily what he does involuntarily. There is evidence
to suggest that what appears to be random movement is actually
organized effort to reach and grasp objects that is unsuccessful due
to muscle weakness (e.g., Bower, 1977). Tomkins (1978) points out
that infants from the first days of life will replace the involuntary
sucking response with voluntary sucking when there is no biological
need to do so, implying an attitude of "I would rather do it myself!"
Tomkins points out that, because this autoimitation is not modeled

for the child, the child must generate both the idea and the affective interest as well as guide the performance of the activity by himself. Tomkins concludes that the child's autosimulation "represents an extraordinary creative invention . . . amplified by excitement in the possibility of improving a good actual scene by doing something oneself. That is why I have argued that we have evolved to be born as a human being who will, with a very high probability, very early attempt and succeed in becoming a person" (p. 215). Research on early development leads to the conclusion that the infant is born not only with an impressive array of cognitive and emotional capabilities but also with the organizational and creative ability to make use of these inborn capacities to form a self. Moreover, it appears that the infant makes use of these capacities to become a self from the earliest days of life.

As the baby develops and becomes a toddler, this motive to do for himself is even more evident. Piaget's (1952) observations showed that three-month-olds will repeat behavior for no purpose other than to have an effect on the environment. Infants of this age spend "playtime" and are motivated to bring activities to completion without the contingency of other rewards (White, 1963). Even more poignantly, toddlers will routinely delay biological gratification to perform independent tasks, such as preferring to use a spoon even though it makes feeding go more slowly. This evidence demonstrates that the child has an autonomous need to do for himself and affect the environment. Although ego psychologists have conceptualized this motive as "independent ego energies" (White, 1963) or an instinct for mastery (Hendrick, 1942, 1943), such language makes sense only within the context of the primacy of drive motivation, a view that has been repudiated. The desire "to do and learn to do" has no connection to the biologically rooted psychoanalytic defini-tion of drive. It makes more sense to conceptualize a motive to utilize inborn functions and capacities for the purpose of having an impact on the environment. The data support the effectance motivation conceptualized by White (1963) and Greenberg (1991).

The developmental data provide evidence for Winnicott's concept of an inborn maturational process that seeks to realize its potential.

Beginning with the "spontaneous gesture" and continuing with the transformation of involuntary reflexes into voluntary intent, the infant strives to utilize and develop his capacities. Whether one conceptualizes this motive as a maturational process in Winnicott's terms, as the "destiny drive" a la Bollas, or as the "nuclear program of the self" in the language of self psychology, the evidence for an inborn motive to become oneself is convincing. Although relational theorists are in theoretical disagreement with the existence of such a motive, the evidence for it is abundant. In brief, it is safe to conclude that developmental research has substantiated a basic tenet of object relations theory—that the child is motivated to realize his potential and thereby become who he is.

Although inborn potential unfolds in a maturational process, the realization of inborn capacities depends on the caretaker's ability to facilitate this process. For example, for the infant to develop a sense of agency, the caretaker must perform two key functions (Demos, 1992, 1994). First, interventions must be timed properly if distress is to be relieved. If the infant is disturbed and the caretaker moves too quickly to supply comfort, the child is given a solution before awareness of a problem. On the other hand, if the caretaker is unresponsive, the child will become overwhelmed with distress, the affect will become punishing, and the infant, unable to prevent the increased pain and intensity by himself, will feel helpless and eventually shut down. In the latter case, the infant experiences the problem but without the belief that he can do anything about it. There appears to be an "optimal zone of affective experience . . . that allows the infant enough psychological space to feel an internal need, to become an active participant in trying to address the need, and therefore to be able to relate subsequent events . . . both to the internal need state and to the plans and efforts to remedy it" (Demos, 1992, p. 220).

Second, the content of the caretaker's responses is crucial. If the infant is frustrated by not being able to reach a toy, and the caretaker responds by comforting the child as though he were tired or hungry, the child's sense of agency is not facilitated. Only if the child is helped to achieve his goal will his sense of agency be enhanced.

These developmental findings show that the infant's distress cannot be separated from the caretaker's response to it. An inadequate response results in an experience of overwhelming pain connected to a neglectful, excessively responsive, or misguided object. Similarly, a helpful response to stress will lead to a positive object experience as part of the transformation of distress into a positive experience. In short, with the caretaker's role being so critical to the outcome of the child's affect, the object becomes inseparable from the affective experience.

The crucial role of the parenting figure is also demonstrated by the work of Bowlby and his colleagues (Bowlby, 1969, 1988; Ainsworth et al., 1978) showing that the security of the infant's attachment to the mother is the critical factor in the child's later behavior. Bowlby and his colleagues found three infant patterns: secure attachment to the mother, insecure attachment, and avoidance. Children who fit the first pattern were happiest, showed least distress, and were best able to explore the world in the knowledge they will be comforted and nourished. The key to this pattern was parental emotional availability with a push toward autonomy (e.g., Ainsworth et al., 1978). Bowlby showed that these patterns continued throughout life in the form of a "working model" of the mother. Thus, Bowlby's findings, like those of Demos, are that the early maternal relationship becomes integrated into the child's experience of the world and that this relationship is optimal when it includes availability and space for the development of autonomy.

Tomkins (1978), emphasizing the importance of affect, believed that the basic unit of the infant's experience is the "scene," consisting of an affect and object. Infants utilize their generalizing capabilities to connect scenes with similar affects. As amplifiers of experience, affects are the basic motivators of psychic organization. Tomkins calls the connecting of scenes "psychic magnification" because meaning is magnified by connection with other scenes. Families of scenes become linked, enhancing magnification into "scripts"—rules for ordering, producing, and controlling groups of scenes with specific positive or negative affects. Two aspects of Tomkins's theory are central to the present purpose. First, all of the child's generalizations are based on the scene—affect and object. Because all psychological experience includes the object, the magnification of experience involves magnification of the experience of the object. Second, scripts are generated either by analogic thinking or by searching for invariants. In either case, scripts are created via a transposition of affect between seemingly different scenes. Script creation by analogue explains why observably remote scenes can become powerfully connected.

Expansion by perceived invariants requires both repetition of at least some aspects of the scene and some new elements. Although a certain degree of similarity is necessary, psychological magnification occurs best when new elements are introduced, whereas identical repetition of scenes leads to habituation, which dulls rather than magnifies.

Tomkins's view of affect spreading is supported by the affect–memory–metaphor connection described by Modell (1996). Relying on Edelman's theory of memory as a potential to refind the category of which the remembered event is a member, Modell points out that metaphor is the means by which the current unfamiliar situation is connected to previous experience. Modell (1996) writes, "Affective memories are encoded as potential categories[;] we remember categories of experience which are evoked by metaphoric correspondence with current perceptual inputs" (p. 4). Modell, employing Edelman's theory of memory, concludes that affects are spread by metaphor—a position virtually identical with Tomkins's concept of affective spreading by analogy.

If the infant is exposed to an optimal amount of redundancy and variation, he learns the distinction between a thing and its background and eventually is able to differentiate the thing from all its contexts (Demos, 1992). The formation of the maternal image is a specific instance of this "decontextualization of knowledge and experience." The child constructs a multifaceted single image of mother so that, if she is distracted or unresponsive, the infant is able to react as though "all is fine." With sufficiently consistent experience, the child generalizes an image of a helpful mother, which he then utilizes in managing distress (Stern, 1985; Bowlby, 1988).

Bowlby called this image the "working model of the mother." Stern believes that the experimental data support the notion that the preverbal infant generalizes and averages his experiences into "representations of interactions that are generalized" (RIGs), which guide his interpersonal navigation. By activating his RIGs, the infant reexperiences ways of being with a self-regulating other. Episodic memory using RIGs organizes and integrates a unique and unitary self as well as a single invariant other.

According to the best developmental data, it would be a mistake to presume that the child "internalizes" only an image of a parenting figure. Studies of infant–mother interactions show that mother and infant adjust their behavior to each other very early in their relationship, as each brings endogenous processes to their interaction (Beebe and Stern, 1977; Beebe, 1986; Beebe and Lachmann, 1988a, b, 1992). Although each partner influences the other, the mother's influence on the infant is clearly greater. Careful studies of mother–child interaction conducted by Beebe and her colleagues show that the couple matches the affective direction of facial mirroring and the timing of interactions. This matching of affective direction and interpersonal timing is an "early infant–mother dialogue" in which the partners share affects; that is, mother and infant are bonded by the emotional sharing that results from their interpersonal matching.

The dyad forms certain predictable ways of relating, so that each child–mother relationship forms its own rules for the way the couple relates. The child stores experiences matched in timing and affect and expects these rules to be followed by three months; if the mother acts in some discrepant manner, the child reacts negatively to the violation of expectations (Beebe, Jaffe, and Lachmann, 1992). For example, in one experiment, mothers were made to mismatch their timing and affects, and the infant's play was disrupted (Stern, 1985). Even more tellingly, the child's cognition and attachment at one and two years of age are not well predicted from the infant's or mother's behavior alone in the first six months but are highly predictable from the interaction between infant and mother (Beebe and Lachmann, 1992). This fact demonstrates that the child absorbs not just the maternal image but the relationship between himself and his mother.

It is clear that the infant encodes the distinctive features of his maternal interaction long before the symbolic capacity develops.

Despite the importance of matching affect and timing, critically important is the finding that matching can be excessive (Beebe, Jaffe, and Lachmann, 1992; Beebe, 1995). The results of Beebe's very detailed studies of mother–infant matching show that the highest and lowest matched mother–infant pairs have the most insecure babies, whereas secure babies tend to be in the midrange of vocal matching with their mothers. Because the most successful couples demonstrated both affective and timing matching as well as allowance for discontinuity and a variable range of pattern matching, it appears that excessive coordination does not provide the child with sufficient diversity. Beebe concludes from these findings that the optimal developmental process is not mutual regulation but an optimal combination of mutual regulation and self-regulation, and mutual regulation includes a variety of matching patterns. These findings are in striking agreement with both Bowlby's and Demos's conclusion that healthy development requires an optimal zone of affective responsiveness.

Beebe and Lachmann (1988a, 1992) argue convincingly that the interactional structures encoded by the infant are the central organizers of the personality. This creation is then used by the child to guide later cognition and interpersonal relating. The child creates flexible, productive ways of relating if provided with proper environmental regulation and given the space to create.

In summary, developmental research makes clear that the child (a) comes into the world with innate potential to become a self that he is motivated to realize, (b) needs an object to achieve his project, (c) requires psychological space to create new meaning, (d) makes creative use of the object for this purpose, and (e) uses affects as the primary bonds with objects and amplifies and magnifies them to create psychological organization. There is abundant evidence that the infant and growing child are powerfully motivated to achieve self realization and inherently drawn to the object relationships that will naturally facilitate the achievement of this goal. The weight of the developmental evidence indicates that object relationships are the

key factor in the formation of psychological organization and therefore in the determination of the success of the child's project to create
a self. This conclusion supports the object relations view, advocated
by Winnicott, Bollas, and Kohut, that people are born with two
motives: self realization and the formation of object relationships.

Self Development and the Role of the Object

These findings shed considerable light on the relationship among
the neonate's inborn capacities, their maturation, and the role of
the caretaker. It is clear that the development of the self is not
interpersonally determined, as argued by relational theorists, and
does not grow from the internalization of functions (e.g., affect
regulation) that are "taken in" by the child, as implied by self
psychology. Rather, the child is born with a range of affects and
capacities, and the caretaker's role is to facilitate their development
with a combination of responsiveness and allowance for individual
experience. Maternal empathy, the mother's intuitive recognition
of optimal responsiveness, provides not "functions" but the opportunity for the creation of meaning. When the mother is able to
allow the child to experience his affect and respond to it, the child
is able to create the meaning he needs.

   To use affect regulation as an example, the child is born with
negative affects that provide him with an opportunity to learn to
regulate these states and thereby to achieve a sense of agency. As we
have seen, the development of this capacity depends on the caretaker's ability to provide an optimal affective zone that will allow the
negative affect and help the child overcome it. The child can learn to
utilize the caretaker's response to manage negative affect, thereby
enhancing his sense of agency, but the child has not taken in the
caretaker's function of providing an optimal affective zone. Rather,
he has made use of it to continue on his developmental path. In
Winnicottian terms, the mother has made herself available as a usable
object, and the child has taken advantage of the opportunity to use
the mother's responsiveness to grow.

Critical to the maternal role is the provision of psychological space for the child to experience affects and develop capacities. The infant and growing child need the opportunity to experience affects and develop capacities so that they can learn to do voluntarily what had been innately reflexive. Self psychology overemphasizes "in-tunement" and affective matching, whereas ego psychology, including contemporary structural analysis, does not sufficiently recognize its importance. The evidence is clear that the child needs psychological space (rather than perfect in-tunement) to develop capacities. If empathy is to be conceptualized as the cardinal maternal virtue, then the concept of empathy must include the recognition of the child's need for experience without affective in-tunement.

Stern's RIGs, Bowlby's "working model," and Tomkins's scripts and their magnification are all creative productions composed from mother–child interaction. Demos shows that the child's inherent organizational behavior includes the creation of plans. Similarly, Beebe and Lachmann's (1988a, b, 1992) meticulous studies of child–mother interaction demonstrate that the child creates self and object representations to guide future behavior. Tomkins's work is even more telling because scriptwriting, the psychic magnification of experience by analogy, is a creative act, the content of which is not predictable.

These findings and conceptualizations substantiate Winnicott's view that in normal development the mother's role is to facilitate the child's maturational process, the true self, and that the child makes creative use of the mother's offerings to realize this innate potential. These same results may be taken to confirm the self-psychological concept of a nuclear program of the self if that concept is broadened beyond Kohut's bipolar self of ambitions and ideals, an expansion advocated by some contemporary self psychologists (e.g., Stolorow, Brandchaft, and Atwood, 1987; Bacal and Newman, 1990). Demos's "zone of optimal affective engagement" is a virtual paraphrase of the self-psychological concept of "optimal responsiveness," a crucial selfobject function that allows the continuance of the nuclear program of the self by helping the child manage negative affective states. Although affect regulation is a key selfobject function, rather than internalizing such a function, the child is able to use the mother to facilitate his growing capacity for distress relief.

The object is embedded in the experience but in a way unique to the infant's use of the object. The mother does not provide meaning to the child; rather, the child utilizes the mother's offerings in order to create meaning (Demos, 1994). The mother's ability to provide the child with this opportunity defines Winnicott's concept of good-enough mothering. The distinction between received and created meaning is the difference between Kohut's and Winnicott's otherwise similar theories of how the child uses the parent. The weight of the evidence indicates that Winnicott's concept of object usage captures the relationship between the child's growing self and the parental object better than Kohut's concept of transmuting internalization. Bollas's view of the self as a unique idiom that seeks expression and elaboration is supported by the finding that infants are inherently motivated to utilize their capacities to do for themselves. Also, Bollas's contention that the idiom of the self is fashioned from innate potential and the process of care is sustained by the findings of developmental research.

The developmental evidence shows that the child is motivated to do for himself to the point that he will choose to perform activities alone that he began doing with others. Relational theory, as I have argued, does not do justice to the child's determination to use his capacities and organize his experience. Greenberg (1991) properly criticized relational analysis for not recognizing that the need for autonomy is as important as the need for relatedness. However, Greenberg's alternative, the dual needs for safety and effectance, albeit a step in the right direction, is too narrow. Beyond seeking effectance, the infant works hard to develop all his inborn capacities, make sense of the world, and amplify, magnify, and organize his experience.

Object relations theories and developmental research dovetail in their view of the infant and growing child as motivated to form object relationships and use them for self realization. As experiences are magnified from scenes to scripts to psychological organization, the corresponding objects become woven into the fabric of the self. In this way, the motives to realize the self and relate to others result in a self structure composed of object relationships. In the object relations model advanced here, these motives replace the drives as the foundation of human striving. How does such a view of human motivation account for the drives?

Drive Theory: A Reprise

It is not that the drives are ignored or rendered unimportant in object relations theories, but rather that they subserve the more primary motives toward self realization and the formation of object relationships. There is no prejudicial assumption here that the biological nature of drives makes them primary to the two fundamental human motivators of object connections and self realization. Furthermore, the evidence indicates that, of the two drives postulated by psychoanalytic theory, only sexuality is a biological urge that motivates behavior for no purpose other than its own gratification. This standard definition of drive includes sexuality along with other biological needs such as hunger and thirst, but it does not fit aggression.

Aggression

Anger, the first aggressive expression, is an inborn affect and, like the other affects, is a capacity that exists from birth and that is evoked by environmental triggers (Tomkins, 1978). Parens (1979), in the most in-depth and widely cited study of the development of aggression in childhood, concluded that aggression is inborn and inherently nondestructive. Ascribing the importance of aggression to motivating play and exploration, Parens found that its purpose is mastery of the environment. Rather than an inherently destructive drive, aggression appears to be an adaptive response, critical to both the growth of the self and its protection and security. In the normal situation, as aggression is employed to these ends, it serves the purpose of self realization.

Parens (1979) found that there is a clear distinction among forms of aggression. Spontaneous, inborn aggression is not hostile and possesses no destructive intent but serves the adaptive purpose of learning about and controlling the environment. If all goes well, this form of aggression, which first appears in almost all infants between eight and 16 weeks, eventually leads to self-assertiveness. When, inevitably, the environment resists the child's unfettered exploration, most poignantly via peer conflict, or there is excessive delay in achieving a goal, the child experiences displeasure, leading to hostile aggression. Parens found that this form of aggression is a reaction to negative experience, most typically threat and endangerment. When the source of displeasure is removed, the hostile aggression stops. For example, if the toddler is busy at play, and a rival reaches for his toy, the child will respond aggressively to the intruder, intending to cause him to back off. If the response is successful, the hostile aggression, having achieved its purpose, abates, thereby allowing the child to resume play, continuing the imaginative exploration of the world that is needed for enrichment and growth.

If, on the other hand, negative experience is not typically removed by environmental provision, it becomes repetitive, and hostile aggression may grow into an automatic and chronic pattern. In this situation, aggression, no longer serving the purpose of learning and mastery, becomes deflected to the continual discharge of hostility. Now imbued with destructive intent, aggression may be excessively prohibited, as by repression, splitting, or denial, and a critical resource for self development will be lost, thus impairing the child's ability to realize his potential. Even more poignantly, when the defense fails, aggression tends to burst forth in a seemingly uncontrolled, disorganized fashion. Outbursts of rage may then appear to be "impulses," but such eruptions are a product of repression or other defense against aggression rather than a breaking through of impulses that have failed to be sufficiently repressed. Under these circumstances, aggression looks like a drive with inherent hostile intent, but, in fact, the hostility is a transformation of the original nondestructive aggression. Furthermore, if there is excessive delay in the expression of hostile destructiveness, its eventual discharge will be relieving, result-ing in the pleasurable destructiveness of teasing, taunting, and sadism.

Parens's (1979) results indicated that children whose distress was not well responded to felt helpless, with no way to relieve the source of pain. Their hostility distanced them from others and thereby protected them from repeated painful, helpless experiences. The chronic, automatic hostility of these children served the critical function of protecting vulnerability. This deflection of aggression from its purpose of self-assertion to the defense of the vulnerable self defines pathological aggression and is precisely the function of hostility described by Kohut. Parens concluded that the automaticity of hostile aggression and the gratification it provides are not inborn but a function of unresponsive object relationships and bear the history of those relationships.

The assumption that aggression is inherently destructive is made not only by drive-based theorists such as Freud, the Kleinians, and Kernberg but also by such nondrive authors as Winnicott, Fairbairn, and even Mitchell. All these theoreticians equate the hostile intent of pathological aggression with normal aggression, failing to distinguish the infant's natural joy in aggression from hatred. Parens's findings support Kohut's concept that assertiveness is inborn, but hatred is a pathological breakdown in response to threats to the self. However, Parens's findings dispute the Kleinian assumption, adopted by Win-nicott and Kernberg, of innate hatred and Mitchell's assertion of a "natural joy" in hatred. Fairbairn and Guntrip have been supported by Parens's work in their view of hostility as a reaction to threat but not in their denial of inborn aggression.

Aggression may be seen as prototypical of inborn capacities. Although having a natural trajectory, aggression requires an object to achieve its purpose. If derailed by unfavorable responsiveness, aggression becomes deflected from its original goal of environmental exploration and mastery to serve other, self-protective aims. We label these deflected purposes pathological precisely because they no longer serve their original purpose, although they leave signs of this deflection in the form of symptoms. For example, Dexter was unable to use his aggression to pursue his ambitions assertively because he feared loss of his father's love and engulfment by his mother. In response to these object-induced anxieties, he buried his aggressive pursuits and defeated his efforts to achieve. His self-defeat and outbursts of rage toward his wife belied the deflection of his aggression from its path toward self-assertion. These two primary symptoms were his ways of signaling to himself and others that his aggression was repressed.

Sexuality

Unlike aggression, sexual desire possesses a biological cycle characteristic of drives. However, to infer that this biological component should be given psychological primacy is to commit the fallacy of "biologism," the prejudice that biology is primary, as though physiological states must be the ultimate meaning of human experience. As we have seen, the motive to attach to objects and utilize capacities is inborn and irreducible to other urges, such as drives. Sexuality, as the most intimate form of bodily contact, can be a powerful and enriching expression of object relatedness. This self-expansion function of sexuality will be achieved only if sexual intimacy is experienced not as impersonal drive discharge but as a form of human relatedness. Sexuality serving only as a tension discharge function tends to be empty and unsatisfying—a fact that indicates that meaningful sexual experience cannot be reduced to drive gratification. Given that people achieve self realization through object contact, sexuality, as the most intimate and enriching form of such contact, has the potential to promote the growth of the self.

The classical drive theory of sexuality does not sufficiently appreciate the fact that all sexuality has meaning, however disturbed it may be. The myth of the drive theory of sexuality is that there is a "natural" form of human sexuality, untamed and without meaning, to which social meaning later becomes attached due to the necessity of restricting sexual impulsivity. Even if one grants for the moment that there are states of pure sexual-tension discharge, they are found only in severely pathological conditions. To liken such pathological states to natural sexuality is a reductionistic equation of sexuality with pathological forms of its expression.

Several studies have demonstrated that human sexuality has a critical function in the establishment and maintenance of gender identity and derives its meaning from this purpose. Simon and Gagnon (1973) demonstrated that there is no aspect of human sexuality that is without social meaning. Employing the concept of "scripts" in a fashion similar to that of Tomkins, they show that all aspects of sexuality involve encoded meanings that organize sexual experiences and, perhaps most important, define the way meaning from nonsexual aspects of life will gain expression in sexual behavior. Simon and Gagnon's conclusion reverses drive theory: Social roles are not vehicles for the expression of sexuality, but sexuality is one critical way in which social roles gain expression.

Person (1980), in her discussion of the origins of sexual identity, points out that early sensual experiences are inextricably linked to early parental relationships, so that sexuality is always an expression of these object relationships. Similarly, Stoller (1985) points out that, because attitude toward the genitals is a core component of identity, sexuality promotes and sustains gender identity. From our viewpoint, it should be emphasized that sexuality not only is key to gender identity but is the most intimate form of the human need for relatedness. Consequently, the early object relationships that form the self will be expressed and communicated through sexual behavior, and this most intimate form of human relatedness is the realization of one of the self's most passionate and powerful capacities.

When sexuality is separated from relatedness, it is reduced to tension release only and loses its capacity to promote self realization. For example, if sensuality and bodily intimacy are not allowed in early caretaking relationships, sexual contact may take on the meaning of illicit, "dirty" contact that must not "soil" positive, tender relationships. In this situation, sex partners must be continually changed to avoid interpersonal closeness, and significant relationships cannot become sexual. Patients of this type use sexuality only for tension discharge but report very little gratification from the experience. In such situations, one observes pleasure seeking done for its own sake, which Fairbairn (1944) identified as a pathological breakdown called ego fractionation and which Kohut (1977) regarded as a breakdown product of a weakened self. In brief, the health or pathology of sexuality is determined not by its physiological function but by its ability to express intimacy and thereby realize a primary potential of the self.

The importance of object relatedness in sexual gratification is acknowledged even by some classical analysts. For example, Bach (1995) refers to sexuality in which the other is only an instrument of physiological gratification as "the language of perversion," to which he opposes "the language of love," in which the other is a whole object. According to Bach, when sexual experience is an expression of bodily intimacy with a loved object, it becomes a means of self realization, but, when sexuality is not allowed to gain expression in this way, it becomes diverted to pure tension relief and serves a pathological purpose. Thus, Bach is implicitly accepting that sexuality subserves the larger motives of human relatedness and self realization.

Both aggression and sexuality are inborn capacities that can serve the purpose of self realization given proper facilitation or that can be diverted to pathological ends if deflected from their natural trajectories. Aggression can become a means for the realization of ambition and the achievement of goals, and sexuality has the capability of becoming the most intimate form of human related-ness. If environmental responsiveness facilitates their develop-ment, these capacities become powerful means for self realization.

Conclusion

The object relations model described in this chapter sees the devel-opment of the self as a creative outcome borne of the inborn maturational process and relationships to objects. Strongly support-ed by developmental research evidence from a variety of traditions, this alternative to the ego-psychological and relational models views psychic structure as the outcome of a complex, creative relationship between the givens of inborn dispositions and environmental responsiveness. Meaning, the generalized categories created from these interactions, is encoded in the form of object relationships, connections between self and object, that guide navigation through the world.

From this viewpoint, the needs for self realization and relatedness are the motivational bases of personality development. This theory of the duality of human motivation is heir to a long but often neglected tradition in psychoanalytic theory. Freud (1915a) believed that the human psyche is subject to conflict between the poles of three antinomies: pleasure–pain, activity–passivity, and self–object. Early psychoanalysis emphasized the pleasure–pain dimension, ego psychology shifted emphasis to the relative activity–passivity of the psyche, and object relations theory may be regarded as recognizing the importance of the third psychoanalytic antinomy: self–object. Rank (1929), Fairbairn (1952), and Bakan (1966), a lesser known but significant analytic theorist, all see the human condition as a tension between the need for autonomous functioning of the self and relatedness, the need for connection with others. Greenberg's (1991) theory of the dual needs for safety and effectance is a more contemporary statement of a similar theme. All these theorists, although differing in terminology and slightly in emphasis, see inherent opposition between needs that draw toward others and needs of the self.

In this model, the needs of the self are not conceptualized as a particular type of experience, such as autonomy or agency. The concept of self realization embraces the inherent movement toward the development of a broad array of psychological capacities, the combination of which is different in each individual. This motive is fueled by inborn affects and the capacity to magnify them into categories of experience. Psychic well-being is a function of the degree to which the individual is able to realize inborn potential, and the development of these capacities is, in turn, dependent on the relationship to the object.

The current theory of the dual motivation for relatedness and self realization differs from previous versions of this model in one fundamental respect. Whereas the other variants of duality theory see inherent conflict between the two motivations, the theory proposed here views relatedness and self realization as mutually necessary and enhancing motivations rather than as inherently conflictual. The optimally responsive object does not conflict with, but promotes, self realization; conversely, the process of self realization does not oppose, but requires, the formation of object relationships to achieve its end. An abundance of research evidence supports this mutually beneficial relationship between the realization of self capacities and the need for relatedness (Blatt and Blass, 1992).

However, if the environment does not respond to the developing child within the optimal zone of affective engagement, the requirements of object contact divert the self from the realization of capacities, and object relationships and self development are at cross-purposes. We have seen an example of this conflict in our discussion of Dexter, whose aggressive strivings could not be realized for fear of threat to the paternal bond. This conflict between self realization and object contact, unless corrected by later development, derails the trajectory of self potential. This principle is the basis for an object relations theory of psychopathology, and it is to this implication of the model that we now turn.

Chapter 3

The Fate of the Buried Self

As we have seen, the child whose affects and interests are not responded to will bury her genuine experience, but authentic modes of being and relating will continue to seek indirect modes of expression which we call symptoms. This viewpoint puts us in a position to define both a general object relations concept of pathology and specific pathological categories. In this chapter we delineate the model of pathology more fully by presenting a more specific account of the failed parental response, the child's reaction, and symptomatic outcome.

The Caretaker

We may begin to define the model by appreciating the results of the developmental research reviewed in the previous chapter. The Beebe, Demos, and Bowlby research findings reviewed in the previous chapter provide a strong evidential basis, across research traditions, for the view that failure of the caretaker's responsiveness to the child's affects impedes the development of the self. The failure may be from neglect (a lack of reaction that does not give the child the necessary aid to develop her potential) or intrusion (a stifling pattern that does not allow the child the opportunity to develop a sense of agency). In either situation, the caretaker lacks appreciation for the child's experience and vitiates the child's belief that she can have an impact on it.

This model is not based solely on the findings of developmental research. Clinicians have reported considerable anecdotal evidence that in childhood the primary caretaker of characterologically disturbed patients was typically unable to provide a stable, positive relationship with the patient (e.g., Winnicott, 1945, 1963b; Fairbairn, 1954; Boyer and Giovacchini, 1967; Kohut, 1971; Giovacchini, 1973; Kernberg, 1976, 1984; Goldberg, 1978; Adler, 1985). Their reports include a variety of unresponsive patterns, such as overt physical and sexual abuse, emotional unavailability, abandonment, sadistic teasing, sexual provocation, hostile rejection, and chronic expressions of disapproval and criticism.

All these forms of parental injury lack both recognition of the child's experience and a helpful response to painful states. Under conditions of disturbance, the parental role is to repair the disturbance by providing the opportunity for a different, nontraumatic meaning to the event. When the child cries after losing a game, the parental arm around the child adds a positive component that takes some of the sting out of the loss, not by denying the distress but by adding a positive connection to the loneliness of the hurt. Or the parent may add a perspective that the child is unable to see at the moment—such as pointing out that the child wins sometimes and that she will always "win some and lose some." Either response conveys recognition of the child's feelings and the belief that the negative event can be overcome—that is, that the child is not helpless to ameliorate her feelings. The transformative parental response is a recognition of the negative side of the experience and the inclusion of this new dimension.

This model implies that the helpful parental response is not best conceptualized as the internalization of parental soothing, the view favored by self psychology (Kohut, 1977, 1984). In most situations, when the parental response is helpful, the child does not do what the parent does but infers from the parental response that the child can be effective in coping with untoward experiences and analogizes this feeling to other situations. Only in unusually disturbing instances do children say to themselves what the parents once said to them, such as, "It will be all right, it will feel better."

The inclusion of the parental viewpoint into the child's experience has significant implications for the child's view of the other. That the parent does not only attune to the child's experience but offers something new shows the child that the mother is not simply an object of her experience but is an other with a separate center of initiative and feeling. "Overattunement" impedes the child's movement toward the recognition of the other as other (Benjamin, 1995). Benjamin has pointed out that the child's experience of the parent who may not see, understand, or be otherwise attuned, if not excessive, is valuable because it shows the child that the parent has a mind different from hers. The mother's leaving does not just help the child separate, it demonstrates that the mother is a separate person and abets the child's sense of intersubjectivity. Benjamin's work is invaluable, but another factor must be added: Positive, helpful parental responses to distress also demonstrate the parent's difference by providing a positive addition to the child's negative experience. Consequently, this type of parental responsiveness also contributes significantly to the development of the child's appreciation of the other as a separate center of subjectivity.

The Child's Response

If the caretaker is unresponsive, the child will attempt to form the relationship according to the needs of the caretaker. A wide variety of defenses is possible, each of which diverts the personality from authentic experience. Because attachments are necessary for survival, the child typically searches for a way to maintain some type of connection, albeit with defensive protection. As the purpose of this defensive construction is to protect against authentic relatedness, the transitional space necessary for the creative play of self development cannot occur. Consumed by self-protection, the child has little opportunity for the realization of potential.

If the child's positive affects are responded to, she develops the confidence to use them as guides for navigating the world. Unless the child's experience is recognized by the gaze of the other, she does not feel her reality is confirmed (Winnicott, 1969; Kohut, 1977). Unable to use her affects as beacons for her conduct, she must turn to others for indices by which to navigate the social world. Indeed, clinically one observes that patients whose affects have not been responded to tend to have a sense of invisibility.

As we saw in chapter 2, the child's affects become magnified by analogic connection with new situations, resulting in affect categories (Tomkins, 1978; Modell, 1996). If the child is helped to transform a potentially negative experience into a positive outcome, she will analogize this experience to other situations so that her affect category of negative feelings will include belief in her ability to effect their resolution. Pain now includes the meaning of potential relief in other situations, a meaning that promotes a sense of agency and reduces the threatening component of the experience. Without this optimal dual response, the child analogizes a wholly negative experience to other similar situations and develops a feeling of helplessness when events turn against her, a process that cripples the development of agency.

Benjamin (1988) points out that the development of subjectivity, the sense of one's own desire, requires recognition by an other whose desire and power can be identified with. If the child cannot be recognized by and identify with such a figure, she will seek desperately for such recognition in later relationships. Such an individual tends to form masochistically tinged relationships in which power and desire are believed to reside in the other. The consequence is an inability to rely on one's subjective states and a lack of agency, an inability to experience oneself as possessing power and desire.

The importance of recognition emphasized by clinicians such as Benjamin, Kohut, and Winnicott is consistent with the research finding that lack of responsiveness to the child's affects results in the failure to develop trust in affects and a sense of agency (Demos, 1983). The unsuccessful effort to be seen or recognized by the other leads to a belief that what one has to offer is inadequate to attract the attention of the loved object. It is for this reason that shame is a common component of much character pathology (Morrison, 1989; Miller, 1996).

Such a child must find some basis other than authentic experience to form relationships. Operating out of the anxiety of needing to secure relationships without the use of her own resources, the child's movement toward self realization is crippled. The sense of "not having a self," or of being invisible is a common experience as patients feel their lives are a sham. Whatever form of defensive compliance the child uses, authentic aspects of the self are buried. The result is an arrested self weakened in its ability to realize its potential and requiring protection by a defensive mode of relating. The psychological organization may now be called presymptomatic.

The complex construction formed by the child to foster connections while maintaining the burial of authentic self potential is the character defense. The specific nature of the character adaptation will depend, in each case, on the degree of self burial, the caretaker's requirements, and the type of defensive adaptation.

Symptom Formation

The child will disavow authentic self-expression if required to do so by parental relationships, but authentic experience denied direct expression will seek an indirect route to be heard. Authentic desires and interests, assuming disguised form, become realized through symptom formation. An index of what cannot be communicated directly, symptoms are the fate of the buried self. The "return of the repressed" becomes the return of the true self (Winnicott, 1960a).

For example, Dexter's aggressive strivings, searching for expression through conventional ambitions, were crippled by the anxiety they evoked in both parental relationships. With Dexter's aggression threatening to both parents, his aggressive potential was aborted by a veneer of compliance that maintained both parental bonds. Both his professional self-sabotage and eruptions at his wife were symptoms of aggression desperately attempting to gain expression and, simultaneously, a signal of arrested potential under his surface compliance.

Bollas's (1989) distinction between "destiny," the inner movement toward the realization of potential, and "fate," an imposed outward-dominated outcome, is crucial to this view of pathogenesis. The child who must comply at the expense of authentic self-expression loses a sense of control over her life. For this reason, it is common for patients removed from their authentic affects to have a "fate fantasy," a deep conviction that their lives are on an uncontrollable trajectory toward misery or even doom. Aborted potential ways of being and relating having lost their destiny, are now fated to gain expression only as symptoms. The destiny of true self realization is replaced by the fate of symptomatic expression.

The object relations perspective advocates a persistent search for the veiled meaning in all symptoms, no matter how uncontrolled and chaotic they may appear to be, thus rendering a wide array of pathological states accessible to analytic inquiry. For example, Dexter's outbursts at his wife were symptomatic of a relationship that allowed no opportunity for the expression of conflict. However frightening to both of them, Dexter's rage at his wife was his only way of giving expression to his anger at feeling exploited, an advance over his relationship with his mother in which the same conflict lay dormant. Although from an ego-psychological perspective one may say that Dexter lacked the ability to control his rage, from the object relations viewpoint his outbursts meant that he had no other way to communicate his aggression over feeling exploited and misunderstood by his wife.

Symptoms are adaptive, but the compromise is not between instinctual discharge and guilt (Brenner, 1979) but between the need for self realization and the strictures of environmentally limited relatedness. The defensive constructions the child creates in response to neglect or overattunement are adaptations, but not creations of meaning. "Creations of meaning" applies only to the elaboration of genuine affective experience, whereas defenses are adaptations constructed to protect affective states. In Winnicott's terms, defenses are focused on the shell, not the kernel.

Zelda, a 23-year-old single woman, to be discussed in detail in chapter 6, entered treatment for help with chronic depression, frequent anxiety states, and a severe binge-eating disorder. Her father had a harsh, violent, and unpredictable temper, which terrorized her as a child to the point that she had become anxious in his presence. By her admission, Zelda's mother had never bonded to her, and, in fact, Zelda had a reaction of disgust to her mother from the time of her earliest memories. Neither parent facilitated trust in Zelda's affective states. Nor did her mother offer the gaze of approval in which the baby could see the mother taking pleasure in her, and her father was too self-centered, volatile, and ill-tempered to recognize her subjectivity.

Unable to believe in the value of her own affects, Zelda organized her behavior around pleasing others and cultivated considerable social charm by adjusting her behavior to what she sensed others wanted. She was terrified that without compliance she would be as vulnerable to others' attacks as she had been to her father's volatile outbursts. While achieving a socially successful external compliance, she hid from herself and others her inability to rely on affects and her sense of shame, inadequacy, and helplessness. Her behavior thus being determined by others' needs, Zelda felt incapable of affecting people and events. The resulting feeling of helplessness led her to complain often of not "having a self." She felt helpless to cope with negative incidents, a reaction that resulted in frequent outbreaks of anxiety in response to seemingly minor events. The consequence was a deep sense of shame and inadequacy that made her feel a need to protect herself from others. In adolescence she had been part of the "popular crowd," developing a haughty, arrogant attitude that served as a character defense against her feelings of shame and inadequacy. While this superior posture defended against awareness of these painful affects, it also distanced her even further from emotional connections with others.

Beneath her social veneer, Zelda felt imprisoned in her identity as "the pretty one," a self-definition that required her to bury most of who she might become, especially her aggression and ambition. Unable to articulate authentic affects or voice directly her dissatisfaction with the stifling of her potential, Zelda protested by binge-eating in front of her family. Her food gorges did not interfere with her apparent compliance but did communicate her emotional and intellectual starvation. By bingeing and purging, she pleaded for both a response to her distress and for her unrealized potential to be recognized, but her parents showed no sign of noticing that she had a problem. Eventually, Zelda's overweight belly became the symbol of her protest against and rage at her inhibiting identity as "the pretty one."

When binge-eating failed to bring the desired response, Zelda became depressed, a state she experienced intermittently throughout young adulthood. Whenever frustration with the paralysis of her life mobilized her to obtain a new job or adopt a plan for a career, she was temporarily buoyed, believing that she had found her niche. Rather than being founded on authentic self-reflection, these plans were concocted to combat helplessness, and they inevitably foundered, restoring the depressed state. New relationships served the same purpose: The escape from loneliness created temporary states of veritable euphoria, but lack of authentic feeling for the man eventually ended the relationship and evoked a new bout of depression. Consequently, Zelda's life was subject to sudden and frequent mood swings, and her emotional life was chaotic. Most importantly, each depressive episode expressed the emptiness underneath her superficial compliance.

The case of Adelaide represents an extreme though not atypical symptomatic response to abusive and nonresponsive early caretakers. An irritable baby, she had cried frequently and at times had appeared inconsolable. Her mother had believed that she did not "like to be held" and left her in her crib to cry until she fell asleep from exhaustion. In early childhood, her father had either ignored or sadistically teased her. When Adelaide was pubescent, he subjected her to humiliating sexual assaults during which he would laugh while touching her genitals. Her father's sadistic exploitation of her vulnerability exacerbated the feelings of helplessness, shame, and inadequacy she experienced in response to her mother's neglect. Feeling her subjective states were either abused or ignored, Adelaide was an isolated, lonely child who related little to either family or peers. In adulthood, she confronted her parents with the abuse, and her mother supported her father's denial and claimed never to have been aware of anything untoward in the household. The denial of the abuse continued the pattern of not "seeing" her.

Thirty years old at the time of treatment, Adelaide had never had an intimate relationship and felt that men were not interested in her. Sadistically abused and grossly neglected as an infant and child, Adelaide believed she was defective and unlovable. Denied the opportunity to rely on her own affects, Adelaide felt helpless to influence her life of pain and loneliness. Ashamed of these "defects," her mental life was organized around the prevention of "exposure" and further insults. Extremely sensitive to personal slights, Adelaide tended to feel that others were critical, devaluing, and rejecting of her. Being easily injured by others whom she typically found insensitive and unempathic, Adelaide withdrew into a life of chronic isolation to protect against constant feelings of shame and humiliation.

Because the unpredictability of the real world evoked the terror of being shamed and devalued, Adelaide's massive self-protective armor required the belief in a world that would operate according to her needs. Frequently making plans on the basis of unrealistic assumptions, she was consistently frustrated when events did not unfold according to expectation. These unrealistic expectations were one manifestation of an illusionary, self-protective belief system that relieved the unbearable anxiety of an unpredictable world. To recognize others as separate centers of initiative who may not wish to respond as she desired would have led to traumatic helplessness. When she did attempt to form relationships, she expected the other to meet her needs as though the two were in a merger, and she often assumed that her partner knew her wishes without having to communicate them.

Not being able to fulfill her expectations, people inevitably failed her, and the ensuing disappointment often ended the relationship.

Although these "entitled" expectations allowed her to have some engagement with the interpersonal world, the relationships so formed were highly volatile and easily disrupted. When her expectations were not met, Adelaide believed that others were attacking her, a perception that resulted in recurrent hostile encounters. Such relating was chaotic, explosive, and usually short-lived.

Although Adelaide's self-protective psychic organization was necessary for survival without constant fear and threat, it also arrested her entry into the adult world of mutuality and negotiated interactions. When her illusory, self-protective world broke down, she fell into states of utter futility ending in severely withdrawn depression. While offering protection from confrontation with feelings of shame, victimization, and helplessness, her defensive posture of withdrawal from the interpersonal world resulted in chronic depression and loneliness.

For both Adelaide and Zelda, the potential to develop according to affect dispositions was arrested by neglectful and assaultive parental relationships. Each adopted a defensive posture in a desperate effort to form attachments without genuine affective engagement. Zelda learned social charm and compliance, a posture that allowed an appearance of interpersonal relating and general normality. Adelaide, on the other hand, feeling desperately helpless and with only a very minimal sense of self, needed to create an illusory world that she expected others to fit. The resulting object relationships of merger or withdrawal left her without Zelda's capacity for superficial compliance. Nonetheless, both women constructed character structures that buried a large share of their authentic experience while finding a way to form relationships, that is to say, both character styles were presymptomatic. When the emptiness of living an anxiety-dominated life became intolerable, both women expressed their imprisonment and dissatisfaction symptomatically.

Theory: Conflict and Guilt

For classical and ego psychology, conflict between guilt and wish is the central pathogenic factor. As can be seen from this discussion of symptom formation, the current self-arrest model does not give conflict a major pathogenic role. The rationale for this de-emphasis is the existence of a fundamental logical problem with the conflict model of pathology: The very ubiquity of conflict means that conflict alone cannot account for symptoms. To explain the eruption of a symptom, another factor must be introduced. This inexorable logic led Fenichel (1945, p. 19), a quintessential ego psychologist, to postulate the existence of an "ego defect" to account for the formation of neurotic symptoms, a grudging but clear concession that conflict alone cannot explain symptomatic outcome.

Sexually based symptoms may be used as an example. As seen in chapter 2, the meaning sexuality assumes will be greatly influenced by the nature of early object relationships (Person, 1980). If sexual seductiveness is part of an early sensuous object relationship, sexual experience may come to mean intrusion and assault, a construction leading to either debilitating ambivalence in sexual relationships or complete avoidance of them. The typical response to this intrusiveness is to defend against sexuality, a result that arrests psychosexual development. The symptom, inability to experience sexual gratification, is not a product of conflict around sexuality; rather, the assaultive meaning of sexuality leads to conflict in sexual expression and the inhibition of sexual experience.

The same reasoning applies to conflicts around aggression. We saw in our discussion of Parens's work that aggression, inherently directed toward mastery, will, under conditions of excessive frustration, become diverted to destructive aims, such as self-sabotage or sadistic attack, and lead to defenses such as repression, denial, or splitting. It may then appear that conflicts with hostility are a source of the pathological outcome; however, the original deflection of aggression from self-assertion to chronic hostility is in itself a pathological aggressive expression and the root of the conflict.

Pathological sexuality is the diversion of sexual experience from its purpose of bodily intimacy, and excessive hostility is aggression diverted from mastery. These are examples of the fact that pathology is a product of interference with the realization of potential, a process that typically results in diversion to another purpose. It follows that the root of symptoms is never to be found in conflict alone. However, "defect" (in the sense of a missing structure) is a metaphor that misses both the arrested potential at the source of all symptoms and their object relational meaning. The defect model is applicable only if the term is understood to mean failure to fulfill potential.

Despite this emphasis on shame, the importance of guilt as a pathological factor in this model is not diminished but is reconceptualized. According to Freud (1923, p. 29), when the sexual object is given up, its place is taken by an identification, typically with the same-sex parent. The need to take in the same-sex parental object is an identification that maintains an internal tie to it and becomes a powerful motive in superego formation. Guilt, being the experience of conflict between wish and superego, always has the stamp of the object of identification and carries out its wishes. A way of maintaining the tie to the object, guilt derives its considerable power as a motivator from this connection. Guilt is an object relationship that signals moral transgression and guides moral conduct, but its power to do this is derived from its connection to the object of identification. "Bad object" guilt occurs whenever the child must feel bad or self-blaming in order to maintain a needed relationship. That is to say, guilt is a vehicle through which the attachment is maintained.

A second category of pathological guilt, existential guilt, originates not from an object relationship maintained by "badness" but from a tie to a caretaker who requires compliance (Summers, 1996). Slavish devotion at the expense of self development in some patients leads not only to a lack of authenticity but also to a profound sense of guilt for having betrayed the self. In both forms, guilt is pathological by virtue of its role in a relationship that arrests the realization of potential.

These theoretical shifts in the role of guilt and conflict force a reconsideration of the way psychoanalytic theory differentiates forms of pathology. In classical psychoanalytic theory, intrapsychic conflict characterizes neurotic disorders, whereas "ego defects" apply to character pathology. This type of distinction being eliminated by the self-arrest model, a classification of pathological conditions must be based on the type of self-arrest and corresponding object relationship.

Categories of Pathology

Given that pathological outcome is an adaptive compromise that maintains a form of relatedness while burying self potential, types of pathology may be differentiated by the way in which authentic self development is sacrificed for relatedness. Each interference in the realization of self potential requires a corresponding object relationship to maintain the defense. Although each case is a unique combination of factors, one can distinguish three broad categories of self-arrest, each of which correlates with a type of object relationship. The "fragile self" seeks a fused relationship, the "defective self" pursues self-protective ties, and the "unworthy self" attaches to bad objects. It must be kept in mind that these categories are only broad groupings of complex individual cases, each of which is a unique constellation.

Fragile Self, Fused Object

The extreme is the patient whose sense of self is so fragile that all relatedness threatens her boundaries. Because seeking the object is so threatening, the patient tends to withdraw from all apparent relatedness, a character defense depicted as schizoid by Fairbairn (1940) and Guntrip (1969). Although Fairbairn and Guntrip were incorrect in their assumption that devouring object hunger is a state of normal infancy, they demonstrate convincingly that patients who are unable to form affectively meaningful object ties become desperate to secure attachments and are so consumed by their needs that the only object ties possible are devouring. Because the function of the object for these patients is fusion, the borrowing of the self from the object, they long to blur the self–object distinction. The protective defense being removal from the interpersonal world, there is no relationship usable for self development, and a massive self-arrest ensues. The price paid for protection by nearly complete removal from the world is an almost total paralysis of the self and a corresponding poverty of usable object relationships, resulting in an affectless, empty life.

The available evidence on infancy, much of which is reviewed in chapter 2, indicates that there is no symbiotic phase, and normal children typically do not seek to devour the object. Such a desire is a product of helplessness so extreme that the separateness of the other is barely tolerable, as seen in the case of Adelaide. Seeking to achieve self-functioning through fusion, relationships are doomed to fail. As we saw with Adelaide, people were inevitably disappointing, leaving her with a sense of disillusionment and futility. Further, although people like Adelaide cannot tolerate separateness, emotional relating threatens the minimal sense of self they have achieved (Summers, 1988). The upshot is that patients at this level form bonds of attempted fusion that become volatile and explosive, withdraw from affective ties to others, or oscillate.

In my view, it is unnecessary to differentiate borderline personality disorders from the schizoid character defense. Both clinging and withdrawn patients suffer from a shaky, undeveloped self, differing only in their reaction to this fragility. The clinging, demanding "borderline" so well described in the clinical literature attempts to use relationships to solidify her fragile self, although she will inevitably resist the connection. The schizoid patient responds to the same threat by withdrawal. The level of self-arrest and object relationships being the same, the two states are dynamically equivalent, despite the difference in external adaptation.

Defective Self, Protective Object

Caretaker responsiveness that is not traumatically assaultive or neglectful but that fails to provide consistent recognition tends to lead to the formation of a self that is not fragile but defective. Not being recognized, the child experiences herself as lacking interest for the other (Demos, 1983, 1988). The feeling that "what I have to offer is not enough" issues in a sense of shame, a feeling of humiliation about one's own capacities. Whereas the borderline patient has only a fragile sense of self, a desperate need to become a self through the object, the narcissistic patient has a coherent sense of self but feels defective, resulting in shame. Deficient but not fragile, the self is able to form a tie with a separate object, but this object relationship must protect a vulnerable self that experiences shame.

Many types of defenses and symptoms may be used to protect the vulnerable self, but the most common reaction is grandiosity, a defense that protects shame by a feeling of self-inflation and that leads to the creation of a narcissistic personality organization (Morrison, 1989). This term refers to a personality organized around the use of grandiosity in an effort to protect the sense of vulnerability and shame from exposure to the world, with a corresponding idealized and/or devalued object relationship to help the defense.

The function of object relationships is to maintain as much emotional connection with others as possible while shielding the feeling of defectiveness. Idealization and devaluation are designed to bolster the grandiose character defense, idealization by the connection with an object that has exaggerated value, and devaluation by enhancing the feeling of self-worth in comparison with the devalued object. The grandiose defense with the corresponding object relationship shields feelings of defectiveness and shame, along with accompanying anxiety and pain, from the world. In their place arise the defensive "narcissistic affects" of self-inflation and denigration of the other.

If the patient is unable to utilize a grandiose defense, or if it fails at some point, the patient is forced into a direct means of gratification in order to soothe shame and vulnerability. Addictions, especially eating disorders, perversions, and delinquencies, are typical efforts to protect against awareness of shame. Zelda is a prototypical example of this class of narcissistic defense: She adopted a haughty, arrogant posture as an adolescent in order to protect her sense of shame and helplessness. When she could no longer sustain this defense, she began to binge. Narcissistic behavioral symptoms (Kohut, 1971) serve the same function as the grandiose defense but utilize physical means of gratification rather than the psychological defense of grandiosity.

Unworthy Self, Bad Object

If the caretaker recognizes the child's experience but conveys consistently that the child fails to meet expectations, the child may feel she is a disappointment to the parent and may believe the relationship is threatened. To preserve the relationship, the disappointed parent becomes internalized as a harsh, disapproving voice so that the child may experience the actual parent as benign. The feeling of being undeserving of achievement and life success preserves the actual relationship at the cost of self-attack. Doubting her right to command the caretaker's interest, the child feels unworthy of achieving goals and becoming successful.

Self psychologists will recognize in this sequence a conceptualization akin to Kohut's (1984) definition of neurosis as the incompletion of the "nuclear program of the self." However, Kohut did not address the importance of the negative object relationships arising in response to the incompletion of the nuclear program. Patients at this level seek to maintain the early relationship by explaining the object's failure, typically unconsciously, by their own inadequacy. In this way, realistically positive aspects of the other can be experienced, admired, and utilized. Meanwhile, the critical aspect of the other becomes an internalized object, a harsh voice within, that the growing child tries continually to please. The patient operates as though, if she could just be good enough, the caretaker relationship would be secured.

The actual relationship, freed from the negative aspects, may promote growth in some areas but at the expense of a pattern of harsh, punitive self-attacks and a tendency to view others as disapproving and critical. It is precisely this self-abuse that allows a nominally positive object relationship to be established. Although guilt may play a role in any level of pathology, it is here that one most frequently sees it being used to maintain object ties. Negative object relationships and their representation in the form of persistent, attacking voices are the product of an effort to redeem a self felt to be tainted and, at the same time, to please the other in the hope of securing love. Potential ways of being and relating that do not fulfill parental expectation evoke guilt, unleashing harsh self-attacks that impede development while the child attempts to please the caretaker.

Dexter's dynamics illustrate the development of an unworthy self with a corresponding bad object to preserve a needed parental tie. We have seen that Dexter sustained his relationship with his father by suppressing ambition to the point of self-sabotage, and he attempted to preserve his connection with his mother by gratifying her need for his success. Unable to experience either parent consciously as interfering with his own aims, Dexter saw both parents as benign, positive figures while feeling himself to be inadequate and undeserving of achievement. The consequence was sabotage of his potential success. In this way, the bad object, experienced as guilt, dominated his life and prevented the achievement of his goals. Dexter's inadequate self interfered with his authentic development in an analogous manner to the way Adelaide's fragile self and Zelda's defective self impeded their growth.

Anna O, Again

There is no case better able to represent this conceptualization of psychopathology and its difference from the classical conflict model and other approaches than the oldest and perhaps most famous case in psychoanalytic history: Anna O. Now that much is known about the life of this fascinating figure and her treatment by Breuer in addition to Breuer's published account (Breuer and Freud, 1893–1895), this case affords the opportunity to see how the object relations model would conceptualize the symptoms and dynamics of this historical case. First, we look at the case history and at Breuer's formulation of it; then, we compare this account to the object relations view presented here; finally, we briefly compare this conceptualization to the self-psychological view of the case recently set forth by Tolpin (1993).

Breuer's Treatment

As is known from Breuer's published case history, 21-year-old Bertha Pappenheim fell ill beginning in July 1880 while nursing her sick father, to whom she was devoted (Breuer and Freud, 1893–1895). Suffering from a persistent cough, weakness, and anorexia, she was forbidden by her mother and older brother from continuing to care for her father. She immediately deteriorated, took to her bed, and developed hysterical blindness, muteness, and paralysis. She alternated between "clear" states in which she seemed rational and "naughty" states in which she was irritable, angry, and agitated. In December, the family called in Dr. Joseph Breuer.

Breuer was impressed by more than the young woman's illness. He was struck by her powerful intellect, articulateness, and imagination, which had been "undernourished" by the severely limited educational opportunities available to her (Hirschmuller, 1989). Breuer immediately recognized that he was in the presence of a prodigious intellect, one that had developed despite limited formal education. For example, Bertha spoke five languages and had an astounding memory for detail. Also impressed with her personality traits, Breuer admired her tenacity, criticalness, independent judgment, compassion, and good nature. Breuer was convinced that her capacity to help people would serve her well in life and that, after termination of treatment, it "should be exercised at the earliest" (Breuer and Freud, 1893–1895, p. 21).

The family, practicing strict Orthodox Judaism, was training her to carry on the Orthodox traditions by becoming a Jewish homemaker. Her father was puritanical and severely restrictive, insisting that his daughter follow the lifestyle dictated by his religious beliefs, and her mother was hypochondriacal and preoccupied with the loss of two daughters to tuberculosis. Breuer observed that Bertha "sought compensation in passionate fondness for her father, who spoiled her and reveled in her highly developed gifts of poetry and fantasy" (Hirschmuller, 1989, p. 276). In Breuer's unpublished case history, he noted that Bertha was in total disagreement with her father's religious views even as she tried so hard to please him and ultimately devoted herself to him. She went through the motions of learning to become an Orthodox homemaker but withdrew into a private fantasy life in order to escape the tedium of her life. Equally important for our purpose, nobody in her family noticed that she had withdrawn from the world of her external behavior; nobody seemed aware that, in a very real sense, she was "not there."

Breuer found her muttering in autohypnotic states. When he echoed her "mutterings," she talked to him about what bothered her; described her states, symptoms, and hallucinations; and embarked on chains of associations that led her to the beginnings of her symptoms. After these evening sessions, she invariably felt better and stayed up late, functioning well. The next day, the cycle repeated itself. In the spring, she got out of bed and began to recover. However, in April 1881, her father died, and her symptoms worsened alarmingly. She suffered from terrifying hallucinations of "death heads" and snakes. Although she continued to do better after sessions, Breuer admitted her to a private sanitorium, where he was able to visit her only once every three days. Another cycle ensued: She did best on the day after Breuer's visits, was distractible on the second day, and deteriorated markedly by the third.

By December 1881, Bertha's condition improved sufficiently for her return to Vienna, and Breuer began to visit her two or three times a day. At this point, "Anna O" relived the year before day by day with astonishing accuracy while simultaneously living in the present. (Independent data confirmed the accuracy of the reliving.) Via hypnosis, Breuer took her back to the period of the first phase of the illness, and she insisted on reliving the events (arriving at the psychic trauma of each symptom) in exact reverse order. According to Breuer and Freud (1893–1895), each such symptom disappeared after the retelling, although he acknowledged that some symptoms disappeared spontaneously and others were not removed until later. The treatment ended in June 1882. We now know from Breuer's unpublished record that the treatment did not achieve the complete result Breuer had indicated and that, in fact, Bertha spent three months after its termination in a Swiss sanitorium and was hospitalized on three subsequent occasions between 1883 and 1887.

In 1888, 29-year-old Bertha moved to Frankfurt with her mother, a move that was a critical turning point in her life (Tolpin, 1993). Bertha became a part of the social circle of her mother's family, the Goldschmidts, wealthy German Jews who were cultured and sophisticated. These relatives, who accepted Bertha and appreciated her intellect and wit, exposed her to their strong values and social purpose, especially the German feminist movement and social welfare. For the rest of her life, Bertha Pappenheim devoted herself to fighting for the rights and needs of Jewish refugees from Eastern Europe, orphans, homeless teenage girls, pregnant teens, and unmarried women. She founded a home for delinquent and pregnant teens over the opposition of Orthodox rabbis. For refugees, she helped establish programs to meet educational, vocational and social needs.

Additionally, Bertha Pappenheim became an outspoken feminist scholar, applying her prodigious intellectual and linguistic talents to the study of the history of Jewish ghetto women and translating the works of former Jewish feminists. She also became a writer of essays on the subjugation of Jewish women, outwardly expressing her convictions in clear opposition to her parents' beliefs. Her strong bond with Jewish feminists from the past is clearly demonstrated by the commissioning of a portrait of herself dressed as a 17th-century ancestor who overcame ghetto restrictions to become educated and a successful businesswoman. There is no indication of any return of symptoms from the time of her move to Frankfurt.

The evidence suggests that Breuer's "talking cure" helped immeasurably but that it did not lead to the total and lasting cure that Breuer had hoped for and that was implied in his published case report. Pappenheim's recovery was not complete until a minimum six years after her treatment with Breuer ended. She found purpose and meaning in her life only after she formed bonds with people who helped her relinquish her compliance with beliefs she opposed and give voice to her authentic self.

It is striking that this authenticity included not only her opposition to Orthodox Judaism and outspoken advocacy of women's rights but also the very character traits that Breuer had identified in 1880 when he first saw her. During the last 40 years of her life,

Pappenheim deployed the natural compassion and kindness Breuer had so quickly identified in the performance of extraordinary acts of social justice. Breuer was also impressed with her obstinacy and critical judgment, two traits that formed the basis of her feminism and opposition to the orthodoxy in which she had been brought up. Her life became meaningful and fulfilled not at the time of her termination from Breuer but when she formed relationships in Frankfurt that allowed her to bring to fruition her talents and personality traits. Her social work was a realization of her natural compassion and capacity to help others, as Breuer knew. Her scholarly studies of Jewish feminists, translations of their works, and essays realized the extraordinary intellectual capacity that had been stifled by her family and given expression only in the pallid substitute of private fantasy in her early life.

Breuer clearly recognized Pappenheim's buried self and the forces that opposed its growth. Deploring the upbringing that had stifled the development of her impressive potential, Breuer listened to her, recognized how unfulfilled she was, and performed an invaluable service to her that her family was unable to provide: He recognized the brilliant but unfulfilled young woman whose outward compliance prevented her from giving voice to her beliefs and fulfilling her potential. Breuer saw that her "private theater" and devotion to her father were compensation for her unfulfilled life. However, because Breuer believed the treatment was about getting affects "unstuck" by reliving the roots of their strangulation, he focused exclusively on the reliving of symptom origin, did not engage her around the meaning of her daydreaming and devotion to her father, and did not regard her unrealized potential as a target of the treatment. It was left to the Goldschmidts to facilitate the realization of her personality traits, intellectual potential, values, and convictions.

The Object Relations View

At the time of her illness, Pappenheim was living in two worlds: an external compliance with her assigned role of becoming a homemaker in an Orthodox Jewish home and a hidden opposition to Orthodox Judaism and this assignment. She could not express her rebellious views or dare aspire to the realization of her intellectual ambitions without fear of losing the one relationship that had meaning to her: the paternal bond. Her mother being hypochondriacal, passive, and unavailable to her, Bertha attached to her father, the patriarch who represented power, competence, and authority and whose love and admiration meant recognition by a powerful figure. However, her father required slavish compliance and a tedious existence that allowed no room for Bertha to pursue her intellectual ambitions, the implementation of her social compassion, or the independent, critical aspect of her personality. She "chose" her father but at the cost of precious talents and traits that lay buried beneath her superficial compliance.

Bertha's prolific imagination found expression in a rich fantasy life that eventually gave rise to hallucinations, and her hysterical paralyses and symptoms were the expression of the unbearable dissatisfaction and pain she felt in living her meaningless existence. Bertha was forced to withdraw into a private theater, where her hallucinations and fantasy life were the only expression of her extraordinary creativity and intellect. Unable to voice direct opposition to the orthodoxy that severely limited her life, she protested with the motoric paralyses that symbolized her emotional and psychological paralysis. That her symptoms were communications begging to be heard is suggested by the fact that, when Breuer echoed her mutterings, she spoke to him about her symptoms and the traumatic events that gave rise to them. What had been considered meaningless gibberish became clearly intelligible speech as soon as Breuer took her mutterings seriously.

From the viewpoint advanced here, Bertha's symptoms were what Breuer implied: the only expression of her unrealized self of which she was then capable. She could not protest directly the stifling of her needs and talents because she needed her father, and her mother was not available. Unfortunately for Bertha, the most important person in her life, the person to whom she was so "passionately devoted"—her father—was most responsible for the stifling of her intellect and core personality traits. The paternal bond required near annihilation of the self for its sustenance. Neither parental relationship provided the transitional space within which her self could develop and find meaning. As a consequence, Bertha withdrew into the space she could create for herself, her private theater.

The only outlet for her compassion was nursing her father. When her mother and dominating brother forbade her from caring for her father, she lost the one mode of self-expression she had been able to find. Her inability to care for her father meant not only separation from the most important figure in her life but also the loss of the single outlet for her compassion. Furthermore, her father's impending death meant the loss of the only figure close to her who took pleasure in her gifts. When her father died, she was not simply grief-stricken over his loss—she despaired over the loneliness of having lost the one meaningful relationship in her life. She still felt constrained to comply with the stifling rules he had imposed on her but without the benefit of his admiration and love. In consequence, her condition deteriorated.

Breuer became the replacement for the father Bertha had lost first psychologically and later physically, but he represented much more than the second powerful figure who appreciated her potential: Breuer not only saw her talents, but, unlike her father, grasped the importance of her being able to use them for social good. Furthermore, Breuer recognized and took seriously Anna's mutterings as an effort to communicate. His recognition of who she was, his seeing her in a way no one else had, accounts for Anna O's coming alive in his presence and subsequent return to her symptomatic and dysfunctional condition after he left.

Breuer seemed to bring her out of her arrested state, but this proved to be only temporary, as he was limited by his view of the treatment as the freeing up of strangulated affects. Consequently, despite all the improvements under Breuer's care, Bertha was still ill when he terminated with her. The incomplete nature of Breuer's treatment can be directly attributed to the fact that, although he saw her need to utilize her potential, he did not regard this need as part of the treatment and thought that the exercise of her gifts could wait until after the treatment ended. By contrast, from an object relations perspective, self realization is the very essence of treatment.

The other people in Bertha Pappenheim's life who saw her potential and encouraged its full realization were the Goldschmidts, her mother's relatives with whom she bonded after her move to Frankfurt. Her symptoms disappeared permanently only after this move had given her the opportunity to become the person she had always potentially been: an independent, outspoken fighter for social causes and someone with serious scholarly interests. Although Breuer grasped this potential, the Goldschmidts helped her to realize it. To her family, she was invisible, but Breuer saw who she was under her surface compliance, and the Goldschmidts helped her become that person.

Despite the fulfillment Bertha Pappenheim received from her work during the last 40 years of her life, one area remained unfulfilled: She lamented the lack of a love relationship and children of her own (Edinger, 1968). Neither Breuer nor her socially committed relatives and friends were able to help her achieve a meaningful love relationship, and, in this arena, her life remained incomplete. Although her life still included a great deal of meaning, that she could not fulfill her desire for personal love indicates the limitations of her bonds with the Goldschmidts. They recognized and facilitated her ambitions and desire for social good, but they did not help her overcome her blocks to intimacy. Perhaps Bertha feared that any meaningful relationship with a man threatened her hard-won independence in the manner that her father had stifled her independent strivings. Whatever the dynamics, Bertha's more deeply personal blocks to intimacy could not be fulfilled by her social and intellectual circle, however meaningful it may have been in other respects.

Needless to say, Breuer had no model of therapeutic action that included the use of the analytic relationship to overcome object relationship blocks and the formation of a new object relationship. Without a treatment that could help her gain such an experience, Bertha buried the desire for love and gave it the only form she knew, battle with the forces of social injustice in favor of oppressed women and teenagers: "I have often thought that if one has nothing to love, to hate something is a good substitute" (quoted in Edinger, 1968, p. 47). Unable to realize her desire for love, Bertha Pappenheim turned hatred to good use. She needed but was not offered a treatment that could facilitate the development of the capacity for an intimate relationship.

Comparison with Self Psychology Perspective

Tolpin (1993) expresses a similar viewpoint from the perspective of self psychology. She too adopts the view that, whereas Breuer helped Bertha, the Goldschmidts provided a lasting "cure." Tolpin's position, framed within the language of self psychology, is that the Goldschmidts provided the "selfobject functions" that Breuer could not provide due to the limitations of his theoretical perspective. More specifically, the Goldschmidts fulfilled mirroring and alter ego functions, and the refugees aided by Pappenheim met her alter ego needs. However, although Tolpin acknowledges that Bertha was developing her gifts, Tolpin insists that the realization of Bertha's potential in Frankfurt was "compensatory." Writing of Bertha's alter ego relationship with the refugees she helped, Tolpin (1993) states, "Forming an alter ego bond with an injured self in need of restoration, she began to expand herself and her horizons. In effect, she was on a compensatory pathway for self-restoration" (p. 169). Tolpin never says what Bertha's struggle for justice, which she clearly admires, is compensatory for. To label Bertha Pappenheim's fight for justice compensatory is to pathologize it as a replacement for something missing. Tolpin is justifiably critical of Freud and classical analysts for their pathologizing of Bertha's courageous social work. However, by designating it a "compensatory structure," she falls prey to a similar if more subtle reductionism. In fact, the evidence suggests that this work was the realization of Pappenheim's authentic self: an independent, obstinately persevering, thoughtful believer in the rights of women oppressed by laws that deprived them of their status as equal human beings. To reduce this fight to compensation is a reductionism that denigrates Bertha's most special personality traits: her independence, her critical judgment, and her compassion.

Tolpin's formulation of Bertha's self realization as compensatory defines a key difference between the self-psychological concept of structure formation and the object relations model being set forth here. The self-psychological formulation proposed by Tolpin sees the exceptional growth Bertha underwent after the move to Frankfurt but does not appreciate that Bertha's achievement of her goals was the expression of an authenticity long denied. From the current viewpoint, Bertha Pappenheim's severe illness represents a prototypical case of symptoms as a communication from the buried self.

Final Comment

The case of Bertha Pappenheim exemplifies an extreme split between authentic potential and early caretaker relationships. To be sure, all children make adaptations to the requirements of caretakers. The current model does not dispute the psychoanalytic insight that some renunciation of individual gratification is the price for societal living (Freud, 1930), but it reconceptualizes this compromise as the balance between the realization of potential and the maintenance of needed relationships. When caretaker injunctions impede the development of the child's most authentic ways of being and relating, the price paid for relationships is too extreme, and symptoms are inevitable. We have seen this arrest as the core pathology not only in Anna O but also in Dexter, Zelda, and Adelaide. Beyond conceptualizing pathology, the case of Anna O is of particular importance because one can observe the limitations of treating her using a pure conflict model. This case is paradigmatic of psychoanalytic treatment. Although successful in certain respects, treatment was limited by a model unappreciative of the importance of unearthing and facilitating the growth of the buried self. In what Bertha Pappenheim needed but did not receive, one can begin to see the clinical implications in a model that regards her arrested potential as central to her pathology. These considerations lead us to the specific treatment strategies that arise from viewing pathology as burial of the authentic self, and it is to these implications that we now turn.

Chapter 4

Transcending the Self

We have seen that pathological symptoms are indirect communications of potential ways of being and relating that have been unable to find a direct avenue of expression in the world. It follows that the aim of psychoanalytic therapy is the deciphering of these veiled expressions to discover self potential and help it become realized. My purpose in this chapter is to delineate the model of therapeutic action emanating from this overriding analytic task. After broadly outlining this object relations model of psychoanalytic therapy, I describe the specific phases of therapeutic action. In the course of this discussion, fundamental concepts of the analytic process are reconceptualized.

The Analytic Relationship as Transitional Space

All relationships are defined by boundaries that determine permissible and forbidden modes of interaction. Implicit rules tell the participants the difference between acceptable and prohibited behavior. The analytic relationship differs from all others by virtue of its aim: the development of hidden self potential in one of the participants.

For new ways of being to become articulated, the analytic relationship must provide the maximum possible space for the patient's self-expression within the limits of the therapist's capabilities. The provision of this space defines the psychoanalytic relationship.

The most useful concept for capturing the unique nature of the analytic relationship is Winnicott's notion of transitional space. As seen in chapter 2, in his early writings Winnicott developed the idea that the transitional area of human experience was a specific developmental phase of "intermediate" experience, neither fantasy nor reality but illusion, a blend of both spheres (Winnicott, 1951). In his later theoretical elaborations, Winnicott (1971) realized that this transitional space defined the very essence of the psychoanalytic relationship. His concept was that the patient in some sense knows the analyst is an "other," a person with real qualities, but treats the analyst as though he were an object of the patient's creation. The analyst's task is to provide sufficient space in the relationship for the patient to create the analytic relationship in the way he needs.

This view of the analytic process signals a shift from interpretation to adaptation as the paramount psychoanalytic value. Rather than being confined to verbal understanding, the therapist's role embraces whatever is needed to promote the development of arrested potential. To the extent that the elucidation of meaning aids in the accomplishment of this goal, interpretations are a necessary part of the process, but they subserve the therapist's facilitation of the unfolding of previously dormant capacities. The analytic arena is conceptualized as a space for realization of new aspects of the self rather than as a dyad organized around interpretation (Summers, 1997).

There is no illusion here of a blank screen, but the analyst's role includes the provision of a certain "formlessness" in the setting (Winnicott, 1971). That is, the analytic task is to be flexible enough to adapt to the experience the patient needs to create. Too much "form" or structure restricts the space the patient can make use of in order to realize the yet unborn self. The analyst attempts to read the patient's behavior as expression of need and then adjust himself insofar as possible to provide an experience the patient can use to articulate new ways of being and relating.

From the classical perspective, the therapist's role is confined to words, the giving of interpretation, and action is conceptualized as a countertransference problem. Once adaptation becomes the paramount value of the psychoanalytic process, analytic boundaries are extended beyond the word–action dichotomy. The criterion for therapeutic activity is not verbal understanding but whatever is judged best to facilitate the process at the moment. This conception of therapeutic activity is akin to Bacal's (1985) concept of "optimal responsiveness": The criterion for the analytic response is the judgment of what is most useful for the patient at the moment, irrespective of whether the response elucidates meaning.

This concept of the process does not imply that the therapist is somehow an "objective" judge of what the patient needs. Although a determination must be made as to how to respond in any given situation, the therapeutic offering is intended to be used according to the patient's criteria. The therapist aims to find something that is potentially "there" as an authentic experience of the patient, but its articulation is not fully known to the therapist. Although not the "judge" of who the patient is, the therapist offers a judgment that is intended to be "played with" by the patient (Winnicott, 1971). If the patient is able to use the interpretation in a way that fits his authentic experience, the therapeutic offering facilitates self development.

The true self is frequently misconstrued by relational critics to imply that there is a homunculus somehow "lying in wait" inside the patient, impervious to environmental influences (e.g., Mitchell, 1993). The distinction between true self and false self is meant to refer to the fact that some ways of engaging the world are genuine expressions of who the person is and others are protective of authentic experience. "True self" does not mean that there is a single way to be that can be equated with the self but refers to any of a variety of possible avenues of self-expression that correspond to authentic experience. The targets of analytic intervention are potential ways of being, not a "fully developed self" lying beneath the surface of social adaptation. The analyst's task is more subtle and difficult: he must "find" potential that is not yet fully visible. This is what makes the art of analysis so vexing and ambiguous: The analyst must have a vision of the patient that fits who the patient is but that goes beyond the reality of who the person has been in order to envision the possibilities of who the patient can be (Loewald, 1960). This double-sided therapeutic vision is a crucial component of the process because, unless the therapist sees potential that the patient is unable to envision, dormant ways of being and relating cannot be brought to fruition.

Transference

Transference is an illusion, a blend of reality imbued with personal meaning—that is, a transitional experience. The "as-if" quality of the transference reflects the dual nature of the patient's experience of the analyst: The patient knows that some of his affective responses contrast with the person he perceives the analyst to be, but the patient treats the analyst according to his feelings anyway. This definition maintains the traditional conception of transference as an idiosyncratic emotional reaction to the analyst rooted in the patient's history. However, it differs from this conceptualization in two key respects. First, the classical concept beginning with Freud (1912) limited transference to the transfer of drive-based wishes from childhood. Neither the addition of aggression nor the ego-psychological modification that included defenses as a transference dimension altered the concept of transference as rooted in drive-originated wishes (e.g., Arlow and Brenner, 1964; Brenner, 1979). The object relations concept of transference as transitional space broadens the transference arena to whatever affects and meanings compose the patient's experience of the therapist. From this viewpoint, any effort to confine the impact of the therapeutic relationship to drives is reductionistic and excessively limiting.

Second, inherent in the notion of transitional space is the creation of the object—rather than the more straightforward view of a "template" that is "placed" upon the person of the therapist (Freud, 1912). In the transitional concept of transference, the reality of the therapist is included in the patient's experience so that the patient never simply "transfers," or reenacts, an object relational pattern from the past but enacts it in some new way with the therapist, thus creating a new version of the old relationship. This novel aspect of the relationship must be understood and not confused with its repetitive aspect. The definition of transference as transitional space gives importance to both the newly created relationship and the repetitive component that tends to define the therapeutic issues to be overcome. Conceptualizing the therapeutic task as adaptation leaves room for both one-person and two-person elements, although it may well be that the object relations approach does not emphasize the two-person aspects to the same degree that relational theorists do. Nonetheless, the ultimate mode of therapeutic action, the analytic object, is a creation of both parties to the dyad, as is shown further on.

Dexter, it may be recalled, idealized the analyst as superior, sailing a smooth course through life, replete with the virtues he found lacking in himself. This perception was not a simple transfer of his experience of his father but a complex creation based on a need to believe the therapist was diametrically different from his father. Nonetheless, the transference experience bore within it the lifelong wish for his father to be successful, and, in this sense, an important component of the early relationship was transferred onto the analyst despite the fact that Dexter had never experienced his father as possessing the virtues he attributed to the analyst. The therapeutic relationship provided the opportunity for an idealized relationship unique in his experience. This component of the relationship illustrates that the transference is a blend of repetition and creation, transferred meaning and a new object relationship.

The creative aspect of the transference relationship reflects the fact that affective categories, not discrete perceptions, tend to be transferred (Modell, 1990). Dexter tended to experience interpretations, whether he found them helpful or not, as my effort to one-up him, proving my superiority, and Dexter often responded by trying to find an area in which he felt superior to me. This component of the relationship was a transference of the affective category of angry, competitive feelings and the need to feel superior, but it was typically experienced as my narcissistic need. That the patient transfers an affect category rather than an individual event or experience explains why the relationship between the patient's history and present pattern is so often murky rather than clear and straightforward.

Therapeutic Boundaries

That the therapeutic space is designed to give maximal play to the elaboration of the patient's maturational process does not mean that the analyst somehow disappears from the analytic encounter and gives the therapeutic space completely over to the patient. The expression of the patient's self is limited by the givens of the analyst as a person. Transitional experience is not absolute fantasy but the creation of personal meaning from a given reality. The analyst works within his limits to provide the space the patient needs, and the patient must find ways to use what the analyst has to offer in order to create the needed experience.

From this perspective, the therapeutic boundaries are the therapist's limitations as a person (Summers, in press). The therapist is not bound by a "rule book" that says certain behavior is prohibited or accepted. To be sure, there are certain defined prohibitions that apply to all psychoanalytic dyads, such as the proscription of a physical relationship between patient and therapist. These "absolutes" define the psychoanalytic relationship: Transitional space requires a limiting reality out of which meaning can be created. Even here, however, the therapist is choosing to abide by these rules in forming the relationship on a psychoanalytic basis.

When the therapist cannot or will not adjust to the patient, a therapeutic boundary has been reached, and this boundary is indistinguishable from who the therapist is. The drawing of boundaries is an expression of the therapist's subjectivity, often the deepest demonstration of it. It follows that interpretation should not be used to set limits on patient behavior. Frequently, analytic therapists hide the subjectivity of their limit setting under the guise of interpretation.

When patient behavior becomes intolerable to the therapist, the therapist often insists that they try to understand the patient's behavior, but the proffered attempt to elucidate meaning then becomes an effort to limit the patient's behavior under the guise of interpretation, and the therapist's subjectivity remains hidden. The more candid response would be an open expression of the therapist's intention to have the patient stop the behavior—rather than the disingenuous, at times even manipulative, use of interpretation to control behavior. If the therapist is direct regarding his unwillingness to adapt to the patient, his response becomes a deep expression of his subjectivity and a limitation of the relationship, the reality side of the transitional space.

Theory of Therapeutic Action

Interpretation

From the viewpoint of transitional space and adaptation, interpretations are not bits of information to be absorbed but offerings to be played with and responded to as the patient needs (Winnicott, 1969; Sanville, 1991). This concept of interpretation has its analogue in the child development research, reviewed in chapter 2, showing that the child uses the parental response to create meaning from the experience. Although in some instances the patient may absorb the interpretation as the analyst meant to convey it, in other situations the patient may make use of the analyst's understanding in a manner different from the latter's intent. The ultimate value of the interpretation is the meaning the patient creates from it rather than the analyst's intended meaning. The veridicality of the analyst's understanding is an issue only in that it must make an affectively meaningful connection with the patient's experience. A "good" interpretation is an analytic offering that the patient can imbue with meaning that adds to or enriches his authentic experience; a "bad" interpretation is an analytic submission from which the patient cannot create a useful meaning.

Even though interpretation no longer holds its place at the top of the psychoanalytic value system, the interpretive process is essential because by illuminating the defenses, it becomes the vehicle for the analyst's recognition of who the patient is and may become. The challenging, often perplexing analytic task is to find in the patient those potential modes of engaging the world of which the pathological picture is a disguised expression. When the analyst interprets the patient's symptoms as indirect communications of potentially authentic forms of self-expression, he is making visible previously unseen object relationships, although he can perceive them only in nascent form (Summers, 1997). The best clues to the patient's potential are indirect expressions of affect and desire, which is why affect has always had a central role in the psychoanalytic process. When interpretation conveys the analyst's recognition of desires buried under the veneer of anxiety-driven external behavior, the patient feels "seen," often for the first time. Furthermore, if pathological behavior is understood as the patient's effort to communicate blocked potential, the patient feels "heard" in a way he never has before. The experience of being seen and heard is the first step toward realizing previously dormant potential and accounts for the relief that so frequently accompanies interpretations even when they are not immediately mutative.

One of the most useful indicators of the patient's object relationships is the countertransference reaction in the broadest sense. The patient will attempt to draw the therapist into his characteristic self and object role patterns and often succeeds in doing so. For this reason, the affects evoked in the therapist are the best clue to self and object roles being enacted at any given time, and the roles the analyst feels drawn into indicate the patient's self state at the moment (Kernberg, 1984). Interpretation of the currently enacted object relationship brings to light an adaptive mode of relating that defends against potential self development. For example, when Dexter constantly compared us and found ways to best me, he stirred competitive feelings in me, a clue to the reenactment of his competition with his father. These interactions hid a desire to love and be loved that had been protected by the continual effort to one-up. A buried desire, the longing for love, was ultimately made visible by an associative theme that began with the countertransference experience of rivalry. The first step to making this aspect of Dexter visible was not something seen "within" Dexter but the countertransference affect.

A simplistic view would see the analyst as either observing the unfolding of an endogenous self or creating the patient according to the analyst's prejudgment. The specific potential that becomes realized and how it develops will inevitably be a product of the therapist–patient interaction, but the possible outcomes are limited by what can be authentically experienced by the patient and the therapist's adaptive capacity. If the analyst's vision does not correspond to ways the patient can authentically be, the patient will not make use of it, and the process will be arrested. If, on the other hand, the analyst sees potential that fits the patient's authentic experience, the "proof of the pudding" will be the development of the process toward new, richer, more invigorating, and more satisfying ways of being and relating.

We can see that interpretation serves two functions: It makes defenses conscious, thus loosening the protective covering of the patient's adaptation, and points to unrealized ways of being that lie dormant beneath them. This dual role of interpretation is illustrated in the case of Zelda, who, it may be recalled from chapter 3, entered psychotherapy for help with bulimia, intermittent depression, extreme anxiety, and a marital relationship on the verge of collapse. As discussed in the previous chapter, Zelda's mother never bonded with her, and Zelda learned to charm her father in order to avoid outbursts of his volatile temper—a pattern that became her primary mode of relating.

Zelda's eating disorder began in adolescence. She binged at home, but the behavior was ignored by her family. Socially poised beyond her years, she had been told by many people including previous boyfriends and her current husband that she gave them an especially good feeling when they were with her. Zelda acknowledged that she knew how to do that, but she felt that pleasing others was her only talent. Having been labeled by her family as "the pretty one," Zelda had never taken school seriously. She considered herself neither intelligent nor competent, had been in her high school's "popular crowd," which "looked down their noses" at others, and had gone to college only to date and pass the time until she married. She believed that she had been able to pass her courses in a low-pressure curriculum only because she was mentored and pressured to study by a friend who virtually coached her through her classes. Similarly, she did not take seriously her current relatively routine, unchallenging job.

Therapeutic foci were her ability to please and manipulate others and her efforts to repeat this pattern with the therapist. Underneath this lifelong pattern, she hated herself for having no value apart from her looks, and she felt insubstantial, believing that she had never accomplished anything. The interpretive efforts at this phase of the psychotherapy were directed at pointing out that Zelda's flirtatious, charming social exterior was a protective veneer that served to keep hidden her threatening but more genuine feelings of ambition, aggression, intelligence, capability, and resourcefulness. As her fear of utilizing these capacities appeared, Zelda realized that she had long been both stifled in the use of her potential and enraged at both her parents for her imprisonment in the identity as the pretty one.

Terrified of direct expressions of anger or even of conflict for fear that she would incur her father's wrath as well as lose her charm and ability to manipulate others, she could not afford direct communication of her dissatisfaction. Zelda feared that, if she openly opposed others or was even unpleasant, she would lose her only way of relating to others, thus risking those relationships she did have. Instead, Zelda protested her unjustified imprisonment with binges meant to convey a desperate sense of "Help! Something is wrong! There is a person in here desperately longing to be loved and valued for who she is! Please recognize there is more to me than my looks!" This disguised scream had gone unheard by her parents, who ignored her bingeing, further imprisoning Zelda in her superficial compliance, and she fell into despair and self-hatred, of which her depression could now be seen as a symptomatic expression.

When, in the therapeutic process, we saw the binges as protests against an identity Zelda hated but to which she felt bound, she felt her plea had been heard for the first time. She felt relieved, and she associated bingeing to her fear of her father's wrath. In adolescence, episodes of binge-eating had allayed the anxiety of her negative affects and communicated them in the only way available to her. Now, as an adult, her presenting complaint that she binged whenever she felt "stressed" or "upset" reflected both her inability to communicate directly her rage and her desperate desire for recognition of her pain and imprisonment.

Recognition of this anger was difficult for Zelda; she could incorporate neither aggression nor ambition into her image of herself as "the pretty one," an identity she felt was necessary in order to make the world safe by attracting men and getting people to care for and about her. Only at this point in her therapy did she realize that this "caring" responded only to her looks and left her feeling empty. When she first began to confront her aggressive affect, she became repulsed, as she feared she was "butch," lacking in femininity. Having a deeply embedded identification with her mother as helpless and inadequate, Zelda knew relationships only as a clinging dependence that provided a feeling, however illusory, of protection. When she did begin to experience aggression or dawning competence, a sense of control over her life, she became anxious and felt threatened. Helplessness and external pleasantry had long connected her to her parents and provided an illusory sense of safety.

Interpretation of her charm and manipulations as defenses against aggressive strivings and feelings of competence led to awareness of a deep resentment that she had neither valued nor fostered her competence and intelligence. The recognition that the charm served a defensive purpose was the first step in overcoming the rigid restrictions of her lifelong self-definition. Bitter that she had never been able to feel proud of her thoughtfulness and cognitive abilities, Zelda became extremely insightful with regard to her motivations and experienced great satisfaction in arriving at self-understanding. Once aware of her social manipulations, she arrived at many of the insights that emerged in the course of the therapy with little help from me. For example, when rage over her identity as "the pretty one" became evident, Zelda realized that the root of her self-hatred was her conviction that her only valuable attribute was her looks. At this point, Zelda was beginning to exercise intellectual and emotional capacities formerly buried under her self-presentation.

The interpretation of Zelda's food binges as a futile protest of rage and dissatisfaction against the inhibition of her ambitions and resourcefulness led her to feel that possibilities existed for her outside the narrow frame of her identity as "the pretty one." Eventually, the exercise of her ambition, insight, and intelligence became a source of great satisfaction to her. How these capacities were developed is a topic for chapter 6, where the case is discussed in greater detail; the point here is that their actualization required the interpretation of Zelda's primary mode of relating as a search for safety through accommodation to the needs and desires of others. Only after achieving this understanding and sharing the therapist's vision of her potential (Loewald, 1960) was Zelda able to create ways of being based on competence and a sense of agency.

Recalcitrance of Pathological Patterns

None of the foregoing is meant to convey that Zelda easily gave up her characteristic modes of relating. Aggression and competence jeopardized her sense of femininity and the belief in her ability to manipulate others. With no way of understanding relationships except on the basis of pleasing others so she could depend on them, Zelda asked with genuine puzzlement, "If I am capable, what do I need a relationship for?" These anxieties led her to remain stubbornly attached to her old patterns even as she tried valiantly to give them up. In brief, Zelda feared that any change in her characteristic manner of relating threatened needed relationships and might bring her to the edge of abandonment.

The stubbornness of pathological patterns reflects the fact that efforts at therapeutic movement threaten old ways of being. The frequent ineffectiveness of repeated interpretations has long been noted and caused Freud (1937) to become pessimistic about therapeutic outcome. Within his theoretical framework, Freud could only ascribe therapeutic stubbornness to resistance, a concept that gave him little that could be used to help the patient overcome recalcitrant pathological patterns. Using the tools of interpretation of drive and defense, Freud believed he had hit psychological rock bottom. Contemporary ego-psychological conceptualizations have responded to the problem of resistance by including ego mechanisms in interpretation (Gray, 1982; Busch, 1995). These ego theorists avoid Freud's pessimism about overcoming resistances with their belief that, by including the ego in interpretive formulations, the resistances can be resolved solely by deciphering their meaning.

The problem with the classical model even in its contemporary guise is its exclusive reliance on interpretation. Although there are many cases in which interpretation plays a major role in therapeutic efficacy, we cannot depend on this relationship to achieve the changes we seek. Far too frequently, our patients tell us, "I understand that, but it doesn't change," or, "I can't change it." This phenomenon has been variously described as resistance, therapeutic impasse, therapeutic stalemate, and even negative therapeutic reaction in extreme cases. Here we see the limitations of the conflict model, which posits that only interpretation has the potential to overcome the recalcitrance of pathological patterns. If the patient is not helped by understanding conflict, the solution is to interpret the "resistance" to understanding (e.g., Busch, 1995). This approach all too frequently results in therapeutic impasse, as patients tell us that they understand but are not changing.

Dexter's treatment illustrates the limitations of an "interpretation-only" therapeutic strategy. Dexter was appreciative that analysis had led him to understand his fear of competitiveness and narcissistic exploitation and their relationship to his self-defeating lifestyle. However, the awareness of these patterns, even within the transference, had minimal mutative impact. For example, Dexter could see that he was competitive with me and feared my narcissistic vulnerability to his possible success just as he had always thought his father would be damaged by his achievements. However, this deeply felt awareness did not significantly reduce his anxiety regarding accomplishment and competition. He remained fearful.

The object relations viewpoint suggests a useful way to understand why awareness of pathological patterns does not necessarily change them. The structural change we seek requires the relinquishment of current object relations and their replacement by new, more authentic ways of relating. Insight can illuminate these patterns, but it cannot by itself effect their relinquishment or replacement. New ways of being and relating require new object relationships, new experiences with others.

The recalcitrance of pathological patterns has led some contemporary analysts to question the mutative impact of interpretation altogether (e.g., Bacal and Newman, 1990; Levenson, 1991). Relational analysts tend to adopt the position that the emotional impact of the analyst rather than interpretive content is the source of therapeutic change (e.g., Mitchell, 1997). However, severely limiting the role of deciphering meaning ignores the importance of relinquishing defenses and glimpsing awareness of new possibilities. Without self-understanding, attempts to overcome the limitations of the self cannot be based on self-awareness. As we have seen, Zelda could not begin to fulfill her ambitions until she was aware that her social behavior had long protected her against the anxiety of becoming competent and aggressive. Interpretation is necessary, although insufficient, for the realization of self potential. Thus, the object relational viewpoint does not resolve the "interpretation-versus-experience" controversy by advocating the replacement of insight with new experience; it assigns a valuable role to both in therapeutic action.

People who attempt to form a new self without knowing what they have been protecting, who they are, and what their genuine potential is develop pathological character structures. Common varieties of these efforts include grandiosity, the manic defense, reaction formation, and what Winnicott (1960a) referred to as the false-self defense. Such attempts to stretch beyond a rejected self structure are ill-fated efforts to transcend the limits of pathological patterns. Such maneuvers cannot succeed because they are disconnected from authentic experience and continually conflict with disavowed realities.

The therapeutic action for both Zelda and Dexter lay in freeing themselves from the constricting limitations of their anxiety-driven ways of being and relating. Zelda could not give up her bingeing and move ahead with her life until her relationships were anchored more firmly in her authentic self-experience than in her coquettish, manipulative, pleasing behavior. Similarly, Dexter could not achieve his goals in life until he could find ways of relating other than competitiveness and exploitation. The key to analytic change for both patients was transcending these confining object relations patterns. Genuine transcendence is the creation of new object relationships that realize dormant capacities rather than impede them. Once Dexter was able to form relationships that helped realize his ambitions and establish affectionate, close connections without fear of exploitation, the old limitations of rivalrous battling and victimization were transcended. Dexter's therapeutic movement is exemplary of the transcendence of old structures that lies at the heart of all genuine analytic change.

Although it is true that patients adhere to the old patterns out of familiarity, previous experience is not a sufficient explanation for the maintenance of patterns that create prolonged pain and dysfunction. We may well ask: Why is novelty so feared when the cost of repetition is so dear? This question is especially poignant given the abundance of research findings showing that there are human (and even subhuman primate) needs for both novelty and familiarity (e.g., Butler and Alexander, 1955; Fiske and Maddi, 1961). There is no simple human preference for the familiar. Pathological patterns appear to be more persistent and less flexible than most human behavior, and it is the unyielding nature of the very behavior that patients need to change that has been the most frustrating aspect of the process for the clinician. This tendency has been a conundrum for psychoanalysts from its inception, and Freud's (1937) final explanation for the phenomenon constitutes a clinical cul-de-sac, a fact that resulted in his ultimate pessimism about therapeutic outcome.

Threat to the Self

At the critical treatment juncture when the patient's unconscious patterns have become known in the transference but change is grudging if it exists at all, one finds perhaps the most important contribution of the object relations concept of therapeutic action, a viewpoint markedly different from the classical model. If the patient is to change his ways of being and relating, his sense of who he is must be altered. By bringing to light the defensive nature of the patient's ways of relating to the world, the analytic process threatens not only the patient's mode of engagement with the world but also his self-definition. For example, when Dexter understood his pattern of construing relationships as competitive or exploitive, he tried to construct a different form of relationship with me but lost the connection. Having no concept of how to relate to me without competing or feeling exploited, he felt lost, embittered, confused, stating simply, "I do not know who I am." When he was able to restore his competitive relationship with me, he was anxious about losing the competition, but his confusion abated, and he returned to feeling organized and focused. In doing battle, he knew who he was.

The threat Dexter experienced illustrates the motive for adherence to pathological patterns despite the pain and dysfunction they cause. What is classically referred to as resistance is the patient's defense against losing such sense of self. From the current viewpoint, resistance is reconceptualized as the analytically induced threat to the patient's experience of himself.

Another example of the stubbornness of pathological patterns is the case of Sharon, who achieved her sense of self by relating to the analyst as either attacker or victim. During one episode of suicidal ideation, she asked that the analyst see her for a second session that day, fully expecting her request to be refused. When it was not, she was shocked and pleased, but then she became despondent and momentarily confused and disorganized until she decided that the analyst was just complying with her request in order to make more money and to deceive her into thinking he cared. She became angrier but less anxious and visibly relieved as she concluded that the analyst was victimizing her.

Similarly, when Zelda began to be less compliant, she divorced her husband, who had expected her to fulfill the role of a pretty, adoring wife, an adjunct to his success. Determined to pursue a life of greater authenticity, she, with her efforts at direct communication and assertion of her desires, especially in opposition to others, typically created a panic that made her wish to flee, often to another part of the country. At these moments, she frequently thought of returning to her ex-husband. On dates, she began to pay less attention to her clothes and appearance and started to articulate her opinions and feelings openly and directly, at times expressing disagreement, with less concern for the effect on her date. This behavior tended to evoke panic, often leading to thought flooding and difficulty maintaining concentration; only with the gravest difficulty was she able to sustain interaction for the evening. In extreme cases, she terminated the date prematurely in order to calm herself. After these incidents, Zelda typically felt that self-assertion was "too hard," and she frequently binged upon returning home, often accompanied by a desire to return to her former husband, on occasion even calling him.

That this anxiety could not be reduced to a fear of killing or damaging the object with her aggression is demonstrated by the fact that it occurred in response to all new forms of interaction. By not being flirtatious with men, she felt threatened and "lost," unable to cope, without any idea what to do or say. When eventually she began graduate school, she became panicked at the idea of becoming a serious student. Any sense of competence or relating to others without a focus on pleasing them was likely to evoke the feeling of being "at sea."

Threat to the self has been recognized as the deepest form of anxiety in all major object relations theories (Summers, 1993). It was called annihilation anxiety by Klein (1957), unthinkable anxiety by Winnicott (1960b), and disintegration anxiety by Kohut (1971). "Annihilation anxiety" is used here to capture the psychological manifestation of threat to existence that Heidegger (1927) referred to with his concept of "dread" (*Angst*). The patient who stubbornly refuses to yield pathological patterns is like the rock climber desperately clinging to the rope as he begins to lose his footing. For Sharon, who can relate only as victim or attacker, the only alternative is the experience of nonbeing. When Zelda had moments of self-assertion that defied her usual feelings of helplessness, she felt anxious and threatened, often finding relief only in the desire to return to her ex-husband, who would expect nothing of her beyond her good looks. If the analyst does not see the patient's stubbornness as a clinging born of the threat to the sense of existence, a crucial moment in the analytic process can be missed.

The phenomenon commonly referred to as transference regression is an effort to return to earlier modes of adaptation in response to the analytically induced threat to the self. Similarly, what is typically called acting-out of the transference can be understood as the patient's desperate effort to obliterate the experience of nonbeing when patterns of interaction are threatened by the treatment process. These reactions must be understood as responses to the patient's threatened sense of self created by the possibility of yielding pathological patterns (Summers, 1993).

Bromberg (1995) discussed this issue in a similar fashion by conceptualizing the patient's resistance to change as a need for maintenance of self-continuity. According to Bromberg, the patient's fear and anger at giving up part of the self are the "conservative tendency of the psyche," representing one pole of the dialectical growth process. Bromberg's appreciation for the patient's need for self-continuity represents the closest theoretical position to the stance advocated here. However, even Bromberg does not address the deeper question of why the patient needs self-continuity, and, therefore, he misses the annihilation anxiety that must be confronted for meaningful change in self structure to occur. Furthermore, Bromberg does not offer a clinical strategy for overcoming the conservative tendency of the psyche.

In response to nascent changes, patients often retreat to the old sense of self that, however pathological, allays annihilation anxiety by providing a sense of who they are in relation to the world. Neither classical analytic theory nor contemporary relational approaches show full recognition of the power of the threat to psychological existence and resulting dread inherent in yielding psychological structure. The central dilemma of therapeutic action is how to overcome the threat to the self while changing the object relational patterns that define the very sense of self. This conceptualization of the recalcitrance of pathological patterns points the way to a clinical strategy.

One of the fundamental object relational contributions to the theory of therapeutic action is the importance of overcoming annihilation anxiety in the relinquishing of pathological patterns. For example, when Dexter returned to the competitive transference, this symptomatic regression was interpreted not only as his need to outdo his father but as a return to his sense of self. Competitiveness restored the relationship with the analyst in the only way he was able to sustain it. It was pointed out that he was terrified of relinquishing the competitive relationship because without it he had begun to lose his connection with the analyst and simultaneously his sense of who he is.

Addressing this anxiety leads inevitably to the question of who the patient would be outside the established transference pattern. When I pointed out his terror of forming a different type of relationship with me, Dexter responded, "I don't know how. What would I do?" At this point in the therapeutic process, the patient has sufficient insight to see the pathological object relations patterns and their consequences, wants to give them up, and may even be willing to give them up, but nothing new has been created.

The void resulting from the dissolution of old patterns without their replacement tempts and sometimes leads to the resurrection of old patterns. The initial therapeutic strategy is to interpret the patient's symptomatic reappearance as an effort to avoid the dread of nonbeing. In this way, the patient is brought back to the void of anchorless existence, but, if the therapist were to confine his role to that, he would only be the embodiment of the patient's deepest anxieties, and the treatment might be confined to an ongoing confrontation with those anxieties. Two types of therapeutic intervention are of inestimable value in reducing the intensity of the patient's anxiety.

First, the therapeutic "holding" function (Slochower, 1996) is necessary to help the patient bear the edge of nonbeing, the "unthinkable" anxiety of nonexistence. The patient's anxiety is such that he requires an other to feel and contain the sense of threat while he explores new ways of being and relating. If the patient finds in the therapist a trustworthy figure, this therapeutic presence provides a sense of safety in the reliability of an other when the patient has little sense of self on which to rely. Without such a holding environment, the patient would be abandoned to annihilation anxiety and likely forced to regress to old patterns to allay the dread of nonbeing.

Second, the double-sided nature of the therapeutic vision helps to diminish the threat to the self. The therapist sees not only the anxiety avoided but also the possibilities that may potentially emerge from the empty space of nonexistence (see Loewald, 1960). When the patient asks, "What else can I do?" the therapist must point out that in this space without the usual guides, the analytic couple has created the opportunity for a new possibility, although its realization must be led by the patient's experience. In the therapist's vision of the void as potential for the creation of new modes of being, the space for this possibility emerges. The "formlessness" of the setting is designed so that the direction for new modes of self-expression comes as much as possible from the patient (Winnicott, 1969; Sanville; 1991). Therapeutic not knowing and the vision of what may emerge create the space from which more authentic ways of being and relating can arise.

As can be seen, the success of this process hinges on the analyst's ability to see as yet unrealized possibilities in the patient and on the analyst's openness to new and unforseen ways of relating to him. Consequently, the therapist's subjectivity is enmeshed in the creation of the analytic space. Each therapist must be willing to extend himself enough to engage unrealized possibilities glimpsed in the patient and ultimately required for the patient's creation of new ways of being and relating.

The psychotherapeutic process is at the point of allowing the new potential to appear, and free association abets the patient's arrival at the "spontaneous gesture." Any thoughts, feelings, images, or sensations that emerge from the void reflect incipient development, and it is imperative that the therapist not interfere with the inborn spontaneous gesture from which the self is created. The role of the therapist is not to impede the patient's struggle but to find the spontaneous gesture when it appears, to attend to it, and to facilitate new modes of self-expression as they appear.

To continue with the example of Dexter, when asked, "If you were not competitive with me, what then?" he struggled and was reluctant to say what came to mind, until he acknowledged that he wanted to be loved. This admission was a spontaneous gesture, an emerging revelation that surprised him even as it appeared. The expression of his longing led to a new arena of therapeutic material—his desire to love and be loved and his feeling that this desire had never been and never would be met. In the process, Dexter acknowledged that he wanted me to love him, and the relationship shifted dramatically at this point. The closeness then achieved in the analytic relationship had not been possible until his competitive strivings and fears of exploitation were recognized as substitutions for these deeper longings.

The importance of annihilation anxiety in yielding object relationships and the need to address it analytically is illustrated in the case of George. This 40-year-old married man entered analysis in an attempt to master lifelong depression, anxiety, and feelings of inadequacy and failure. From a long and complex analysis, one crucial component, the paternal object relationship, is discussed here in order to illustrate the importance of annihilation anxiety in response to the relinquishment of object relationships. In the beginning of treatment, George expressed a feeling of conflictless love for both parents. In the first two years of analysis, the interpretive themes were his disavowal of considerable verbal and sometimes physical abuse by his father, feelings of helpless dependence on him, recognition that his chronic verbal self-flagellation was the internalization of his father's voice, his father's usurpation of any recognition he achieved, outward compliance with this "thievery," and a lifelong need to please others as a symptom of his frustrated desire to please his abusive father. He felt that his mother had been his only source of nurturing but saw her as weak and ineffectual, as she was helpless to control the father's frequent attacks on both her son and herself. Indeed, George felt that his mother was afraid to protect him for fear the attacks would be turned on her.

As painful as his relationship with his father had been, George realized that the older man was the only source of strength in the family, and part of his attachment to his father was fueled by the wish for his father's strength. Despite feeling that his maternal relationship was blocked by fear of his father's angry response, he did become aware of a thwarted desire to be close to his mother and receive her love and nurturing. This desire was a source of his intense need to win his father's approval, as he feared that his father had the power to keep her from him. Thus, the oedipal constellation included intensely ambivalent feelings toward both parents: He longed for his mother but was angry at her weakness and inability to protect herself or him from his father; he feared his father but sought his love and approval. He also felt an identification with his mother in his submission to his father.

George developed an intense transference attachment with a strong desire to please and be loved. Nonetheless, he believed he was disappointing me by not doing the analytic work well enough and feared overt expression of my disapproval. Pleasing me as the father-analyst became very important, but he felt that I would appropriate any analytic gains to my sole credit, thus exploiting his treatment progress. On the other hand, he feared that to give himself any credit would end the relationship. In the third year of analysis, we addressed what it would be like for George to give up his belief in my thievery of his analytic gains and caustic disapproval. In response to this line of inquiry, George felt that he had lost his father, as though the older man were dead. Despite his father's biological death, he was very much alive inside George. Making harsh internal judgments and experiencing others as taking credit for his success were his only ways of keeping his father alive. Repeated discussion of these transference themes felt emotionally powerful to George but had little mutative impact. This failure led to another transference paradigm: When the analysis seemed stuck, I was the inadequate mother helplessly watching as the father (now internal) abused the child. The interpretation of this and other oedipal themes of identifying his father's attacks as guilt over his preference for his mother and identification with his mother in fear of the father-analyst's attacks resulted in only slight alteration of these transference paradigms.

As these issues were discussed, in one session George asked rhetorically why his "father inside" stopped him from enjoying life, and he spontaneously related some positive experiences that he had never mentioned before. Saying that he was then much more aware of his father inside than when he began treatment, George expressed frustration at his inability to stop this voice from controlling him. When he was able to have moments without his father's voice, his burden was relieved, but the loss of his father left a void. Only when his father's voice returned was the emptiness filled. He reported a recent incident of feeling good with his son in his bedroom in a moment of self-recognition when his father "came back." George promptly quit listening to his son, became dissatisfied with himself, and felt compelled to leave him. He realized that his father, being wholly consumed by work, had never seemed to enjoy any experiences. At that moment, George came to the deeply felt realization that he had never separated psychologically from his father. When he enjoyed an experience, such as a quiet interlude with his son in the bedroom, he felt guilty, but, more than the guilt, he felt an anxious moment of separation from his father, and this feeling led him to escape such intimate encounters.

In the next session, George became aware that any negative experience triggered his father's attacking voice. However, in the absence of this voice, he felt an emptiness that he sometimes tried to fill with frenetically driven activity. On these occasions, he tended to overexert himself physically, frequently in contradiction to medical advice, a pattern that at times resulted in injury. I interpreted George's desire to return to driven activity as a reaction to the void resulting from the loss of his father's re-presentation. George equated the emptiness with uncertainty regarding who he was, and he then became aware of his father's eyes as he felt his father's harsh judgment that "real men know what they want." I pointed out that in the emptiness he had no sense of who he was, he became afraid to give up the paternal representation, and either he was driven to activity, or his father's image filled the void. George replied that, whenever he was uncertain of anything, he envisioned his father's stern gaze upon him, a look that at times drove him to avoidant activity.

He realized that his paternal re-presentation was of a predator preying upon his lack of certainty. Whenever he felt uncertain or ambivalent regarding a course of action, he heard his father's voice screaming within, "You're inadequate! Stupid! Weak!" In any situation without an immediately definable course of action, he felt weak and unmanly. In childhood, his father told him what to do with great certainty, but he realized the recommended action was always in his father's best interests. I commented, "Instead of letting you emerge out of the uncertainty, your father filled the void with himself." George replied, "It's still filled. My self development has stopped."

One can see from this brief description of a key juncture in the analysis that George suffered from a harshly judgmental paternal representation who was unrelenting in his attacks on both joyful experiences and states of doubt and ambivalence. George was desperately trying to free himself from this painful object relationship, but brief moments of such freedom imperiled his emotional connection to his father, leaving a void in his sense of self. As a consequence, he tended to escape such experiences either by frenetic activity or by embracing once again the representation of his father. He knew the paternal voice was painful, but he preferred it to an experienced loss of self. The analytic process then became an oscillation between the endangerment resulting from yielding lifelong object relational configurations and the attempt to regain the sense of self by clinging to the old patterns. Each movement forward evoked annihilation anxiety and a return to former pathological patterns. This anxiety of nonbeing is an object relations formulation of what would be called resistance from a classical viewpoint or the conservative tendency of the psyche by Bromberg (1995).

George's intense, stubborn attachment to both his real and representational fathers illustrates Fairbairn's (1943) formulation that abuse strengthens rather than weakens the attachment to the object because trauma intensifies object need. Even more significantly, recent proponents of Fairbairn's thought have pointed out that the attachment to the bad object preserves the sense of self (e.g., Ogden, 1994; Rubens, 1994). In Fairbairn's theory, because the self is composed of object relationships, it follows that object loss is experienced as loss of self. This principle is borne out by the intensity and resilience of George's attachment to both his actual and representational fathers, a connection that provided a precious sense of self he feared giving up.

Critical here is the relationship between annihilation anxiety and analytic regression, a difference frequently blurred in clinical discussions. Experience of nonbeing is a threat to the self that can lead to regressive behavior as the patient desperately attempts to cling to the sense of self he can muster. The psychoanalytic setting does not necessarily imply such a regression; it is but one common response to the anxiety of relinquishing patterns that configure the self. From this viewpoint, analytic regression is the simulation of an earlier form of adaptation (Bettelheim, 1971) in response to a therapeutically induced danger to the self. There are many possible responses to the imperiled self, only one of which can properly be termed regression. For example, some patients repress or deny the experience of endangerment and preserve their current patterns; others develop new defenses and symptoms; some experience the "lost" feeling of nonbeing without defending against it. The last group suffers intense anxiety, but this potentially growth-promoting dread should not be confused with regression. George's return to the representation of his father and his frenetic activity were both regressions evoked by threats to the paternal object relationship. When the patient defends against annihilation anxiety by simulating a return to an earlier form of adaptation, as George did in this case, the analytic task is to point out the connection between such regressive behavior and the threat of nonbeing.

We can now see that the time-honored concept of working through has a specific object relational meaning. Each step of potential therapeutic progress imperils the existing ways of being and relating, a process that inevitably leads to anxiety and defense, classically conceptualized as resistance. The therapist's role is to address the defense continually in terms of avoiding the potential loss of the feeling of selfhood. As the analytic process repeatedly brought George back to the paternal representation, he would attempt to give him up, reexperience the void, and then regress. This oscillating process between patient and therapist is the first phase of the working-through process from an object relations viewpoint.

The persistent interpretation that George was clinging to his father's voice in order to maintain his sense of self did not remove the guiding paternal image because understanding by itself could not give rise to alternative ways of being. In order to establish a new self structure, a new object relationship had to be created. Here we find the limitations of a purely interpretive clinical strategy: The familiar ways of being and relating continued to provide a sense of self even while their meaning was elucidated.

Creation of the Analytic Object

At this point, Winnicott's (1971) concept of the analytic process as transitional space becomes crucial. As we have seen, the analytic relationship is characterized by a "formlessness," the purpose of which is to provide the therapeutic space for the patient to create a new object relationship, the analytic object, out of the givens of who the analyst is, his adaptations, his interpretations, and the analytic setting. The establishment of this new object relationship, partly created and partly given, out of the transitional space provided by the analyst is the essence of therapeutic action. The analyst must make himself usable in this way by the patient, and the task for the patient is to find a way to use the analyst to create the needed object. The analytic object is neither patient nor analyst but what the patient creates from what the analyst offers, an "analytic third" (Ogden, 1989).

The term analytic object is preferred here to new relationship because the creation is not simply a new interpersonal relationship. Although there are many types of enriching and useful relationships, the analytic relationship differs from all others in that the analyst's role is to make himself as usable as possible by the patient for the creation of new ways of being and relating. People will grow to some degree from any satisfying relationship, but most such growth occurs by chance, as a by-product of the relationship. The analytic relationship differs from all other such relationships in that it is created by "art" in the Aristotlean sense—that is, by the conscious design of the analyst to facilitate new ways of being and relating for the patient. This analytic purpose is what ultimately differentiates the analytic object relationship from all other interpersonal relationships.

Because the concept of transitional space is necessarily vague, its value is best appreciated by a description of how it is used in the analytic process. We return to George to consider in detail how transitional space may be used for the creation of the analytic object.

Recognition of the tenacity with which George held onto the painful paternal object relationship issued in a protracted period of oscillation between increasingly lengthy moments of authenticity, often accompanied by a sense of inner peace, and the return of his father's harsh judgmental voice. In one session during this phase, I pointed out that George equated separation and destruction. He excitedly agreed, "That's it! Otherwise, I *could* separate!" He went on to say, "I am driven by fear of separation, and I avoid all conflict—I have no self. I want you to make all my decisions for me. Why am I not okay without you? After all this time, I can't risk feeling okay by myself!"

I made two interpretations. First, the risk involved is the threat to George's father inside, the father from whom he could not separate and without whom he did not know who he was. Second, the intensity of his attachment to me reflected the anxiety of separation in our relationship. George replied that he indeed felt empty without his "father inside," but this thought evoked anxiety because he was "fearful of the predator waiting to take advantage of my softness. Don't I have to be certain to fight the predator?" I noted that he was, in fact, frequently uncertain regarding the proper course of action to pursue and that this feeling made him anxious. George replied that recently he had been having experiences of difference from his father, but the older man lurked nearby and could not be warded off for long. Here is the sequence he described: "Right now I feel so peaceful . . . I do not feel him inside me [long pause] I'm thinking about a business situation—anxiety, uncertainty, lack of recognition—my thinking about it: That's him."

In this session, one sees a transition between George's initial effort to overcome the paternal image by becoming self-certain enough to win a titanic struggle against the haunting predator and his emerging realization that acceptance of his uncertainty could bring inner peace. His original idea was his ill-fated lifelong effort to transcend himself by denying doubt and ambivalence, by convincing himself that he always had a definite course of action in mind. Such a defensive strategy is an empty attempt at transcendence. Later in the session, however, as George began to feel indecisive without his father's intrusive judgments, he gained a sense of himself as being different from his father and experienced a peacefulness with the analyst that might be called a "moment of being." Freed from his father's burdensome voice, George tentatively embraced a new attitude toward his states of uncertainty. However, this development threatened his sense of self, and he reverted to the paternal representation of uncertainty by thinking of an unpleasant business situation in which indecision worked to his disadvantage. This process is exemplary of the second phase of the object relations concept of working through: George began to create a new analytic object relationship and then stepped back from that new way of being in reaction to the anxiety of the newly emergent state. The clinical value of this concept of resistance, as noted, is that it suggests interpreting the regression as a reaction to self-endangerment.

For increasingly lengthy periods, George felt a clear separation between his own experience and his father's voice, and, on many of these occasions, he began to have fun in analysis. He not only told me about good and enjoyable times, but he also told me jokes, related humorous incidents, and even teased me on occasion. At times, entire analytic hours were consumed with this "play." I felt that this behavior, rather than being a resistance or defense, was a much needed, highly effective use of the analytic space. My experience of George, at these times, was of being in the room with a different person, someone who could take genuine pleasure in life. In my view, this play was an attempt by George to find ways of being without the intrusion of his father's voice, a voice that had never allowed him enjoyment.

It should be emphasized that George's play appeared only after we analyzed his fears of pleasurable experience. Although the understanding of his previously powerful paternal representation did not result in transcending the inhibited self attached to his father's voice, it did create a new space in the analytic relationship within which enjoyment became a possibility. The inclusion of positive experience as part of the analytic relationship gave rise to a self that embraced pleasurable experiences as an acceptable component of who he was. For my part, I greatly enjoyed these playful encounters and felt I was experiencing a new, freer George who was overcoming burdensome lifelong inhibitions. To have interpreted his playfulness as defensive or acting out would have denied him the positive, life-enhancing experience that he required in order to overcome his constraints. Enjoyable moments previously ejected by the return of his father's voice were now becoming an integral part of his self.

In moments of freedom from his father's harsh judgments, George experienced uncertainty as a peaceful state, although he knew it would be anxiety-provoking to his father. He had begun to create a new attitude toward his doubts, an outlook that was tantamount to the creation of a new self state, another step in the development of the analytic object relationship. At this point, George was engaged in a struggle between his joyless self (attacker of uncertainty and ambivalence) and his increasingly emergent new self (capable of experiencing joy and tolerant of ambiguity and uncertainty). During one session in the midst of this conflict, George realized he feared tolerance for ambiguity, despite the peace it often brought. I reminded him of his previous experience: As he began to gain his own sense of self, his father died inside, and, in this slippage of influence, he feared the void of nonbeing. George replied that he recognized a sense of loss coincident with his moments of freedom. The battle waged between the pull of his intolerance for ambiguity and the emergence of a new self-acceptance of ambiguity constituted a dialectical growth process (Bromberg, 1995), another dimension of the second working-through phase.

A key moment in the abolition of the haunting, judgmental father occurred one day when all of George's most important coworkers and consultants were absent in the midst of a business crisis. He had hired a consulting group to reorganize his manufacturing plant, but, on this day, with the consultants and his partners gone, major snafus had ground the operation to an almost complete halt while an order was pending. Feeling abandoned and helpless, George felt that he should be able to resolve the crisis, but he was uncertain of what to do. The problem was beyond his expertise; only the consultants knew enough about their system to repair the damage. Previously, the need for help had been "discolored" by George's belief that he was not entitled to assistance and should know how to solve problems by himself, a feeling easily traceable to his father's voice. George's reflexive response to the daunting task before him was to feel ashamed that he was unable to overcome it himself.

Upon reflection, George connected his reaction to me, recognizing that needing business help felt similar to his desire for analytic help. So, while feeling deserted and powerless at work that morning, the association with the analysis made him aware that he was entitled to, and could make constructive use of, assistance from others. Despite feeling helplessly alone in the business situation, George recognized that his uncertainty in managing it was a negative only from his father's viewpoint. Absent the dominating paternal voice, his indecision was a reflection of his capabilities at the time. His father's judgmental voice did not enter, and he arrived at a reasonable decision: He called his consulting group and told them they had to send more people. He also made a realistic assessment that receiving help was not a panacea but a positive step toward problem resolution.

I commented later that, at that moment, he had "emerged." When he expressed enthusiasm about all this, I commented that the enthusiasm was his. George responded that the anxiety, frustration, and feelings of powerlessness, uncertainty, and desertion were also his. Although he still felt unsure of his ability to accomplish his business goals, doubtful of his future success, impatient, and frustrated, George found that, without the intrusion of his father's voice, these feelings were not threatening. In fact, he noted that their appearance would usually be "prime area for my father's voice to come in," but, at this juncture in the treatment, he experienced no such interference. Instead of the paternal representation, he was aware of a close bond with me and an accepting attitude toward his dubious business situation, a major step in the creation of the analytic object.

George was eliminating his father's presence not by abolishing frustration but by adopting his own attitude toward his very real frustrations and doubts. Indeed, it was in the very experience of frustration, ambivalence, and doubt that he was most free of his father's influence and, ironically, at greatest peace. In the void, which he had hoped would be filled with nurturing and which had previously been saturated with his father's voice, he was creating an attitude of self-recognition and acceptance based on his experiences of joy and uncertainty in the analytic relationship.

During this time, George experienced noticeable relief from his recurrent bouts of depression. States of indecision and doubt no longer led to the harsh self-flagellation that had previously resulted in painful depressive episodes, and moments of enjoyment and success no longer resulted in retreat to the paternal image. George attributed these changes to the completion of mourning for his father and the separation he now felt from the paternal image, a separation that permitted experiences previously found unacceptable. It must be underscored that, although this separation was made possible by insight, it transpired only after George had made considerable progress in the creation of the analytic object relationship.

George replaced the unconscious magical expectations of euphoria with the excitement of finding new ways of relating to the world that fit his sense of who he was. Although this self did not comport with the fantasy of inner peace, it was enriching and gratifying because it was his creation and enabled him to function effectively. Even the recognition of his need for business help was satisfying because it was an aspect of his newly emergent self, and it made use of the analytic object relationship. Having used the analytic object to achieve self-definition, George no longer felt the burning desire for nurturing; the question of who received "credit" for analytic progress was no longer relevant. He was now using the analysis to create new ways of being and relating rather than to achieve a state of euphoria or dependence. He had shifted from object relating to object usage (Winnicott, 1969).

To create the analytic object, George did not simply "identify" with the analyst or even internalize him; he created a new relationship from the space remaining after the old object relationship was cleared away by interpretation. Where his father's harsh judgments had been, George now had a new object that regarded uncertainty as a signal and enjoyment as desirable. I submit that this is what Winnicott meant by object usage. In utilizing analysis in this way, George experienced a form of gratification he had never before known and had not expected: the joy of self-transcendence.

Conclusion: The Analytic Result

On the basis of an object relations model of development and pathology, a four-phase model of therapeutic action has been delineated: interpretation, threat to the self, a battle between the old ways and an emerging new self, and, finally, the creation of the analytic object. This concept of the process issues in a reconceptualization of fundamental concepts such as transference, resistance, and working through. This model differs decisively from both the ego-psychological and relational models in conceptualizing the analytic stance as a posture of finding potential and adapting to the patient's need to create new ways of being and relating. The Winnicottian concepts of transitional space and the analytic object have been utilized to show that the patient is a creator of a new object relationship. According to this view, the essence of therapeutic action is ultimately the analyst's adaptation to making himself usable and the patient's ability to use the analyst to realize arrested potential. We have seen an example of this process in the way George employed the analytic space to develop a new attitude toward uncertainty and enjoyment.

In some object relations theories and versions of self psychology, the internalization of the analyst is regarded as the mutative factor (e.g., Fairbairn, 1958; Kohut, 1971). Such a passive view of the patient is to be contrasted with the current model in which the critical therapeutic moment is the patient's inventive use of what the analyst offers.

Currently, there is considerable debate over the relative roles of interpretation and the therapeutic relationship in therapeutic action, the extremes of which are the classical view of "interpretation only" and a questioning of any role for interpretation in favor of the importance of the new relationship between therapist and patient. The object relational model sees a critical role for both aspects of the analytic process. In this view of therapeutic action, the role of the analyst is to provide the conditions for the creation of the analytic object relationship, conditions that are created largely by interpretation. Although this interpretive function does not overcome pathological patterns, it does create the conditions for its occurrence. In this sense, the role of the therapist is not unlike the depiction of the change agent in Fellini's film, *Juliet of the Spirits*. In this story of the liberation of a woman who has spent her life in a kind of inhibited martyrdom, Juliet remembers and fantasizes about her grandfather, who represents the spirit of freedom, symbolized by his flying an airplane. At the end of the movie, as Juliet is determined to transcend her martyrdom, she has a fantasy of running up to her grandfather and asking him to take her with him on the plane. He refuses, replying, "No, this plane existed only to bring you here."

In a very real sense, the analyst exists to bring the patient to the point of transcendence by his adaptation, interpretation, and recognition of threats to the self, but, because the act that transcends is ultimately an act of freedom that must come from an inner voice, the patient cannot "go with" the analyst. The patient uses the analyst to create ways of being and relating that are unforeseen and sometimes unknown to the analyst. Only if the patient takes the step to create something new that is truly his own can the joys of freeing and transcending oneself be known.

The capacity to transcend the self can be used throughout the patients' life and is perhaps the most enduring result of successful analysis. Long after the content of particular changes may fade in memory, the patient will be able to use the analytic object relationship to create ever new ways of being and relating as human growth continues throughout life. In this sense, the concept of therapeutic action as self-transcendence leads us to disagree with Freud's pessimistic statement that analysis can only transform neurotic misery into common unhappiness (Breuer and Freud, 1893–1895). It is not only that Freud was limited by his theoretical model to a restricted concept of what analysis can be; he also had a problematic concept of happiness. If one looks for happiness in a state of nonfrustration, as Freud did, disappointment in its achievement may well be inevitable. The happiness George sought came about not because he was without frustration but because he had transcended the limits of his old self and had created a new way of being of his own making. The English social philosopher John Ruskin put this most poignantly when he wrote, "Happiness is not wealth, nor property, nor achievement; not even virtue. Happiness is not any particular thing. We are happy when we are growing." Patients like George can and do learn to transcend themselves in psychoanalysis. By facilitating the process of overcoming limits and developing the capacity to create oneself ever anew, psychoanalysis can indeed help people achieve this uniquely human form of happiness.

Chapter 5

Fragile Self, Fused Object

One day I received a call from a psychologist not of my acquaintance who asked if a I was interested in seeing a case he "would not refer to my worst enemy." Apologizing profusely for the referral while giving me every opportunity to turn it down, he called me because a colleague had told him of my interest in severely disturbed patients. The therapist recounted the story of seeing Sharon and her husband initially as a couple to discuss their indecision regarding having children. After a period of time, Sharon asked to see him individually and not long thereafter began to call him at night, more and more frequently late, at midnight or after. Often she was completely silent on the phone, and the calls consumed 30 minutes, longer, or even hours on occasion. During this period, her functioning deteriorated. Fired from her job, she was so devastated that she was unable to motivate herself to search for another. Increasingly immobilized, she found performance of her normal routine more and more difficult. In the sessions, Sharon's demands escalated: She often refused to leave therapy sessions, expecting their extension immediately upon request, and she asked to be held physically. Her therapist lengthened the therapy hours when he could, but, when he ended them on time, she became enraged. He complied generally with her request to be held, but, whenever he refused a request or suggested they try a different approach, she became enraged. Her angry outbursts were becoming more frequent and intense. During one attack of rage, she reported the fantasy of wishing to kill the therapist, who became frightened and suggested hospitalization. Sharon ran from the room, and it was at this point that both decided it was time to end their relationship.

While listening to my overwhelmed colleague, the word borderline kept repeating itself in my mind, an appellation that he used as part of his warning. My reaction is not atypical but nonetheless unfortunate, as "borderline" has come to be equated with severe emotional drain on the therapist. All too frequently, "borderline" is used as a pejorative label to dismiss patient behavior that is difficult to manage. In another sense, such reactions are instructive if they are listened to and used as a vehicle for understanding.

Upon hearing this story, I was convinced that Sharon would be a difficult, demanding patient with whom I would likely engage in control struggles requiring all the patience, forbearance, and frustration tolerance I could muster. My reaction of trepidation and his of utter futility seemed to be readily recognizable reactions to patients who tend to be labeled borderline. I believed that my colleague's desire to end the therapeutic relationship was the extreme though not infrequent manifestation of hopeless resignation that I have almost inevitably felt at some point in the treatment of these patients. Indeed, one wonders if "borderline" becomes the diagnosis when the therapist has this reaction.

The Borderline Personality Organization: An Object Relations Formulation

The key question for the clinician is: Why do such patients evoke such intense, aversive reactions? Sharon's situation is illustrative: She made demands on her therapist with which he felt impelled to comply, whether he wished to or not. Feeling himself to be the victim of emotional blackmail, he believed insurmountable problems were created with any decision he made. "Limit setting" evoked reactions of rage to the point of homicidal ideation, and gratification of requests led to ever-escalating demands he feared would never end. My colleague's dilemma is one form of the problem I have faced with every borderline patient with whom I have worked: There is no winning. If I gratify a desire, I have the fear of becoming drained, being taken advantage of, and losing control of a therapeutic process in danger of becoming dominated by demands and my responses to them. Refusal to comply evokes such intense reactions that efforts at understanding are futile. Because patients such as Sharon feel so easily misunderstood and abandoned, their despair leaves no room for dialogue. I then fear I may become just one more unempathic, unavailable figure in the patient's life. Both "yes" and "no" create so many problems that the attempt to provide a productive response feels futile. My colleague experienced exactly this dilemma: Holding Sharon, he fell into a situation from which he could not extricate himself, and setting limits evoked such extreme depression and rage that she became dangerously immobilized, and he became fearful. The resulting therapeutic pessimism, felt by both therapist and patient, defines the predicament of treating the borderline patient.

As the therapeutic relationship evolves, the patient's expectations escalate until there is little space in which the therapist can operate as a separate center of initiative. The relationship sought is a blurring of the boundaries between patient and therapist, a bond that may be characterized as a desire for fusion. The intolerance for the therapist's separate existence in itself creates breaking-point strain on the therapeutic relationship, but, when the therapist–patient interaction does reach the patient's goal of blurring self–other boundaries, her minimal sense of self is threatened, resulting in annihilation anxiety and defense against the therapeutic bond.

Because the very existence of the therapist's subjectivity implies a difference from the patient, the therapist's subjectivity must be denied. In her effort to break down therapeutic boundaries, the patient pressures the therapist to deny her own subjectivity, to function as a part of the patient. However, the sense of self can be found only in the recognition by an other experienced as a subject in her own right (Benjamin, 1995). The borderline patient, unable to recognize the therapist's subjectivity, cannot find her own. By denying the therapist's subjectivity, the patient eliminates the possibility of being recognized as a subject in her own right, and her minimal sense of self begins to erode. Gaining no sense of self from the fused relationship, she must oppose what she seeks.

Because the borderline patient has contradictory needs, the treatment at some point must become a perpetual cycle of conflicting demands that can never be satisfied. The therapist's feeling of "never winning" indicates that she has been pulled into this contradictory world. What makes the treatment so emotionally draining for the therapist is precisely the feeling of living in a world in which no satisfactory response appears to exist.

Sharon's experience with her former therapist is illustrative of the escalation of demands when an emotional tie begins to form. When she was in couples therapy and had little emotional connection to the therapist, she appeared to be a woman who, although depressed and under stress, had normal relationship boundaries. When she began to have feelings for the therapist, the treatment switched to individual psychotherapy, her emotional tie intensified beyond her capacity to control it, and her boundaries gradually eroded. Finding the therapist's separate existence to be unbearable, her demands escalated in desperation until both patient and therapist felt out of control and feared where their relationship was leading. Patients like Sharon appear to have no way to sustain an emotional bond other than a connection so close that it threatens to blur self–other boundaries. Nonetheless, Sharon formed a reality adaptation that served her well apart from emotional relating. She had been effective at work, for example, where she had been able to maintain distant, impersonal contact with others.

The borderline syndrome is characterized by this combination of fused boundaries in emotional bonding, which can lead to delusional or nearly delusional interpersonal states, and reality adaptation in other situations (Kernberg, 1975). This definition of the syndrome renders the designation borderline applicable to a specific group of patients who live on the "borderline" between psychosis and reality adaptation. No symptom or group of symptoms defines this group of patients; the decisive characteristic is the tendency to merge in emotional bonding while maintaining the reality sense in other situations.

This tendency to organize relationships by either fusing boundaries or withdrawing to defend against fusion is the defining characteristic of patients whose sense of self is fragile, a group that includes patients typically categorized as both borderline and schizoid. As discussed in chapter 3, I regard both groups as suffering from the same "fragile self," the difference between them being in the response. Whereas patients commonly labeled borderline oscillate between seeking and fearing the two states, patients typically diagnosed schizoid have given up the search for the object and withdrawn into a position of isolation from others.

Because sustained affective contact with another evokes the desire to make the object a part of the self, for the borderline patient, personal relationships are limited to demands for constant availability and "givingness," threatening the fragile sense of self that does exist and generating annihilation anxiety. As seen in chapter 4, any patient will suffer this debilitating dread when her ways of being and relating are threatened, but the borderline patient feels it in response to any emotional contact. The nature and variety of interpersonal relating being so constricted, such patients lead impoverished emotional lives. Complete withdrawal results in such a strong sense of disconnection that the very sense of self is once more threatened, and, most typically, the patient seeks a compromise in which some degree of emotional relating is possible. In this respect, the borderline patient's addictions, although refractory and difficult to treat, constitute a positive sign, an indication of continued hope that the sought-for object may yet be found. This disavowal of the need for others while searching for the experience of "oneness" is the source of many of the florid symptoms endemic to the borderline personality organization, such as substance abuse and food disorders, symptoms that constitute a derailed search for the longed-for object tie. Because the substance can never provide the sought-for transformation, the patient is fated to a futile but endless cycle of addictive behavior in a desperate effort to find gratification by nonhuman means. However, it is important to remember that these symptoms can manifest other types of character disorder; they are indicative of borderline pathology only when they reflect longing for a fused object relationship.

By contrast, in the schizoid form of borderline pathology, the patient cannot bear the pain and futility of pursuing the longed-for object and tends to withdraw from emotional connections. In consequence of having abandoned this search, this group tends not to develop substitution symptoms, such as substance abuse or food disorders, the lack of which reflects resignation, apathy, and lack of hope. Although the absence of addictions in this schizoid group removes the treatment obstacle of having to overcome dependence on a nonhuman object, it also indicates a sense of futility, a lack of belief that there is something in the world worth seeking.

Unable to utilize transitional relating, the borderline patient responds to frustration of the need for fusion by seeking a merger in symptomatic form. The ensuing symptoms achieve a temporary illusion of a merger in the nonhuman world while communicating the inability to tolerate the distance between self and other. The drunken episode, drug state, or food binge is a respite in which the illusion is created of an unbounded connection with the world, however temporary. In the human world, the sought-for merger may appear as illusory expectations of others. Additionally, as Bach (1995) pointed out, sadomasochistic relationships are frequently rooted in denial of separation from mother. These relationships must be repeated endlessly in a futile effort to achieve the restoration of the lost maternal bond. Being another desperate effort to experience a merger, such reactions are typical symptomatic expressions of the borderline patient's frustrated longing for fusion.

It should be emphasized that this definition of borderline psychopathology excludes many character disorders commonly labeled borderline. Too often, patients who present particularly difficult problems receive the appellation borderline. As we have seen, indicators of severe psychopathology, such as substance and food abuse, do not reflect this level of personality organization per se. Similarly, symptoms such as violent behavior, lack of impulse control, schizoid lifestyle, and suicidal impulses are symptomatic of the borderline personality organization only if they reflect the tendency to fuse self–object boundaries or the disavowal of such fusion.

Origins

The borderline patient's search for a fused relationship has led some theorists to conceptualize the disorder as an incomplete resolution of an early symbiotic bond with the mother (Mahler, 1971). However, we now know from a variety of independently conducted programs of infant research that there is no symbiotic phase (Stern, 1985; Demos, 1994). The infant has no experience of fusion but is aware of the reality of separate objects almost from birth, albeit in a primitive way. As seen in the review of developmental research in chapter 2, the child gradually sharpens and broadens her knowledge of the world rather than differentiates from it.

Why these patients have such a fragile sense of self is a complex matter to which there is no definitive answer. These patients do, however, bear a striking resemblance to the babies and children described in the developmental literature (see chapter 2) as anxiously attached and avoidant. For both groups, the mothers have not made themselves available for a secure attachment. It is recalled that the former group clings to their mother out of chronic fear of being left alone, and the latter group has given up trying to engage the mother, withdrawing into a protective distance. Like children who are products of problematic early attachments to their mothers, these patients are unable to form relationships without feeling threatened and either suffer intense anxiety in attempting to form the relationship or avoid relating completely. The similarity between children lacking secure maternal attachments and borderline and schizoid patients suggests that these patients are the adult version of children who have not formed secure attachments to their mothers.

Clinical evidence supports this hypothesis. Of these patients whom I have treated, each has reported a lack of bonding with her mother, an observation often confirmed by the mother's reports of her relationship with her infant and child. For example, Adelaide was told by her parents that she was a child who did not like to be held, and, because of her distaste for physical contact, they offered little and frequently let her cry for hours at a time without intervening. On a typical night, she cried continuously in her crib until she fell asleep.

It might seem that borderline patients are constitutionally unable to form such bonds. Yet, therapeutic experience indicates that they seek desperately to achieve the connection absent from their childhoods. Clara, to be discussed in detail further on, was brought up in an isolated, rural area and had little contact with the outside world until she went to school. Both parents had great difficulty adjusting to the birth of this baby. The mother, a creative, energetic woman, focused on her own work and achievements and had little time to attend to Clara except when she could derive a sense of accomplishment. She was careless with her infant to the point that, when Clara was prescribed medicine for an infection, her mother failed to read the instructions and gave the medicine at full potency even though the message on the bottle clearly stated that there should be a four-to-one dilution. Clara screamed relentlessly at each administration, but her mother continued to give it at full strength for seven days until the doctor pointed out the clearly marked directions. This incident is important not only for whatever lasting effects it may have had but also because it reflects her mother's neglectfully self-absorbed attitude. She simply did not have the time or interest to pay attention to her child. Like Adelaide, Clara was left to cry in her crib for hours until she finally fell asleep. At other times, her mother became overconcerned. For example, when Clara presumably developed a vaginal rash, her mother rubbed ointment on her genitals on a daily basis, a sexually exciting contact that Clara later regarded as sexual abuse.

Clara's father was probably psychotic. His talk seemed to have little relationship to the presence of other people. He was either silent and uncommunicative or talked at length in free association, seemingly oblivious to the fact that his speech was incomprehensible to others. He was obsessed with saving to the point that the resources that did exist could barely be used. If products and goods were not used until completely worn out, he would fly into an uncontrollable rage. One roll of toilet paper was to last the entire family a month. Aluminum foil had to be used repeatedly until it was so threadbare that it disintegrated on contact. Mistrusting banks, he kept tens of thousands of dollars in bundles of cash inside the house. He refused to spend money on the family home, and so Clara grew up without a bathroom. If she needed to relieve herself at night, she had to do so in a chamber pot in her room and then smell the feces or urine for the rest of the night. Having no playmates in her isolated rural existence, Clara's most salient childhood memory was of swinging for hours and hours on a tree swing by herself. She can recall telling her mother, "Mom, I feel so empty," and running to the well in hopes that water would fill the emptiness.

Sharon reported her mother to be completely cold and unfeeling, with virtually no capacity for warmth, spontaneity, humor, or enjoyment. One of Sharon's prototypical childhood memories was of giving her mother a surprise birthday party with her older sister and eagerly awaiting her mother's reaction. Upon entering the secretly decorated room, the mother frowned in disgust and complained that the children had created a mess that would be difficult and burdensome to clean up. Despite the estrangement Sharon felt from her mother all her life, she longed for the nurturing, caring attachment she had never experienced in the relationship. The depth of this longing renders unlikely the hypothesis that she had somehow been unable to respond to her mother's normal ministrations.

All of this is not to deny that there may be constitutional factors, at least in some cases, and the relative contribution of such factors and environmental deprivation is difficult to judge. However, developmental research, clinical reports, and patients' persistent longing for relationships never actually experienced all converge to suggest that an unresponsive or assaultive environment is likely a primary reason, if not always the primary reason, that the early relationship with the mother is so aborted.

Whatever the ultimate source of pathology in any individual case, it bears emphasis that the longing to obliterate the difference between self and object is not the arrest of a developmentally normal desire but a result of the failure of the early relationships to facilitate self development. The resultant helplessness to influence one's destiny is the most painful and intolerable experience of the borderline patient. Without the fused relationship that provides the illusion of complete control over the object, the patient feels unable to manage the dangers and frustrations of life. Not believing that the responses she needs from the world will be forthcoming and lacking a sense of an ability to control her destiny, such a patient feels fated by circumstances. The longing for fusion is a desperate effort to avoid the terror of such helplessness.

Transference and Countertransference

The emotional relationship between therapist and patient stimulates the desire for dissolution of therapeutic boundaries and the accompanying fear of boundary loss. To protect the boundaries of her fragile self, the borderline patient will inevitably distance herself from the therapist. The longing to dissolve therapeutic boundaries, the anxiety it generates, and defenses against it define the borderline transference, and the therapist's response to both the pressure to enact such a fused bond and the withdrawal from it is the countertransference dilemma.

To call this patient–therapist relationship a transference is to use the concept in a way different from the classical conceptualization of transferring an already formed image from the past onto the person of the therapist (Freud, 1912). What is transferred is not a template but unmet needs from the past for which the patient seeks gratification in the therapeutic relationship. Green (1975) pointed out that such a patient does not have a formed image ready to project but seeks a relationship out of which an image may appear. We saw in chapter 2 that the child requires a facilitating object in order to recognize and meet needs for the realization of her potential and in chapter 3 that the consequence of failure in this relationship is the expression of needs in symptomatic form. The borderline patient's unmet need for a facilitating object results in a fragility of self—a self helpless to control its destiny and subject to erosion upon emotional contact. This sense of fragility and helplessness leads to such intense longing for a secure object tie that only fusion with the therapist seems able to serve the purpose.

Such a patient does not simply express the desire for fusion but actively seeks to form the desired relationship. Not satisfied with therapeutic understanding of her longing for fusion, the patient tries to have the therapist provide the experience, but movement toward this longed-for goal threatens the patient's fragile boundaries and is opposed. This dilemma is played out in the transference–countertransference: The therapist is caught between the patient's dual feelings of threat and despair in response to limit setting and fear of engulfment in response to compliance. The resolution of this dilemma is the central task of the therapeutic process.

Borderline patients such as Sharon leave little room for therapeutic space, the area between the patient's and therapist's preexisting subjectivities that has no predetermined meaning but that allows for the emergence of new meaning. These patients are quintessential representatives of Freud's (1915b) statement that some patients respond only to "the logic of soup with dumplings for arguments" (pp. 166–167). Being linguistic communications, interpretations signify a gap between patient and therapist, and, therefore, interpretation often feels more like deprivation than gratification to the borderline patient. Unlike neurotic and other characterologically disordered individuals, the borderline patient easily becomes enraged or despairing at the therapist's interpretive or symbolic response and attempts to obliterate it. The patient's rage at awareness of differences from the therapist explains the frequent negative responses to accurate and empathic interpretations, a phenomenon understood as "envy" by Kleinians.

The assertion of self boundaries via withdrawal allows for no more therapeutic space than efforts to coerce a merger. Because the withdrawal repudiates all emotional contact between patient and therapist, the patient in this mode cannot use therapeutic offerings, such interventions being representative of the affective connection that threatens the patient's boundaries. The defensive wall preserves the sense of self by denying the possibility of affectively meaningful verbal exchange. Thus, in both borderline states—merger seeking and defensive withdrawal—potential therapeutic space is erased. The patient's insistence on forming a relationship without therapeutic space defines the unique nature of the therapeutic dilemma in the psychotherapy of the borderline personality organization. A major goal of the therapeutic process is the creation of a relationship within which psychological phenomena can be given meaning—that is, the creation of therapeutic space.

The patient's opposition to the creation of therapeutic space leads to the therapeutic pessimism held by many that borderline patients are simply not amenable to psychotherapy (e.g., Grinker, Werble, and Drye, 1968; Kohut, 1984). However, as shown in this chapter, the patient's need for fusion can be utilized to create the "analytic third" (Ogden, 1986), the transitional space in which therapist and patient can create a meaningful therapeutic dialogue.

Clinical Illustration of the Borderline
Transference

This denial of the therapist's subjectivity and oscillation between merger and withdrawal are illustrated in the therapeutic relationship created by Clara. This 29-year-old middle manager of a large corporation came to therapy, as Sharon did, after a breakup with a previous therapist. An intensely emotional but small, thin woman who looked younger than her age, Clara had been in therapy continually with two previous therapists since graduating college seven years before in an effort to overcome lifelong feelings of emptiness, loneliness, depression, severe mood swings, and chronic anger. Feeling chronically victimized in many areas, including all her jobs, she tended to believe that she worked harder and more assiduously than her coworkers only to have her labor go unappreciated while others survived doing far less. Despite her loneliness and depression, she was dramatic and emotionally intense in her presentation of even the most prosaic events, most of her feelings being "peaks" or "valleys" with little in between. Even in the first session, she was on the verge of tears and outbursts of rage. She had some friends but had never had a sustained romantic interest; she felt that men were not attracted to her, and she had been lonely throughout her adult life. Continually angry about the lack of affection, caring, and romance in her life, Clara was openly both envious and jealous of other people, especially women whom she felt attracted men easily.

Clara's former therapist had offered her milk and cookies in the therapy sessions and hugged her at the completion of each therapeutic hour. Deeply gratified by both these routines, Clara found herself looking forward to them, and they had come to dominate her therapy experience. The breaking point in the therapeutic relationship was the therapist's decision to cease providing the milk and cookies because she believed Clara had grown to the point that she no longer needed them. When told of this decision, Clara flew into a rage and ran screaming from the office. She then called the therapist daily to harangue her about the deprivation and accuse her of unprofessional and persecutory conduct. In their last meeting, the therapist told Clara that Clara was not simply depressed, as she thought, but a borderline who had a poor prognosis and who would require many years of intense psychotherapy before improvement could be expected.

The early phase of her twice-per-week therapy with me was consumed with rage at the previous therapist and the extension of this anger to the sense of victimization throughout her life. She associated to the gratuitous "poverty" imposed on her during her early life and became painfully enraged at the brutal conditions under which she had lived. The memory of smelling her urine and feces all night while she tried to sleep made her especially embittered. She also became enraged at a recovered memory of being held upside down in the outhouse for punishment. Clara realized that fear of her father's violent outbursts had led to intense anxiety about using virtually all consumable products. Still fearing his reaction to her "wastefulness" and greed, she kept her eating to a bare minimum.

As Clara recalled these events, she expressed bitter sarcasm at the lives of others, including mine, which she perceived to be far more comfortable. In sessions, she engaged in lengthy diatribes against what she presumed to be my comfortable lifestyle and preference for other patients, whom she believed I found more attractive than her. Dramatizing the difficulty of her current job, which she felt required extensive sacrifice, she began to leave long, melodramatic telephone messages on my answering machine recounting painful work situations in minute detail. These extensive soliloquies often ended with a dramatic flourish, such as, "Damn this is a hard job . . . damn," as the phone was hung up. Most of the time, no request for a return message was made, but, when Clara felt she had been wronged, she engaged in lengthy telephone conversations designed to prove the injustice perpetrated upon her.

As her anger mounted, so did her requests for more contact. Although she was receiving a reduced fee to accommodate a twice-weekly schedule, she now demanded a still lower fee so she could have more weekly sessions. When I told her the fee was already as low as I could comfortably offer, she flew into a rage and accused me of ruining the therapy out of greed. On one occasion, she told me the metal clock in my consulting room represented my wasteful spending, as I could surely buy a plastic clock and see her more frequently. "I don't care what kind of clocks you have; I want you!"

The intensity of her desire for "me" was equaled only by her rage at being deprived of "me." Clara began to investigate my personal life, drove by my home frequently, and referred to my wife and children by their first names, as though she knew them. Vitriolic in her bitterness, she complained unremittingly of the unfairness of my seeing my family more than her. Any effort to understand the intensity of her relationship with me or the need to blur the boundary between the personal and professional was met with an acerbic outpouring of rage and sarcasm in which I was accused of pushing her away and being unable to tolerate a normal therapeutic relationship. She now became infuriated at the ending of each psychotherapy hour, frequently slamming the door so loudly that the noise reverberated for several seconds thereafter. Often she refused to leave, claiming that she had been cheated out of minutes or even seconds and referring to her watch as the arbiter of the official therapy time. When Clara finally did leave, she claimed the therapy was over and said she would never return. Many times, she left long, dramatic phone messages detailing her victimization at my hands and expressing regret that I had ruined what could have been a beautiful relationship.

I frequently acknowledged her need for more continual contact, commenting that she needed seven sessions per week and that it was unbearably painful for her that I did not allow the session frequency we both knew she needed. Relieved by the recognition of her need, she tended to reconnect with me, and she longed for a blissful oneness that she experienced at times by looking soulfully into my eyes. When this idyllic state was disturbed, such as by the ending of the hour, she blamed me anew for the disruption. I also empathized with her frustration and rage at the boundary between us, pointing out that, given her need for oneness, any awareness of our difference was excruciatingly painful. Again, she could be relieved at the acknowledgment of her pain, a recognition that helped her reestablish a feeling of union with me, but any sense of difference revived the accusation that I was creating distance where none need be.

In response, I felt the typical borderline countertransference dilemma: If I gratify it, it is never enough and is eventually rejected; if I say "no," I am depriving her and damaging the relationship, and none of this can be communicated. Feeling suffocated by the lack of a space in which any of this could be talked about, I felt that I was being held hostage by Clara's intense reactions of rage. The most painfully arduous task was to realize that my job was to "hold" these burdensome affects without comment (Slochower, 1996). Because verbalization disturbed both fusion and withdrawal, I felt that I was balancing on a very narrow "tightrope," and the knowledge that this was the tightrope of the patient's life helped me a great deal in maintaining my balance (Summers, 1988). Here, Winnicott's (1963b) concept of the therapeutic task as "holding the situation" and Slochower's (1996) recent application of Winnicott's idea are helpful. Both theorists have emphasized that the most useful therapeutic technique is often to hold intense affects rather than to formulate verbalizations.

I regard Clara's therapeutic pattern as typical of borderline patients. Her feeling of deprivation and need for contact was so intense that she could only feel connected to me in a oneness that allowed no separation. When emotionally bonded, she blurred the therapeutic boundaries by attempting to intrude further and further into my life and seemed to have little control over this desire. Her histrionic dramatization of work situations also served to fuel this type of bond: The emotional embellishment of difficulties, deep sense of victimization, and accompanying plea for rescue legitimized her desire to erase the boundaries between us. Behavior that traditionally would be categorized as hysterical typically functions for the borderline patient to erase boundaries and create the sought-for oneness. Awareness of difference made Clara feel that the relationship was useless and should be terminated. Consequently, the transference was "all or nothing": She either felt connected to the point of boundary blurring or experienced no attachment at all.

Forms of Transference

Transference may be defined as the patient's patterns of expectation of the therapist (Basch, 1985). Desiring fusion, the borderline patient expects the therapist to be as available and knowledgeable as if she were an extension of the patient's self, a state Kohut (1971) referred to as the "archaic merger transference." Such a patient has a set of assumptions and beliefs about the role of the therapist that she believes to be rational and reality based, although to meet them would require magical knowledge of the patient or extraordinary therapeutic ability. It is the magical nature of these expectations that makes the transference of the borderline patient so perplexing and difficult to manage. Attunement to the patient's thoughts and feelings may make the therapist unaware that the patient is forming the illusion of an unbounded relationship in which the therapist operates as an extension of the patient's self. In the context of such a relationship, the patient fully expects the therapist to match her affects and thoughts as well as comply with all requests and desires. Unmet expectations evoke awareness of separateness, causing the patient to feel the intolerable helplessness of facing the world alone, a state that often erupts into uncontrollable rage and anxiety. The intensity, irrationality, and apocalyptic nature of these reactions belie the patient's belief that her survival requires fusion and often give the therapist her first awareness of the depth of the patient's expectations. This dynamic explains why the treatment is often quiescent and may even seem superficial until it erupts in an explosion.

These expectations are of three general kinds (Summers, 1988):

1. The therapist is to be there for the patient whenever the wish or need arises. Although the patient almost inevitably experiences distress at having to adapt to the therapist's schedule, she expects the therapist to be able to accommodate her whenever the desire for contact is felt. Refusal to leave the office at the end of a session is not uncommon. Or, the patient may miss an appointment but may call the therapist at another time, fully expecting to be seen at that moment.

2. The therapist should understand without having to be told. Requests for explanation are often met with reactions ranging from annoyance to rage. Often, the patient will simply inform the therapist of a problem, feeling no need to elaborate or aid in the therapist's efforts to understand, but then will be offended by any gaps in the therapist's understanding; or the patient may complain of the lack of resolution of a problem that has not been mentioned.

3. The therapist is to help or even take responsibility for all manner of tasks and needs in the patient's life. The patient may expect the therapist to help her find employment, lend her a car, take her out on a date, hold or caress her, give or lend her money, or meet any number of other similar requests. It does not spontaneously occur to the patient that these requests are outside the boundary of the therapeutic relationship. Recognition of relationship boundaries is a major achievement of therapy, not an assumption on which it is predicated.

Unlike the neurotic, the borderline patient sees no place for delay of gratification in her relationship with the therapist and cannot conceive of any value in it. The borderline reacts to unmet expectations, such as the failure of the therapist to provide for extratherapeutic needs, as though her survival were threatened. Typical reactions are traumatic anxiety, severe depression to the point of suicidal ideation, and rage that may at times become murderous in intent. The magnitude of the reaction to an unfulfilled request suggests the survival meaning it holds for the patient. Here is one example. Sharon asked that I initiate phone calls to her at home When I replied that I would return but not initiate a call, she fell into tearful despair and suicidal ideation. The severity of the reaction, its barely controllable affect, and its association with death indicate that the denial of the request was experienced as a threat to survival. Years later, Sharon was able to articulate her feeling that I was telling her that I did not care about her, had abandoned her in her hour of need, and was evicting her from treatment.

Whenever I refused to comply with one of Clara's requests, she flew into a rage in which she accused me of intending to injure her. For example, she expected me to see her for whatever fee she could pay and, when I did not do this, concluded that I must be trying to torture her. Convinced that I hated her, she hated me. The fantasy of the therapist's disapproval is common to many patients, but the borderline patient is convinced that the therapist intends to injure her, a feeling typically accompanied by a belief in the therapist's hatred of her.

The other common form of transference is the patient's certainty that she has been abandoned by the therapist. The need for fusion is such that the patient experiences any awareness of difference or separateness between patient and therapist as desertion. Anxiety at the prospect of abandonment occurs with many patients, but the belief that it has in fact occurred is unique to the borderline patient. Reassurance of the therapist's continued existence is sought via continual telephone contact, but at times desertion is experienced even within sessions. As discussed later, during our therapy sessions Sharon frequently asked me if I was "still there."

With some patients, the issue is not as readily apparent because shame over the need for fusion is so great that crises or imaginary reasons for telephone contact will be concocted to hide the fact that the purpose of the call is the search for reassurance that the therapist is still alive. For example, Clara's melodramatic telephone messages and conversations had multiple meanings, one of which was justification for the contact she sought in order to reestablish connection with me. In her rageful outbursts, she felt she pushed me away and lost her sense of connection to me. Panicked by her belief that I had abandoned her, Clara would then call me in crisis in response to an outside injustice she believed had been perpetrated against her. The intensity of her affect recreated the sense of connection, as though there had been no rupture. Clara's dramatic tales of victimization and persecution were designed not only to "bring me back" but also to evoke the affect necessary for the reestablishment of contact. In this emotional bond, she temporarily relieved her belief in abandonment.

These two forms of fusion transference, which may be succinctly labeled "You're trying to destroy me" and "You have left me," are closely linked. The borderline patient who believes that the therapist has abandoned her feels so much pain that she can understand the "desertion" only as an intentional effort to destroy her. Analogously, the patient who feels that the therapist has evil intentions toward her also believes the hatred is so great that the end of the relationship is near. The primary manifestation of the fusion transference is the patient's belief in the therapist's hatred of and intentions to harm and abandon her.

Some borderline patients respond to rupture in therapist–patient rhythm with abandonment despair, others with paranoid ideation, and still others with both. Which reaction is overt is largely a function of whether the patient's focus is concentrated more on the therapist's "hatred" or on the loneliness of "desertion." A typical example occurred in the treatment of Adelaide, who had attended psychotherapy for only a few weeks when she began to ask for advice. Instead of complying with the request, I suggested we look together at the reasons for it. Adelaide became inflamed, her first overtly negative reaction in the treatment. In the midst of her anger, she said that she had felt alone her entire life, that her parents had paid her little attention, and that perhaps psychotherapy could do nothing about this. I remarked that my failure to grant her request for advice provoked her abandonment feeling once again, and she affirmed this interpretation.

Early in the treatment of Lawrence, he asked me why he had behaved so erratically in his workplace. I thought about the question for a few seconds, decided I could not answer it at this point in the treatment, and said, "I don't know yet. Do you have any thoughts?" The young man became enraged. He mocked me with "Oh, I don't know. What do you think?" in a bitterly sarcastic tone of voice and screamed at me for "manipulating" him. He believed that I had not thought about the question but rather had consciously been silent in order to hurt him and "teach him a lesson." The gap between question and answer had forced him to acknowledge separateness between us, but, unable to accept even this degree of difference, Lawrence attributed his anxiety to my conscious intentions. This accusatory response proved to be the first revelation of a series of persistent paranoid beliefs about me: that I hated him, designed plans to injure him, and enjoyed his suffering. In this case, the patient focused on my "evil intentions" in order to defend against the pain of loss and thus had a paranoid rather than a depressive transference.

The expectations of the borderline patient are frequently wishes of many neurotic patients at various points in treatment. The difference between the wish of the neurotic and the expectation of the borderline is the difference between these two character structures. What the neurotic patient wishes for, the borderline patient demands and even requires. When the neurotic patient's wish is not gratified, the patient is often disappointed and angry; however, it does not occur to such a patient that the frustration of the wish would in any way interfere with the therapeutic relationship. The patient's reaction is experienced as part of a complex therapeutic process including an ambivalent reaction to lack of gratification. Characteristic of the neurotic reaction, along with frustration and disappointment, is satisfaction and relief in limits because the patient sees the potential for both disaster in unclear boundaries and growth in a clearly defined delineation between patient and therapist. By contrast, the borderline patient, who experiences limitation as threatening, has no understanding of either of these possibilities. As we have seen, Clara became enraged whenever she was made aware of differences between her and me. Finding any potential space between us to be intolerable, she attempted to destroy this possibility at every opportunity. The difference between the ambivalent wish for magic and the belief that magic is both possible and necessary defines the distinction between neurotic and borderline psychopathology, between transference neurosis and the fusion–withdrawal transference.

The patient's hatred, often expressed in unremitting rageful attacks, is directed not only at the therapist but also at the therapeutic space on which the process relies. Although the therapist attempts to understand the patient's needs and desires, the interpretive process comes under assault because, as already noted, it points up the separation between patient and therapist. For this reason, the patient may erupt in rage at an interpretation that is accurate, well-timed, and empathic. This intense anger is typically not a product of envy but an attack on the fact that the interpretation is an interpretation rather than a direct gratification of need.

It has been pointed out that defenses against the fusion desire are needed to establish boundaries. Although withdrawal is the most direct path for achieving the distance required for boundaries, also serving this purpose are rage, projection of rage, and devaluation. The explosive, rageful outbursts of borderline patients not only are directed at the fact of distance but paradoxically restore distance between patient and therapist, a separation that averts the threatened fusion. After a rageful attack, the patient feels the relief of having constructed a boundary that defines a sense of self and escapes potential psychological disaster. Thus, the patient will become rageful as a result either of frustration and "separateness shock" or of the opposite, gratification and threatened fusion.

Projection of rage turns the therapist into an angry object who may intend to do the patient harm, a perception that justifies the maintenance of distance. Devaluation serves a similar purpose: By depreciating the therapist, the patient legitimizes the needed detachment. The fault finding and continual negative evaluations of the therapist that are so typical of borderline patients, behaviors commonly categorized as the negative transference, maintain boundaries between self and object and preserve such autonomy as the patient can possess while sustaining an object relationship. Because the negative relationship is self-preservative, the patient cannot accept good experiences with the therapist and finds ways to spoil them. The borderline patient who continually reconstructs interventions to construe them as negatively as possible is typically acting not out of envy but out of a desperate need to preserve her sense of self. Mary, a patient discussed in more detail later, provides an instructive example. She demanded loosening of the therapeutic boundaries and found fault with every therapeutic comment, frequently attacking the therapy as a waste of time. When I attempted to empathize with how difficult it must be for her to be seeking help from such a disappointing enterprise, she heaped scorn upon me for denigrating "the most important thing in my life." Mistakenly believing I was finally "getting it," on other occasions I pointed out the important role therapy played in her life, and she attacked me for my self-serving need to believe in the importance of a process that had no value to her.

The negative affects allow a connection that would not be possible with positive feelings because the latter threaten self–object boundaries. In this sense, attacks on the therapist represent an achievement because the negative connection is the way the patient has found to sustain an object relationship, whereas positive affects threaten this tie. The intensely chronic, negative feelings toward the therapist are a compromise between blurring of boundaries and withdrawal from object contact. This solution to the fusion–withdrawal dilemma explains the phenomenon commonly called "hostile–dependent": The patient evinces behavior labeled "hostile" in order to preserve the distance needed to maintain the object tie.

Although each patient presents a unique clinical constellation, at some point the borderline's equation of both separateness and connection with psychological death becomes the focus of treatment, and annihilation anxiety must then be addressed. Whereas this most threatening type of anxiety takes center stage with other patients when the process achieves a depth that threatens old patterns of being and relating, for the borderline patient any emotional contact can evoke this sense of endangerment. The persecutory anxieties, devaluation of others, and rage of the borderline are all products of annihilation anxiety. As Klein (1957) pointed out, persecutory anxiety is more bearable than annihilation anxiety because the source is felt to be external, rendering the danger more concrete and less disruptive. Borderline paranoia and its resultant rage are responses to psychological survival threats and the need to fuse with the object.

The intense oscillation between merger and withdrawal issues in conflicting, mercurial affective shifts that are so dramatic, provocative, and florid that the countertransference now enters the relationship in a new way. Although the therapist may have previously been angry at the patient's rage and devaluation, now, in response to engaging in these repetitive cycles, she feels pulled in by the patient's demands, quickly cast adrift and devalued by the distancing maneuvers, and then suddenly drawn back to the emotional intensity. Flooded with a bewildering array of rapidly oscillating emotions, the therapist feels that nothing she does is right. There is no winning, and it is easy to blame the patient. Some degree of despair about the treatment is inevitable, and resentment of the patient is a common response. This inevitably painful phase of the process answers the question, raised at the beginning of this chapter, as to why clinicians have such intense negative reactions to borderline patients.

The hopelessness and helplessness of the therapist result from walking the fine tightrope on which the patient lives. The therapist despairs of the narrowness of the rope and of her ability to walk on it for any period of time without a harmful fall, just as the patient does. As one side of the relationship emerges, the other swings to the fore, until it reaches its own point of anxiety, and the cycle begins anew. The therapeutic process is typified by the cycles inherent in the dilemma of need–fear fusion.

This self-perpetuating oscillation and negative countertransference, rather than being cause for ending the process, are the very soul of the treatment. With her subjectivity now mirroring the patient's, the therapist can "taste" the patient's life as she could not before. In fact, the countertransference experience is the most useful indicator the therapist has of the patient's life-world.

At this crucial phase of the process, the therapist is understandably tempted to decide that the patient is "not treatable" or requires some form of extra-psychotherapeutic intervention, such as medication or hospitalization. Decisions of this type are often made to reduce the intensity of these heated interactions. Indeed, before ending treatment, Sharon's previous therapist had recommended both medication and hospitalization—a suggestion that caused Sharon to flee the room in a panic. Rather than viewing the patient–therapist dilemma as the very essence of treatment, he regarded it as grounds for termination of the relationship. Such a response constitutes a rejection of the patient's most vulnerable feelings. On the other hand, by holding the most painful parts of the patient's existence, the therapist demonstrates a willingness to experience the patient's most feared parts.

The therapist's despair is an instructive part of the treatment process; to act on it is not. Patient and therapist have reached this juncture because the patient has allowed another person to see and know longings previously removed from human interaction for fear they would be intolerable to others. Extra-therapeutic responses, implying agreement with the patient's worst fear, can be immeasurably harmful to a patient who has spent a lifetime afraid of being rejected for who she most deeply is. Of course, this is not to say that there are not times when hospitalization or other measures may be indicated for the protection of the patient, but the danger must be clear, and the therapist must be careful not to rationalize difficulty tolerating the patient's emotional turmoil with "protecting the patient." Because of the danger of colluding with the patient's deep lifelong fears of unacceptability, the purpose of extra-therapeutic measures must be carefully thought out and conveyed to the patient. Far too frequently, such interventions communicate to patients what they most fear hearing: that their deepest longings are, indeed, intolerable to others.

Comparison with Kernberg's Views

The intensity and pervasiveness of these negative reactions to the therapist has led Kernberg (1976, 1984) to conceptualize the negative transference, rooted in excessive oral aggression, as the key pathognomonic factor in borderline pathology. Although Kernberg is most certainly correct that the transference of these patients becomes inevitably negative at certain points in the process, the drive conceptualization ignores the fact that the patient's rage and even hatred are responses to frustrated expectations. Such moments evoke awareness of separateness from the therapist, indicating failure in the patient's efforts to fuse. Conversely, when the patient is able to sustain the illusion of fusion, the relationship tends to be positive or even idealized.

Although it is true that the patient who asks the therapist "Are you still there?" is asking "Have I killed you with my hostility?" inquiry cannot be ended at this point. Clinical experience indicates that the patient's hostility is traceable to the therapist's not fulfilling an expectation, whether implicit or explicit. Clara's therapy behavior was typical. She tended to push therapeutic limits, such as by trying to stay for extra time or demanding information about my life. Her rageful reactions inevitably occurred in response to my refusal to comply with these demands. Her emotional response, representative of such patients, assumed the following form: "You have not acted in accordance with my wish, therefore my wish and your deed are separate, therefore you and I are separate, leaving me abandoned and alone, and alone I face unbearable anxiety and feel helpless to cope with the world." The drive conceptualization of aggression loses the capacity to understand the patient's rageful reactions in this way. Kernberg (1975) and Kleinian theorists (e.g., Rosenfeld, 1978) contend that excessive aggression leads to splitting, the active effort to keep good and bad perceptions apart, to protect the good object. They emphasize that the therapist is viewed alternately as replete with exaggeratedly positive qualities (e.g., brilliance, highest integrity, charm, excellence in many areas) or extremely negative qualities (e.g., stupidity, corruption, moral bankruptcy, venality, malicious intentions). Although these split-off, disparate perceptions are indeed characteristic of the borderline personality organization, they do not reflect endogenous processes but oscillate in conjunction with the fusion or rupture in the self–object tie. When the patient is able to experience the illusion of merger, she views the therapist as possessor of magically beneficent qualities, but, when the therapist makes known the difference between them, wittingly or not, the patient blames the therapist for inflicting intolerable pain on her and perceives the therapist as an evil and hated witch. Whereas Kernberg and the Kleinians view splitting as a defense against excess aggression, from the current viewpoint splitting reflects the state of the self–object tie.

This difference also applies to the addictive behavior of these borderline patients. For Kernberg, substance and food abuse are the acting out of excessive oral aggression in order to preserve the good object by keeping it split off from the bad one. To regard the symptom as an effort to "split" does not explain why the anger is expressed by the ingestion of substances and does not address the source of the anger. These symptoms are not defenses against the transference but manifestations of its very nature and desperate attempts to communicate ruptures in it. By viewing these symptoms as reactions to disruptions in the needed merger, the therapist is able to understand the patient's seemingly inexplicable abuse of substances within the context of the therapeutic relationship. When the relationship affords the safe, stable bond the patient seeks, the substance abuse dissipates; when the relationship is disrupted for whatever reason, the substance-prone borderline patient will ingest something in order to obliterate the intolerable pain of separation.

Mary, an exquisitely sensitive, paranoid-prone borderline patient, was a binge-eater given to severe alcohol and substance abuse. She frequently perceived slights, insults, and incipient abandonment from events so minor I usually did not notice them. Typically, she would fail to mention the incident in therapy but would leave a message while in a drunken stupor later that night, often stating that she now understood that I did not care about her and that suicide was an inevitability. For example, one day her watch was slightly off, and, while incorrectly thinking I had ended the session one minute early, she later became intoxicated and left a message saying that she now knew that I did not "really" want to see her. At times, she was fully aware of and acknowledged her overwhelming anger, but her wrath was inevitably a reaction to feeling abandoned by me; to miss this source would have been tantamount to misunderstanding both her anger and her resulting addiction. The state of inebriation drowned out this feeling of intolerable "separation" and gave her an illusory sense of the soothing she was now missing in the therapeutic relationship. Mary often said that ingestion of alcohol was the only way she could calm her despair and feel safe. The very fact that alcohol and drugs produce soothing and a sense of safety indicates that the purpose of the substance abuse is to feel a safe, reliable, calming connectedness when the human environment fails.

Finally, Kernberg's clinical strategy relies on the interpretation of splitting and aggression in order to integrate split-object perceptions (Kernberg, 1975, 1984; Kernberg et al., 1988). Such an interpretive stance implies the existence of therapeutic space that belies the patient's need for merger. For the patient to use understanding, she must already accept some degree of distance between patient and therapist, an assumption challenged by disruptive reactions to awareness of difference and constant attacks on the therapeutic space. The conceptualization proposed here suggests that the patient's need for merger must be resolved before such a space can appear. We now turn to the description of this clinical approach.

Therapeutic Action

The therapeutic challenge is to make an adaptation to the patient's need for fusion within the context of a psychotherapeutic relationship normally designed for verbal exchange, so that transitional space can be created. A literal response of holding, although apparently attempted by some analysts in certain situations, erases the therapeutic space. The therapist's task is to find a way to adapt to the patient's need for fusion within the psychotherapeutic context—that is, in a way that maintains therapeutic boundaries.

The inability of such a patient to use empathy marks the decisive difference between the borderline patient's need for fusion and the narcissistic patient's need for "archaic merger" so well depicted by Kohut (1971). Although Kohut referred to the merger transference of the narcissistic personality disorder, he saw the therapeutic action with such patients to lie in empathy and its ruptures. The mirroring transference is the patient's need to be recognized and validated and is best responded to, according to Kohut, with empathic attunement because understanding provides "optimal frustration," partially satisfying the need for mirroring. This capacity to use verbal communication is absent in borderline patients for whom empathy tends to whet the appetite for gratification. The latter group continually searches for the "real thing," a fact that explains the frequency with which they resort to addictions and perversions.

Instrumental to the success of this therapeutic project is the management of the countertransference. The patient's oscillation between contact and withdrawal is wearing on the therapist's patience and strains her emotional tolerance as the hopes generated by contact continually give way to despair in response to withdrawal. But this discouragement is necessary, because only in the experience of this painful sense of hopelessness can the therapist understand the patient's anguish. Nonetheless, if the therapist sees only repetition of hope and disappointment, she may succumb to her frustration, the patient's worst fear. The process is best served if the therapist is able to see that these shifts are not an endlessly repeating treadmill but cycles that include a trajectory in the direction of connection. Awareness that the hopelessness is a necessary component of the process—that it must be shared by the therapeutic couple—is an invaluable aid in the therapist's battle to sustain the relationship while fully engaging the despair. If the therapist disavows or rejects the intense emotions generated within her by the patient, she repudiates the patient and colludes with the patient's worst fear.

Ultimately, the success of the process depends on the therapist's ability to maintain this long view and continue the therapeutic relationship in the midst of ever repeating cycles of despair and hope. The patient experiences the therapist's convictions and comes to rely on them. It is justifiable to say that the process hinges on the therapist's believing enough in the patient's potential to contain hopelessness and to sustain belief in the process in the face of apparently insoluble therapeutic dilemmas.

Because the patient will defend against affective contact, there is no magical solution of saying "the right thing" or gratifying the patient in a way that will be found acceptable. Nonetheless, the patient longs to have her buried needs seen and legitimated. When the therapist shows awareness of the kind of relationship the patient needs and appreciates its survival value, the patient will have a rare moment of visibility even if she becomes anxious in the process. The patient may later dispute the importance of the therapist's recognition and will use a variety of defenses to protect against awareness of it, but this defensive maneuver fends off an important therapeutic moment that must be returned to again and again.

If the process were limited to recognition–defense–interpretation-of-defense, it would not be radically different from the typical analytic process with less disturbed patients. However, the borderline patient will not accept interpretation of defense, and recognition of her needs is insufficient. Although some relief may be found in the therapist's appreciation of her need for fusion, the verbal response leaves an intolerable emptiness, an unfulfilled longing for the actual experience. For the patient to feel an emotional connection, the needed relationship must be created. Although the fusion experience threatens boundaries, the temporary episode provides a moment of contact. The patient will quickly retreat from this connection, but the fact that she survives such moments with an intact sense of self provides the basis for a relationship. Having control of these moments of merger and withdrawing from them as needed allow the patient to titrate the anxiety of emotional connection. If the therapist tries to push in either direction, anxiety will be exacerbated rather than attenuated. The borderline patient able to test the waters of emotional relating without traumatic disruption will gradually move toward the long-sought bond of fusion.

The patient will attempt to concretize the relationship, as Sharon did by seeking physical holding, because an emotional bond is experienced only within a physical relationship. Such demands are an inevitable outcome of the patient's inability to experience what Winnicott called ego relatedness, a purely psychological relating to the other. The therapist must formulate a response that allows some degree of fusion without concretizing the relationship in a way that eliminates the therapeutic space. The therapeutic art is to go beyond recognition of the need to provision of the needed experience without colluding in the boundary blurring sought by the patient. When Sharon was held physically by her former therapist, this line was crossed, the opportunity to use the relationship for therapeutic purpose was lost, and eventually the relationship had to be ended.

In each case, the manifestation of the fusion need and the process of its resolution will depend on the patient's unique way of feeling connected and on the therapist's limitations and capacities. For Mary, verbal understanding of her despondency and alcoholic responses to perceived slights had no impact, and no amount of discussion of her admitted rage at me affected her addictive behavior. After many episodes and months of work on this pattern, she saw that she was using the substances instead of relying on me because of her inability to tolerate disruptions in the therapeutic bond. I told her that the therapy could not work if she sought the relationship she needed from me in substances. This idea terrified her because she was both fearful of depending on me and anxious that relying on me would be futile. Being unable to imagine how discussion could soothe her catastrophic anxiety, Mary was amazed to find that telephone contact calmed her by restoring the therapeutic connection, but the increased dependence created a new danger. The phone calls escalated in frequency and duration. Eventually, I found that her merely hearing my voice was no longer enough to reassure her: Mary required a deeper sense of my presence. In a voice trembling with fear, she would implore me: "I don't think you're there! I need to know you're there!" To calm her, I started repeating "It's meeeee" in a soft, almost melodic tone until she felt my presence. This almost chanting, repetitive chorus became the way she felt connected to me not only on the telephone but also in sessions. Successful episodes of this type almost magically transformed her immediate state from catastrophic anxiety to a beatific calm in which her face lit up with a smile and she was totally relaxed.

Mary referred to these experiences as "moments of being," by which she meant a sense of genuinely experienced personal existence. During these moments, Mary felt that the separation between us had vanished and that she experienced a moment of oneness with me. Although temporary, these instances became the transformative experiences of her therapy. By stringing together these powerful moments, she began to feel a sense of calm between sessions and eventually gave up telephone calls. The substance abuse was relinquished completely during this phase of the treatment and never returned. In my clinical experience, Mary's substance abuse is typical of the borderline patient: it reflects disturbances in the therapeutic bond and abates when that relationship achieves the strength the patient needs.

As Mary "strung together" these isolated bits of genuine experience, she felt that she was taking me "inside" her. When she became disturbed outside of sessions, she talked to the "Dr. Summers in my head," and the sense of my presence provided her with the calm she sought. Mary told herself what she imagined I would say to her, and this capacity to relieve her anxiety provided a sense of freedom to pursue interests for the first time in her life. Her "moments of being" created a positive synergy as her calm, strengthened self states led to successful life experiences that, in turn, alleviated her paranoia and exquisite sensitivity, affording the opportunity for more positive life experiences.

When she found her first job in her newly chosen field, Mary felt she had made the first important conscious decision of her life. Becoming gainfully employed after a dysfunctional life, she was proud not only of doing her job but also of pursuing work that she desired and that gave her purpose. When her calm sense of self was sufficiently continuous that therapeutic contact was no longer required for its maintenance, she terminated therapy. The fragile self who had been unable to make emotional contact without annihilation anxiety had been transcended.

Sharon, for her part, became "little": She engaged me in childlike behavior and games. My acceptance of her need to do this and my willingness to relate to her as a "little" person in need of nurturing provided the conditions for her feeling of merger. However, instead of complying with her persistent request for physical holding, I insisted that we find a way for her to feel a sense of fusion without physical contact. In this nurturing situation, we found the way for her to feel a oneness that provided a purely emotional connectedness unique in her experience.

When coming twice per week, Clara was unable to feel a useful bond with me. Filled with envy and jealousy, she complained bitterly of my greater privileges and comforts and attacked me for preferring other patients, especially women, all of whom she presumed to have lives of greater luxury. She persistently accused me of preferring my wife and family and giving to them in a way I would never do for her. Vacations were so traumatizing that, for months before and after, sessions were consumed with anger and with accusations of my irresponsibility and unfairness for abandoning her.

When the sessions were extended to four weekly, the therapeutic tone shifted dramatically, as Clara felt a new continuity and increasing peacefulness in the therapeutic bond. Envy, jealousy, and rage began to recede as she allowed herself to feel understood by my acknowledgment of her needs. Gratified by the growing emotional connection with me, when she began to get angry, she would calm herself and say, "I don't want to be crazy today." One day, she said nothing as she entered the consulting room, quietly lay her head down on the couch, and rested for the entire session. She later referred to this experience as a blissful sense of oneness with me in which she was for that session entirely unaware of herself as a separate person. Although she had briefer merger episodes thereafter, she cited this session as the pivotal experience of her therapy, having trusted me enough to feel a closeness that felt real rather than overdramatized.

Separations continued to cause severe anxiety for a long time, but Clara responded to interruptions with a longing for the lost contact rather than with rage, jealousy, and envy. During this time, Clara began to date a man with whom she felt immediate rapport, and the relationship quickly developed into the romance of her life. At this writing, the couple is married with two children. Although there is little doubt that she had finally met the "right man," the relationship was made possible by Clara's emotional availability. Knowing that emotional connection with another was possible, she allowed herself to be given to, and, in turn, she was able to be caring and sensitive to him. By this point, rage, envy, and jealousy had ceased to play a prominent role in her life, and they have not interfered in the relationship with her husband.

Without directly focusing on her rage, Clara had transcended the self who had been able to relate to others only by anger, envy, jealousy, and victimization. Once the therapeutic relationship achieved the "unity" for which she longed, her intense anger, along with the other affects that had interfered in her relationships, died off. Her intensely negative affects were reactions to frustration of the longing for emotional relatedness that could only be felt by moments of merger, and, once this need was responded to within the therapeutic context, these affects abated. The psychotherapy of Clara illustrates the fact that "excess aggression" in the borderline patient is not psychological rock bottom but is secondary to the frustration of the longing for fusion.

In all three cases—Mary, Sharon, and Clara—the key transforming experience was the shift in the therapeutic relationship from the oscillations of threatening contact to the meeting of the need for a merger experience. Although the form of the experience was different in each case, the decisive therapeutic step for each patient entailed trusting me with her deepest longings, the most vulnerable parts of herself. In order to be available for the needed experience, I had to absorb painful and almost overwhelming feelings. That is, the first therapeutic ingredient in each case was my "holding" the intense affects generated by the interaction. As each patient came to believe that I was willing to undergo whatever experience she needed in order to feel a genuine emotional connection within the limits of a psychological bond, she began to take steps toward the formation of the needed but feared relationship.

For Mary, my encouragement of her reaching out for contact and my willing availability for extra-session contact provided enough safety for her to begin using me (rather than alcohol) to calm her anxiety over separation. Building on moments of soothing, we eventually found a stable substitute for alcohol in melodic reassurance of my presence. Sharon began therapy with an attitude of angry mistrust, but this outlook began to shift when she saw that I understood her need to push me away out of fear of her longings. When I showed my genuine willingness to contain both her needs and fear of them, she began to show me how "little" she felt inside. Clara was able to experience the oneness she sought only after we increased the session frequency to four weekly. This change made possible the continuity she needed in order to feel a psychological bond and simultaneously allowed me to demonstrate my willingness to contain her rage, envy, and jealousy. In each of these therapeutic dyads, I felt, at various points, the despair of ever being able to achieve any movement, helplessness in my efforts to do so, and anger at the patient for pushing me away. I understood these responses to be communications from the patient of what their life-worlds were like and sustained a vision in each case of untapped potential. Although each patient needed a different concrete experience, the transformation of the therapeutic relationship hinged on my willingness, in each case, to contain my affective response sufficiently for the patient to feel safe enough to expose her most vulnerable longings. The therapeutic action then shifted to my engaging the specific form of the merger experience with each patient. To illustrate more precisely how this model works, I consider in detail the psychotherapeutic process with Sharon.

Sharon: An Illustration of
Transcending the Fragile Self

Because the previous therapeutic relationship had become a "tug of war" around Sharon's demands for holding and nurturing, I had anticipated that Sharon and I would engage in control struggles, and

Sharon did not disappoint. In our initial phone contact, she demanded that I read some informational material before our first meeting. When I told her that I prefer to have my initial impressions of her formed by direct contact, Sharon angrily hung up on me, and I never expected to talk to her again. To my surprise, she called for an appointment four months later—without mentioning the written material, which I later received without notice from her, and we never did discuss it.

The initial presentation of this 31-year-old in psychotherapy was of a woman appearing somewhat older than her age, tightly held, casually but neatly dressed. She described herself as practical, preferring tasks and concrete activities to the world of feelings, a world she found mysterious and perhaps unapproachable. She explained that she had chosen her vocation for the sense of immediate, practical achievement it brought but that had been without close friends all her life because she was unsure of how to form relationships that were not task oriented. Sitting with uncomfortable tension, Sharon talked without affect about her lack of functioning and difficulties with her previous therapist. She appeared to be clutching her chair tightly and, when asked if she was anxious, replied in the affirmative. Stating that she rarely was aware of what she felt, Sharon discussed her difficulties with anger and anxiety in a neutral, emotionless manner.

Entering psychotherapy on a twice-weekly basis, Sharon spent the first few months discussing her husband's emotional unavailability and uncertain financial future. The focus of her complaints tended to be on her spouse's professional and financial passivity, a trait that led her to feel insecure about his income potential. Despair at his inability to change and her incapacity to change him grew into a general hopelessness regarding her own condition, her ability to influence the events of her own and others' lives, and, above all, her aptitude for an emotional relationship.

As Sharon's despair began to consume her life in and out of therapy, the sessions were filled with anxiety and tension. She was often silent for long periods of time—on one occasion, for an entire therapy hour. Frequently, she entered the room in an almost paralyzed state, standing motionless for several minutes, uncertain what to do. Outside of therapy, phone calls became frequent, although their purpose remained unclear, and verbal exchange during them was often minimal. During one entire session, Sharon sat with her back to me and spoke only when spoken to, although she did acknowledge my comment that she wished to be pursued; another time, she stood silently in the center of the consulting room, apparently immobilized, for almost the entire session, eventually sitting on the floor.

During this phase of psychotherapy, when asked her feelings, Sharon replied in a soft, shaky voice, "scared." Her only elaboration was that she was frightened of me and that I was "dangerous." She also began to ask "Are you still there?" during both sessions and phone calls, often more than once in a given session. Each time I reflected her fear of abandonment or anger, Sharon would ask "Are you still there?" either in the session or later in a telephone call. The fluctuations in Sharon's anxiety and depression could be assessed by the timing and frequency of this question. When she felt our relationship was endangered, she asked it; during moments of connection to me, she might still become anxious, but she did not ask the question. When I asked what made her wonder about the existence of someone who was sitting before her, Sharon became sullen and withdrawn and said with great irritation, "I need you to say it." Although she realized questioning the existence of someone sitting in front of her made no sense, she needed reassurance. After the question was answered, Sharon was more amenable to discussing this need, explaining that, without this verbal confirmation, she believed I would leave her. My affirmative answer allayed her anxiety temporarily, although she still feared abandonment. Eventually, she was able to connect the fear of my leaving with her father's desertion of the family home and her mother's emotional withdrawal.

Earlier, I noted that one of Sharon's most striking memories was of giving her mother a surprise birthday party with her sister. The children were enthusiastic about the event and eagerly anticipated their mother's excitement, only to be crestfallen when her response was annoyance at the "mess." Her current despair had a quality similar to the profound disillusionment she felt when her mother derived no pleasure from her birthday party. Sharon associated her lack of emotionality to a persistent childhood anxiety that, if she did not act in a completely "proper," emotionless manner, her mother would abandon her. As a child, she had often thought to herself, "Are you still there?"

On the basis of the disappointment and frustration in both parents and her childhood memories, I pointed out that she had an unmet lifelong desire for an emotional bond that scared her. Although she found this interpretation threatening, she knew it was true, and she was then able to relate her yearning for connection with me while being aware of separateness to the nearly paralyzing anxiety she experienced in sessions. There ensued a period of depression as Sharon mourned her unfulfilled longing for fusion, an awareness that made her acutely aware of being alone.

Sharon's hopelessness and depression frequently followed positive therapeutic moments. If she was not making progress, she complained about that, and, when gains were evident, they were not enough or the wrong kind. When she felt I did understand her, she often despaired, frequently falling silent. When I pointed out that these reactions were her reenacting her relationship with her mother and avoiding a potentially new experience with me, Sharon was then able to say that she feared having good feelings toward me for fear of losing herself in me. Now when she was silent, I interpreted her longing to be understood without having to communicate. Although she agreed, Sharon was frightened by this understanding because she felt that I could "see into" her head. Aware that her despondency was not simply a reenactment of her disappointment in her mother but a defense against a deeper longing that threatened her sense of self, Sharon struggled with her desire for and fear of fusion.

By establishing a routine, Sharon found that she could reduce her anxiety during sessions while maintaining a type of connection with me. She would bring over my desk chair, sit with her feet on it, cover her body with an afghan, and either remained silent or spoke in a low, soft, almost pleading voice, often expressing the need to be taken care of. When asked how she was feeling, her usual reply was a barely audible "scared."

When Sharon discussed her lack of mothering and isolation, her affect and voice began to change into that of a little girl, and she would ask to be "played with." Frequently, she requested extension of the session beyond our allotted time. At the end of one session, she refused to leave until I told her I would have to call the police. When I responded verbally to her wishes for nurturance rather than comply with her desires, Sharon felt I had left her "all alone," a response she associated to her abandonment by both mother and father. With her voice changing into that of the little girl appealing for help, Sharon would often refer to this behavior in the third person, pleading for what "she" wanted. Feeling no control over this part of herself, Sharon also felt that she needed a safe place to be her "little-girl side." Experiencing verbal responses as implying that she was "wrong," Sharon felt rejected by my efforts to understand, a reaction she identified with her mother's coldness.

I felt controlled by Sharon's demands and often wanted to say "no" simply to affirm my autonomy. Nonetheless, I also became increasingly aware of the depth of her pain, isolation, loneliness, and depression. Experiencing her demands as desperate efforts to receive nurturing without feeling vulnerable, I wanted to give to her, but I was not sure how. I viewed her desire for nurturing as the emergence of a formerly buried, terrifying part of herself. Although I responded verbally to this need and her fear of exposing it, I had no conviction that such comments would diminish her longing, and I was right. When I told her that she was seeking comfort for the baby in her that had been so long unattended, she was moved and often cried, but it was clear that such comments neither met nor altered her need to be cared for.

I did my best to provide an environment in which she could be as much of a "baby" as the framework of the therapy sessions permitted. I stayed with her physically and emotionally even when she was silent for the entire session. When I did talk, I said that she seemed like she needed to be in a place where she could "let go" and not feel any sense of burden and that she needed to know that I was there to go through this experience with her. I made an assiduous effort not to let my attention wander from her (although it did sometimes happen) because I felt that she needed to be held, not forgotten. My experience was that, if I wandered from attentiveness for a sustained period, I would be abandoning her. My concentration on her even while she seemed removed, unaware of me, and sometimes even asleep was an adaptation to her need to be held, a connection in which there was no burden on her to do anything other than be there.

In the midst of this deep therapeutic regression, Sharon asked if we could read books together. She brought in children's books, such as *The Velveteen Rabbit,* and I was so moved by the genuineness of her request that I wanted to respond to it. As I read, she was moved, often to tears. My experience was that the emotions generated by the books were a way of meeting her need for a nurturing emotional bond without physical holding. We were becoming emotionally bonded by sharing the experiences and the feelings evoked in her by the children's stories. There were also celebrations. On birthdays or anniversaries of major events, she brought cake she had baked, and we shared it together. On these occasions, I ate with her as we chatted. There was no need to discuss the obvious fact that these experiences were of critical importance to Sharon, who had never before had a participatory sense of celebration with another person. Indeed, such a discussion might well have created distance from the experiences.

During one session in which she seemed to feel especially "little," Sharon asked in her little-girl voice if I would physically hold her. Although this request did not surprise me, it disturbed me because I did not want to meet it, I knew I would not meet it, and I feared for the ruin of all we had accomplished by my unwillingness to comply. I did, however, feel coercive pressure from her. Fearing that physical holding would blur my sense of boundaries and with it my connection to a therapeutic process, I felt that my sense of identity, even my sanity, depended on the maintenance of a firm boundary between the physical and the psychological.

Nonetheless, I knew she would be injured by my refusal, and I hesitated to give it. I said, "No, I will not. I want to hold you but not that way. In fact, I feel that you are being held. I cannot touch you without feeling that I am losing my sense of what this is and even who I am." Although Sharon was distressed at my refusal of her request, she was surprised at and pleased with the candor of my reply. My explanation gave her pause, and she seemed to think about it for a moment. Nonetheless, she indicated that she needed holding and did not know how "this was going to work" if I could not provide what she needed. I replied that, although I would not physically hold her, I had the impression that she had been held in other ways. Although she agreed, Sharon still felt she needed the physical experience. I guessed aloud that she was not sure of my holding, my "really being there," without the physical sensation, and that our work was about helping her to feel my presence, the reality of our relationship, without the physical reassurance of it. Initially, she voiced skepticism and was not sure I was not rationalizing an unwillingness to help her the way she sought, but she found a way to adapt to my limitation: Whenever she felt the desire to be physically held, Sharon curled up in her afghan and rested, sometimes even slept, while I watched over her. She later told me that she felt like a "babe in arms" and experienced the most peaceful moments of her life during these sessions.

It is striking that this woman, who had been so easily injured when her requests were rebuffed, did not have a catastrophic reaction when her most sensitive request was denied. She showed none of the depression, despair, and hopelessness that had characterized her previous reactions to disappointments. I believe her relatively benign response can be attributed primarily to three factors: She had by that point felt given to enough that she did not feel totally rejected or empty; the candor of my response made her feel that the refusal was an authentic expression of who I am, and this point of genuine contact made her feel connected to me in a new way; and my unwillingness to hold her physically set our relationship clearly apart from the relationship with her previous therapist. The critical therapeutic experience was the maintenance of the emotional bond despite the setting of a limitation. My refusal did not interfere with her connection to me and in fact enriched it by providing a relationship she had never had: an affective tie without physical contact. This boundary setting put the relationship into the realm of realistic human intercourse, but she did not lose the attachment because emotional contact was made with her longings, her little-girl side.

After a phase in which she was mostly silent in sessions, Sharon began to talk more frequently, and play became a primary medium of our interaction. During this period, she brought her kitten in, and, although I did play rather lightly with it, I was not as engaged as she wanted me to be. When she questioned my limited interest, I told her that, although I found her kitten cute, I did not have a passion for cats and was not as excited about it as she was. Although chagrined at my limited interest in the kitten, she was surprised and pleased that I was happy to read her stories, played other games with her, and showed genuine enthusiasm for accomplishments of which she was proud. I felt maternal toward her, but I also knew that she was navigating around limitations in my "motherhood."

The uniqueness of this relationship, which included genuine emotional bonding within limits, led to her renewed interest in the world. Her ability to accept my limitations without loss of the bond began her journey back to the give-and-take of normal human intercourse. During this period, Sharon began to show more energy in and out of sessions, performing long-neglected household chores and making efforts to see people with whom she had not been in contact. Feeling a new desire to find employment, she applied for a job, but, after a series of interviews, she was refused. Despondent, Sharon experienced the refusal as rejection and felt the emotional drain to apply for employment to be so extreme and the "failure" so painful that she could not go through the process again. Although she continued to perform domestic chores, Sharon lost much of her energy and returned to feeling despondent.

The disappointment in the job possibility again evoked her despairing feelings of abandonment and isolation from the world. For the next two months, her hopelessness returned, and she needed constant telephone contact and, at times, extra sessions. Despite the increased therapeutic contact, Sharon felt deprived of support and emotional relatedness with me. Continuing to be afraid that I was disappointed in her because of her job "failure," she feared that I would abandon her by terminating the relationship outright or, less directly, by suggesting medication or hospitalization. I pointed out that she felt that the same process had occurred with each parent: She interpreted her mother's emotional abandonment to mean that she could not handle her needs and her father's leaving as an indication that she was a burden to him. Analogously, she feared that I was encumbered with her problems to the point of leaving her. Sharon readily agreed with this interpetation but also felt that she had some realistic basis for her fears given her experience with her previous therapist. Nonetheless, repeated experiences of my living through her disappointment and feelings of rejection, my persistent availability outside of session, and my continued psychological holding of her despair and regression in sessions eventually restored her faith in the therapeutic connection.

Once again, Sharon felt restored to energy and optimism, issuing in the motivation to seek employment; this time she was successful. Her success at finding employment improved her mood still further, and she found that she could work well despite lack of guidance from her employers and an initially problematic supervisory situation. She performed so well that she received excellent evaluations, raises, and a promotion.

This improved functioning extended into other areas of her life. Sadness over the mother she never had and will not have abated as she found emotional connection in the therapeutic relationship. Sharon regained the pleasure she had once derived from domestic activities such as baking and cooking. When she and her husband bought their first home, Sharon was excited about the house and the new suburban area to which they moved. Most important to her, Sharon formed friendships, not just acquaintances, with some of the people she met in her new neighborhood or at work. For the first time in her life, Sharon felt she had a group of people who were important to her. Her relationship with her husband also became closer and less conflictual. Although improvements in his business life were a factor in this shift, Sharon's capacity for emotional relating contributed to their new intimacy. At the time of termination, her mood fluctuated without extreme lows or highs, although she was still given to sporadic feelings of temporary sadness, but with much decreased frequency and intensity.

With regard to the major life decision of motherhood, which had spurred her initial interest in therapy, I can happily report that Sharon was pregnant with her second child when she terminated our seven-year therapeutic relationship. At that time, she reduced her employment to part-time so she could care for her children. When I last saw her, on a chance encounter, she had three children, was continuing part-time employment, and seemed happy and comfortable with her new suburban, family-oriented lifestyle.

Conclusion

The psychotherapeutic process with Sharon illustrates the value of this object relational concept of borderline pathology. Sharon's overwhelming anxiety, depression, and paralysis of functioning resolved only after she underwent a therapeutic regression that allowed her to form an attachment based on her little-girl side, the buried emotional potential of her self. However, this pivotal therapeutic experience was possible only because the interpretive process moved the therapeutic relationship past Sharon's social veneer to her more authentic but long-buried desires. In this way, interpretation "tilled the soil" in which her new self could grow. Together we "reached back" beneath her social adaptation to her vulnerable, protected, fragile self. When these long-buried needs were responded to, not merely acknowledged but "met" in a way that fit the therapeutic context, she felt a new life begin to grow inside her. Critical to the success of this process was my response to the most vulnerable aspects of her self. When she became her little girl, referred to herself in the third person, and participated in childhood play, I engaged her.

In a very real, emotional sense, she gave birth to a "new" self who had the ability to relate and feel close to others. As this formerly buried aspect was realized in the therapeutic relationship, Sharon's depression and isolation disappeared. This process typifies the psychotherapy of the borderline patient: The symptoms are relinquished when the therapeutic connection meets in some way the buried longing for fusion. With the realization of her potential for emotional connectedness, Sharon transcended her fragile self and gave birth to her potential for emotional connection.

The therapeutic action in this case demonstrates the value of a theoretical posture that views psychopathology as arrested development due to the failure of early objects to facilitate self development. With the borderline patient, the technical implication is the provision of the fused relationship sought by the patient within the limits of the psychotherapeutic context. That my affective bonding with Sharon occurred without physical holding and without full collaboration with her wishes maintained a boundary between us that preserved therapeutic space. The therapeutic relationship was Sharon's first experience of an affective connection without physical contact. Once this type of relating was established, Sharon began to find new investment in the world and other people, and her functioning eventually returned but this time without the sacrifice of emotional contact with the world.

No parameters were ever used to block acting out. Sharon's angry, despairing reactions to disappointment were understood as symptoms of her separation–fusion dilemma, and, when the relationship achieved the balance of emotional connection without fusion, both responses evaporated. As her capacity for "ego relatedness" increased, disappointments became temporary disturbances in the relationship rather than threats to it. Her rage and despair were relinquished when the relationship achieved the depth of emotional relatedness she sought without loss of self. The growth of the arrested self required the "nutrients" of adaptation to her need for fusion. Within this facilitating relationship, Sharon was able to gain contact with her long-buried desires for affective human contact, which mobilized the creation of a self that enjoyed relating to others. This new self transcended the fragile self that avoided affective connection out of anxiety of boundary loss and hid behind practicality and superficial social adaptation.

The process of meeting the need for fusion within the therapeutic context was pivotal to the transcendence of the fragile self for both Clara and Mary. When Clara was eventually able to feel a continuity in the therapeutic bond, she experienced a peacefulness that gratified her longing for fusion enough that her desperate clinging demands and chronic rage abated. This relationship, unique in her experience, extended to the world as she formed her first bond of human intimacy. As with Sharon, no "parameters" were ever set to limit the acting out of her rage. When the relationship achieved the needed tie, she no longer required anger to protect her sense of autonomy. Her fragile self was transcended in favor of a continuous self with a strong sense of autonomy not threatened by intimacy. For Mary, my melodic, soothing sounds were the medium for her feeling of fusion. She perceived my repetitive refrain reassuring her that I was with her as an experience of blissful union sufficient to gratify her desire for fusion. When these moments were "strung together" enough for her to feel a continuous connection with me, she was less vulnerable to disappointments between us, and she relinquished her substance abuse. As with Clara, her chronic anger abated in the same process. In both cases, interpretation aimed the therapeutic relationship toward the "target" of buried self potential, but symptom relief occurred only when the relationship achieved sufficient strength that the self no longer needed protection.

By contrast, the ego-psychological framework, even in its object relations form as proposed by Kernberg (1976), views the pathology as ego defect and implies adherence to interpretation as the crux of therapeutic action. Contemporary ego psychologists rely on interpretation of resistance and defense to uncover unconscious fantasy and tend to attack the object relations view of provision of a new relationship (Busch, 1995; Sugarman, 1995; Wilson, 1995). Such a model opposes the offering of just the relationship that catalyzed Sharon's movement from isolation to the world of human relationships, Clara's journey from clinging desperation to adult intimacy, and Mary's shift from substances to human contact.

Opposition to the concept of therapeutic action with the borderline patient as the formation of a fused relationship is not limited to ego-psychological theorists. For different reasons, the relational model of therapeutic action as proposed by Mitchell (1988) also precludes precisely the relationship needed by patients such as Sharon. This foremost proponent of relational theory criticizes object relations theories for "infantilizing" the patient by offering gratification, an approach Mitchell claims results in a "splitting off of the analytic relationship from the rest of life, as the only domain in which one's desires are truly taken into account" (p. 164). In the therapeutic process undergone by Sharon, Clara, and Mary, the opposite occurred: In each case, the gratification in the therapeutic relationship that Mitchell opposes led to the first genuine affective connection with the world. For example, only after Clara established a continuous affective bond with me was she able to sustain her first stable love relationship. In the case of Mary, the soothing melodic chant of my voice provided the gratification that solidified our bond and made our human contact ultimately preferable to substances. The clinical process with borderline patients for whom a gratifying therapeutic relationship is formed invariably goes in opposition to the direction predicted by Mitchell. Further damaging Mitchell's position is the fact that he offers no examples of seriously disturbed patients whom he has successfully treated according to his preferred approach. Set against Mitchell's absence of clinical evidence are the cases of Sharon, Clara, and Mary, three examples of profoundly impaired patients who successfully transcended a fragile sense of self through a therapeutic relationship in which they experienced their sought-for bond of fusion.

Although all borderline patients, by definition, seek a merger relationship, each patient has a uniquely individual manner of creating the needed form of attachment. Unlike Sharon, Clara never asked to be physically held; however, she expected to be told of my private life, a request never made by Sharon. Whereas Sharon had to be "little" for a protracted period in order to experience the needed fusion, Clara was able to feel the unity in brief moments of emotional sharing and did not require my participation in childlike activities. Mary differed from both in her need to have a soft, calming, melodic chant continually repeated in order to feel a sense of "being" that she was eventually able to build into a new self. The therapist's role is to understand that the patient's need is for a merged relationship, to find the unique way of forming it, and to create with the patient the needed relationship. Provision of this experience is the requisite adaptation that makes the treatment of such patients fundamentally different from that of other patients and that renders possible the transcendence of the fragile self.

Chapter 6

Defective Self,
Protective Object

Zelda came to treatment in a panic. Her 18-month marriage was in a shambles, and she feared leaving but could not tolerate being home. Having impulses to leave town and abandon the marriage, hating her job, and yet fearing change, she suffered from overwhelming anxiety alternating with severe depression, both of which gained symptomatic expression in a severe binge-eating disorder. Her life was so chaotic and given to such extreme mood swings that her family and friends thought she should be evaluated for manic–depressive disorder.

In the midst of discussing all these problems in the first interview, Zelda stated with bitterness, "I hate myself. I always have." This statement was not a revelation for her but a fact of life she accepted and never expected to change. Despite her feeling that she suffered from low self-esteem, Zelda had never given thought to why or how this negative self-evaluation might change. Unable to specify any attributes that justified her self-loathing, Zelda stated simply that she hated "everything about myself." The one positive quality she knew she possessed was her looks. As may be recalled from chapter 4,

Zelda believed she was able to manipulate most people, including two previous female therapists, with her coquettish charm and social grace. But this deviousness only left her feeling "fake," as though she were navigating her way through life as a fraud. Her ability to manage people by pleasing and flirting was one more reason to hate herself.

Zelda's problems can be fit into many diagnostic categories, but striking in her self-presentation was her assumption of self-loathing: She believed she had no commendable qualities except her looks, and even that was used for purposes she detested. Her deepest conviction about herself being that she was defective, Zelda believed everything she did was somehow wrong: her husband was inadequate, but she needed him; her job was menial, but she feared doing anything else; she had no friends. Unable to imagine influencing events in her life, Zelda tried to hide from the interpersonal world, and her relationships with others were designed to protect against the visibility of her "defect." Her husband, who would not question any aspect of her behavior, took care of her basic needs, a fact that minimized her need to interact with others. Fearing confrontation with any component of the world she could not control, Zelda had retreated to an existence of virtual sequestration. Although she functioned at work, Zelda felt her job was so far beneath her training and skill that it was tantamount to another way of "hiding" from the world. Her object relationships being organized for protection against visibility and feeling helpless to influence her fate, Zelda tended to lie in bed and sleep for lengthy periods in a nearly paralyzing depression.

Despite the bingeing and severity of symptoms, Zelda did not have the fragility of self that characterized patients discussed in chapter 5—like Mary, Clara, and Sharon, all of whom sought contact through merger. Zelda's symptoms could be understood either as direct expressions of this shameful feeling of defect or as defenses against it. Her sense of worthlessness and of her helplessness to alter this fundamental view of herself was manifested directly in her chronic depression. When such feelings became intolerable, she attempted magical "solutions" to overcome them by fantasies of escape or sudden changes in her life, each of which provided a dramatic momentary euphoria that allayed her depression. Frequently in search of some new "cure" or suddenly different life situation she hoped would relieve her pain, Zelda attempted a variety of "new age" cures, becoming elated at the prospect of being helped only to despair each time the relief she so desperately sought did not appear. The fantasy of escape to a rural or mountain area gave her a sudden rush of excitement and temporary relief, which only dissolved when she confronted her fear of traveling alone. When no magical solution seemed at hand, she attempted to relieve depression and anxiety by bingeing, overwhelming her feelings with a temporary sense of "fullness." Thus, Zelda's feeling of defectiveness was the root of her mercurial mood shifts, nearly paralyzing depression, catastrophic anxiety, and eating disorder.

Needless to say, a variety of personality structures and clinical pictures may emerge in response to such a defect, and Zelda's symptom pattern is only one such outcome. The protection of a stubborn, persistent feeling of diminished or nonexistent self-worth organized her personality. The protection of this deep conviction about one's self, which may be called a narcissistic defect, is the basic motivating principle of the narcissistic personality. The anxiety of having this defect exposed may be called a narcissistic tension state. Because exposure of this "defect" would be experienced as shame (Morrison, 1989), narcissistic tension entails the constant fear of a shame experience.

Of all the problems confronting clinicians, intractably low self-esteem is perhaps the most vexing and ubiquitous. Although many patients typically include in their list of problems the complaint, "I do not like myself," or "I have low self-esteem," for patients like Zelda anxiety about experiences "confirming" their feelings of inadequacy organizes their interpersonal world. Nonetheless, in apparent contradiction, they recruit experiences to fit this preformed idea. If they make a mistake, however mild, or do not succeed at a task, even temporarily, such "failures" are taken as incontrovertible evidence of their inadequacy, but successes are barely noticed and have no discernible impact on their feelings about themselves. It is this "psychic magnetism" for negative experiences that makes the low self-esteem of patients such as Zelda so stubborn, resilient, and refractory to psychotherapeutic intervention.

The narcissistically vulnerable patient has two apparently contradictory needs: On the one hand, he insists on maintaining a persistently negative view of himself; on the other, he works assiduously to prevent the recognition of this "defect" by others. Continual vigilance regarding this possibility puts a burdensome strain on relationships and interactions with others, resulting in a life of chronic narcissistic tension. When this tension becomes too much to bear, seemingly routine events can threaten exposure and precipitate a rageful reaction. Such eruptions being the "last-ditch" defense against shame, the state of continual narcissistic tension explains why apparently minor events can provoke uncontrollable explosions. When the patient is willing to "go to war" over being cut off by another car on the roadway, his scream contains both a plea and protest, "I will not be shamed one more time! I will fight to be recognized! You will notice me!" These explosions reflect the constant narcissistic tension that lies just under the veneer of social existence.

Origins of the Sense of Inadequacy

As seen in chapter 2, we are born with core affects that become part of self-affect-object experiences, and the complex elaboration of these object relationships becomes the self structure. Affects are not simple states; they include our ways of experiencing the world, and that experience in turn affects our affects, a process Spezzano (1993) has described as the "circle of human experience: affect-perception-representation-affect" (p. 52). Thus, affects are at the very center of our subjectivity, our personal idiom; they are the psychic motivators that make us care (Tomkins, 1962; Spezzano, 1993). Because affects are complex and changeable, each person has a wide variety of affective potential, but a core of object relationships based on affective experience becomes our self structure, although the potential for continued elaboration continues throughout life. Ways of being and relating based on these affects express the very heart of who we are, our true self.

Development

For authentically experienced affective states to become articulated into a self structure, they must be responded to and facilitated by early caretakers (Demos, 1983). Kohut (1977) pointed out that the birth of the self occurs in the parents' treatment of the baby as though it were a self. The parent's responsiveness to the child's states elicits and stimulates the child's potential to elaborate those states into a self-organization. Only in the recognizing gaze of the other can the child's potential become an organized self. When the child looks into the mother's gaze, "what she looks like is related to what she sees there" (Winnicott, 1969, p. 112). That is, the child finds himself in his mother's recognition.

Demos (1984, 1988) has shown that competence and trust in affective states are requirements for a stably positive view of the self. Development of these capacities depends on the caretaker's facilitating positive affects and helping in the regulation of negative states (Demos, 1984). As seen in chapter 2, the evidence from Demos's studies of affect development, Beebe's work on mother–infant dyads, and Bowlby's attachment studies suggests that competence is facilitated by a caretaker who provides an "optimal zone of affective engagement," allowing the child to have the negative state but responsive enough to help him cope with it.

Learning to regulate negative affects abets the child's trust in his ability to transform untoward experiences and events. This sense of competence provides a fundamental belief in his resources to manage negative experience. Conversely, children who receive insufficient help with negative affects are overwhelmed by them and, being threatened, tend to withdraw from conflict. Such children do not believe in their competence to manage difficulties, and this lack of faith in their ability results in a sense of inadequacy that in turn leads to avoidance of negative affects.

Interest and enjoyment are inborn affects (Tomkins, 1978); if these states are facilitated, encouraged, and enhanced, the child will come to believe that his positive feelings and excitement are worthy of others' interest, that he is an interesting person. If, on the other hand, the child's interests and enjoyment are ignored or actively discouraged, he will likely believe that his naturally arising positive states are unacceptable, not worthy of others' attention. He is likely, then, to conclude that his positive affective states are somehow "defective," as though he were fundamentally lacking in what others find valuable. Not believing that his affects will be acceptable to others and can be relied on to provide meaningful relationships, such a child looks for other guides in relating to others. In contrast, the child who believes his spontaneously arising affects make him interesting to others will believe that the expression of those affects can be relied on to attract others' interest. Such a child trusts that he can form and sustain relationships by acting on his authentic affects and interests, even if those preferences are different from or in opposition to those of others. Believing in the value of his genuinely experienced affects, such a child uses his affects as criteria for making the judgments that direct his behavior. His judgments, opinions, and values are derived from his affective depths.

With this confidence, positive affects can be enjoyed and experienced fully, and negative affects are met with the belief they can be overcome, both of which issue in a positive feeling toward one's core subjectivity. This belief in the appeal of one's affects constitutes trust in the self, or confidence, healthy self-esteem. Confidence is literally "with faith" or "having faith in." The child who possesses this confidence trusts that his genuinely experienced affects, the core of his subjectivity, are attractive to others and therefore have value. The child who does not believe his affective experience is acceptable to the early caretakers tends to feel defective to the very core of his being.

If the child lacks faith that his spontaneous affects are worthy of others' interest, his affects then feel "shaky," as though relying on them will lead to danger. Rather than being based on genuine affects, relationships become organized around protecting the sense of inadequacy that forms the core of subjective experience. Others then become either sources of gratification, by helping to protect against awareness of the defective feeling, or objects of mistrust, if they threaten to "expose" inadequacy. The paranoic tendency of many relationships formed by such patients is rooted in the fear of such exposure.

From the time of Freud's discovery that hysterical patients defended against the awareness of strangulated affects, psychoanalysis has distinguished between authentic affects and experience that is designed to hide awareness of threatening feelings. The latter type of experience, although it may include affects, is anxiety-driven, whereas authenticity consists of the feeling states that lie at the very center of our subjectivity. It is this "affective truth" that psychoanalysis has always sought (Spezzano, 1993, p. 215). When Winnicott (1960a) distinguished between "true" and "false" selves, he gave new terms to a distinction that has always been at the heart of psychoanalytic thinking. The problem is that authenticity is not easily discerned when defended against by an affectively laden facade. Only after extended therapeutic exploration could Zelda see the emptiness hidden beneath her veneer as well as her anger at those whom she felt driven to please. That is, Zelda recognized that her superficial affects of friendly flirtatiousness were motivated by the need to defend against painful feelings of inadequacy. Anxiety-driven affective states lack authenticity; any feeling that emerges without such threatening motivation may be regarded as authentic. Furthermore, Zelda's underlying affects of anger, frustration, and imprisonment made sense of her bulimia, depression, and cyclic mood swings. That these affects fit her symptom picture (whereas superficial friendliness did not) indicates that her negative affects were genuine (whereas her social appearance was defensive). Goodness of fit with behavior and symptom picture is an effective criterion of affective authenticity.

Benjamin (1988) has pointed out that there can be a specific gender meaning to the lack of parental recognition that results in the feeling of defectiveness. She suggests that, in the traditional family constellation, the father represents the source of power and desire, but he often has great difficulty recognizing his daughter's subjectivity. Not having her subjectivity validated by a source of power and desire, she may feel defective—a conviction of her inadequacy that is often concretely represented as penis envy. She will then seek idealized, masochistic attachments to men in a desperate effort to become recognized.

All of the narcissistic patients whom I have treated, some of whom are described in this chapter, report clear memories and feelings of being ignored, not responded to, or overtly devalued by significant early figures or, alternatively, of being so attended to that they had little opportunity to grapple with their own experience. Furthermore, none of these patients trusted his affective states in the formation of relationships.

As noted in chapter 4, Zelda had a virtually nonexistent relationship with each parent. Her early focus in psychotherapy was on her father's harsh, violent temper, the unpredictability of which terrorized her in childhood until she had become anxious in his presence. It was not until later in the treatment that Zelda began to focus on her lack of connection to her mother and the disgust she felt in her presence from the time of her earliest memories.

Her affects not having been responded to in a way that facilitated the development of positive and regulated negative affects, Zelda had no faith in her subjective states and frequently did not even know what they were. Unable to use her spontaneous affects, Zelda learned to mold her behavior to what pleased others. For example, she admitted that she had never been attracted to her husband but had married him because her parents "chose" him for her. Her college major was suggested by others, and she went along without giving the "choice" much thought. In fact, Zelda could think of no major decisions she had ever made herself and had few opinions of her own, being easily swayed by the views of others.

Not believing she possessed capacities on which she could rely, Zelda felt inadequate to the tasks of life. Feeling incompetent, she was easily overwhelmed by adversarial events. To navigate her way through the world, Zelda became adept at flirtation and social grace. Having constructed this false self, she was especially threatened by the possibility that negative states could disturb her only way of relating to others. By receiving positive responses from others, she protected her feeling of defectiveness, but the approval of others never felt real, and she was chronically depressed. Achieving narcissistic tension relief only temporarily by binge-eating, Zelda's lack of trust in her authentically experienced affects issued in a core feeling of defect that could not be shaken by social adaptation.

Four interrelated points regarding the effects of Zelda's unresponsive early family relationships are salient:

1. She could not trust her feelings as guides to action.
2. Unable to regulate negative affects, Zelda felt helpless to manage them. As a result, she either disavowed negative experience or became so overwhelmed by it that she binged to obliterate unpleasant affects.
3. Lacking faith that her affective states could be utilized as guides to action, Zelda felt that her very core was inadequate, and she had little confidence in her ability to control events in her life.
4. Having buried her genuine affects, she remained emotionally disconnected from other people; she loathed her false veneer but knew no other way to make genuine interpersonal contact.

Adaptive Strategies and Symptomatic Outcomes

Although the narcissistic "defect" tends to be characterized by different patients in similar ways (e.g., as having low self-esteem), the problem may be manifested in a variety of symptoms and relational patterns. The particular clinical constellation in each case is a product of the defenses and adaptations used to protect against awareness and exposure of "defect" while providing such self-esteem and relating as the patient is capable of achieving. These psychological maneuvers are not only defenses but also efforts to navigate the interpersonal world. The constellation of strategies designed to avoid shame, or the exposure of defect, is the narcissistic character structure.

These repair efforts fall into two broad categories: (a) attempts to relieve narcissistic tension by finding a means of gratification to substitute for the missing esteem and (b) attempts to hide the feeling of defectiveness without concrete efforts at tension relief. The latter attempts, utilizing psychological means to defend against awareness of defect, aim to achieve their goal via the way they construct relationships, whereas the former attempts often resort to nonhuman means to relieve shame anxiety. This bifurcation is similar to Kohut's (1971) distinction between narcissistic personality disorders and narcissistic behavioral disorders except that Kohut's division is a categorization of patients, whereas the current distinction applies to psychological strategies, any combination of which may be used by an individual patient. This approach is preferable because many patients use both types of maneuvers to achieve narcissistic balance.

Behavioral Adaptations

One can distinguish three behavioral means of attempting to relieve narcissistic tension, however temporarily: perversions, addictions, and delinquencies (Kohut, 1971). Addictions create an illusion of well-being in which "all is right," so that the anxiety about one's sense of value temporarily abates. When the drug, alcohol, or binge wears off, the narcissistic tension begins to reemerge, and the desire for ingestion resumes as the only known means to soothe it. A good example is Zelda's binge-eating. In the midst of her uncontrolled gorging, her anxiety over her value disappeared. After the binge, she would feel disgusted, often vomiting, hate herself for her uncontrolled gluttony, and resolve not to repeat the pattern. However, when conflict evoked her sense of inadequacy, her narcissistic tension was unbearable, and she yielded again to the urge to binge.

The most common type of narcissistic use of perversion is sadomasochism. As already mentioned, Benjamin (1988) has pointed out that the child whose subjectivity is not recognized by the desirable parental object may submit masochistically to figures of power, a submission that provides the illusion of being recognized as a subject of desire. From this viewpoint, masochism is a perverted attempt to achieve visibility and the soothing of narcissistic tension by submission to abuse. The sadist is equally desperate to be recognized but attempts to achieve this goal in the victim's painful plea. Winning this gaze, the sadist's self-doubts are magically obliterated, and the anxiety of defectiveness is gone for the moment. In this way, the sadomasochistic enactment provides the temporary abatement of narcissistic defects for both parties to the "relationship."

That certain forms of "antisocial" behavior can be a search for a missing object has been recognized at least since Winnicott (1956) pointed out that the feeling of something "missing" can lead to a desperate desire to "fill up" by stealing an object. The stolen object represents the reclaiming of what is gone in an effort to "patch" the defect. For this reason, patients of this type tend to feel a triumphant glee as they successfully outwit authorities. Indeed, the matching of wits becomes a game in which each "victory" ends in a moment of elation, as the patient feels the defect erased and a sense of triumph over the world. However, because the stolen object does not in fact repair a defect, eventually the narcissistic tension builds to the need for triumph once again. In this way, the search for the lost object becomes the addiction we call kleptomania.

This is not to say that these behaviors are invariably efforts at narcissistic repair. Addictions, perversions, and some forms of delinquencies can and often are symptoms of more severe disorders, such as the borderline personality organization discussed in chapter 5. Only when the behavior is used for relief of narcissistic tension is it symptomatic of a narcissistic personality disorder.

Psychological Adaptations

Turning now to efforts to defend against the sense of defectiveness via the construction of object relationships, clinical experience indicates there are five such defensive strategies: compliance, grandiosity, devaluation, idealization, and clinging attachment.

Compliance

Compliance with expectations of others is a strategy that tends to be used by patients whose early caretaking figures required specific behavior from their children that fulfilled narcissistic needs of their own. These patients are imprisoned in a narrowly circumscribed orbit of expectation to obtain parental admiration (Miller, 1981). Because the parental need is often for a high degree of or even spectacular success, such patients are often driven to and succeed in achieving lofty goals and are frequently regarded by clinicians as grandiose. However, their desperation to achieve ambitious goals reflects not an inflated view of themselves but a need to hide a sense of defectiveness through the fulfillment of parental ambitions. When their successes meet parental expectations, the sense of defect abates in response to the glow of parental approval, not self-inflation.

For compliant patients, the illusion that their lives are in synchrony with their affects breaks down when tolerance for an unauthentic life gives way to the plea of the buried self for recognition. A good illustration of the breakdown of a compliant but apparently almost ideal life is the case of Dick, a highly successful real estate developer who amassed considerable wealth at a relatively young age. He entered treatment for help with unbearable anxiety over an upcoming negotiation, a surprising precipitant to the symptoms given that the impending deal was relatively minor compared to many of the contracts he had already successfully negotiated. Visibly distressed as he entered the office for the first time, he looked wan, tired, and overwhelmed. Reporting insomnia and debilitating anxiety and unable to understand why a routine business transaction should evoke such severe symptoms, he sought psychotherapy even though his life from an external viewpoint seemed good. Not only was his work successful, but he was happy in his marriage and family life, which included three children. Reporting no gratification from his work despite his fabulous success, Dick felt relief but little satisfaction after the completion of each project. As he discussed this puzzling fact, he became aware that he was always anxious about failure before business negotiations, a feeling that he had previously been able to disavow. Now that the severity of his anxiety made defense impossible, Dick was consciously panicked over the possibility of the failure of the current deal, even though the realistic consequences were minimal. His anxiety was beginning to interfere with concentration at work, and all areas of his life had become infused with fear of catastrophe.

Reflecting on his life of single-minded devotion to success, Dick realized that in both college and graduate school he was so terrified of imperfection that he overworked to the point of obsession. An unblemished record had become an emotional necessity because he feared catastrophe from anything less. Finishing at the top of his class in both undergraduate and graduate schools brought him not a feeling of accomplishment but a small sense of relief that he had not failed.

Now employing his prodigious intellect for self-understanding, Dick associated his intense anxiety over failure to fear of loss of approval and love from his father, for whom material and professional success were all-important. A highly successful businessman who missed the opportunity for higher education, his father had insisted that both his sons succeed materially and surpass his success by becoming the educated professional he had always aspired to be. Dick and his younger brother had both devoted themselves to fulfilling their father's rigid but lofty ambitions. Expressing undying admiration for his father's work ethic, success, and competence, Dick regarded him as the major, almost sole, influence on his life, spoke with him almost daily, and discussed all of his life decisions with him. By contrast, Dick viewed his mother as weak and ineffectual and accorded her minimal importance in his life. The nonexistent relationship with his mother intensified his fear of losing his father, the only source of strength and competence in the family. The thought of disappointing or even opposing his father in any way terrified him, a fact that led to a life narrowly focused on fulfilling the ambitions his father sought for him.

This adaptive strategy of compliance "worked" in the sense that he was unaware of feeling defective, he was highly successful from an external viewpoint, and, up until the day he was home with the flu and unable to work on the deal in question, he had been able to manage his anxiety. After his return to work, his anxiety over the deal persisted and kept him awake most nights. Conscious now of feelings of inadequacy, Dick feared his entire life might collapse in failure. He associated to his current illness several traumatic childhood episodes in which he was badly injured or ill. His memories of these events were filled with terror and anxiety of death. In both situations, his mother became highly anxious and withdrew from him, exacerbating his feelings of helplessness and loneliness. The recent flu episode, by bringing back these childhood feelings of trauma, evoked his long-buried feelings of inadequacy and fear of failure, stimulating the awareness that this fear had dominated his life and ambitions.

The pressure on his psyche from numerous deals, each of which he feared might collapse in failure, finally took its toll when his illness stimulated his sense of inadequacy. Anxiety, although manageable, and work dissatisfaction had been the voice of authenticity that Dick had long ignored to his peril. His fear of noncompliance with his father's goals was so intense that he had not been able to listen to these voices until they emerged in catastrophic form.

Dick's obsession with perfection in work and academic perform-ance would be regarded by some analytic theorists as grandiose (Miller, 1981). However, Dick's response of relief rather than elation at the carrying out of his goals suggests that his pursuit of perfection was motivated by a terror of failure, not grandiosity. Specifically, his perfectionism was rooted in his terror of losing the love and admiration of his father, his only connection to effectance. Any slipup threatened what he experienced as a precarious paternal bond, the continuation of which he believed was necessary to relieve his sense of defectiveness. His compliance was an anxiety-driven maneuver to protect against loss of the relationship he needed, and his perfectionism was an extension of this compliance, not a symptom of grandiosity.

Grandiosity

Although compliant perfectionism is not grandiose, grandiosity is an organizing defense for many narcissistic patients. When self-esteem sinks to the point of desperation, and little environmental approbation is forthcoming, grandiosity is sometimes an effective defense against the sense of defectiveness. Patients like Dick fulfill parental ambitions at the price of their autonomy and integrity, but high parental expectation provides some sense of recognition. By contrast, when parents are unresponsive and expect little or nothing, the child does not even receive the compensatory gratification of having expectations placed upon him; he faces a rejecting world wholly devaluing of his potential. Without even compensatory means of self-esteem enhancement, narcissistic tension can reach the point of catastrophic anxiety, threatening total self-esteem collapse. In response, the patient may create an inflated image of himself in a desperate effort to disavow his sense of defect.

To believe in the reality of the grandiose image, the patient must have it confirmed and bolstered by others, resulting in a personality organized around the desperate need to sustain the feeling of self-inflation. Environmental responses other than approval and admiration threaten the grandiose defense with awareness of defect. Drive for achievement and perfectionism in these cases represent desperate efforts to alleviate narcissistic tension by bolstering grandiosity.

For example, Terrence, a junior-level manager in a large corporation, was in danger of losing his job partly because of behavior found objectionable by his coworkers and bosses. He was told that he would not listen to others, did not take feedback, and only wanted others to accept his viewpoint without acknowledging theirs. Continually trying to impress me with the people he knew and the power he held in the organization, he explained away the many blemishes on his work record and justified his procrastination on the basis of contributions to the company that were unappreciated. In a highly intellectualized and self-important tone, Terrence embellished his job performance, conveying the impression that the company depended greatly on his exceptional effort. It is this continual search for approbation and the exhilaration of receiving it that distinguishes Terrence's grandiosity from Dick's anxiety over failure. Unlike Terrence, Dick did not seek admiration and felt no excitement when he was complimented.

With Terrence, I felt that I was in the room with a person who was desperately, even pathetically, pleading with me, as though to say, "Please recognize that I am an important person!" Trying to believe in his self-image by having others confirm it, Terrence attempted to foster an inflated image of himself as an exceptional manager in hopes that others would gain this impression of him. If he could create this picture in my mind, as with others, he might defend against the anxiety that he was not good enough.

Devaluation

A third and related strategy to ward off the sense of defectiveness is the use of devaluation to boost one's sense of value relative to others'. This strategy may appear to emanate from grandiosity; many patients, however, use the devaluing defense without the assumption of a grandiose posture. For example, Molly's consciously stated reason for entering psychotherapy was to resolve problems in her third marriage. Her litany of complaints about her current husband made him appear to be a wholly unsuitable mate: He was disorganized, an inadequate provider, a sloppy dresser, and he lacked a sense of humor. Inquiry into her marital choices revealed a long list of complaints about all three husbands. Viewing her job as an impossible situation in which to succeed, she regarded her employer and coworkers as self-involved, unhelpful, competitive, envious, and impossible to work with. Convinced that the people on the job made her situation intolerable and unworkable and that they did not want her to succeed, she assumed that she would soon be fired.

To appreciate the virtues of her husbands would have led her to acknowledge that they might be correct in an argument or conflict and that they might even compare favorably to her in some areas. These possibilities terrified her because they threatened awareness of limitations, and such awareness in turn led to the feeling of defect. To convince herself that she was not inadequate, Molly obsessively attacked people close to her. Each such attack served to allay her anxiety immediately, but, when the effects wore off, she needed to find new flaws in order to gain reassurance.

Idealization

Just as devaluation can easily be used as a defense against defectiveness, so too can its opposite: idealization. Some patients attempt to obliterate a sense of inadequacy by seeking out and attaching to figures believed to possess exaggeratedly positive virtues, such as leadership, intelligence, skill, competence, or beauty. Identification with such exceptional figures boosts one's sense of value and thereby temporarily mitigates anxiety over the feeling of inadequacy. Glenn, who sought the ideal woman into middle age, spent a lifetime searching for a partner who would transform his experience from painful defectiveness to a sense of potency, masculinity, competence, and value. He dated countless women for more than 30 years but found each to possess unacceptable flaws. The elusive magical woman for Glenn served the same function as binge-eating for Zelda: denial of the defect while attempting to heal it.

For Glenn, being acceptable to others, fitting in so as to be beyond reproach, was a lifelong obsession: Status, clothes, and success took on all-consuming importance. Cultivating tastes in areas he felt would be impressive to others, Glenn became a connoisseur of fine wines and gourmet foods. His search for the ideal woman was a symptom of a character structure designed to ward off his sense of inadequacy by identifying himself with anything "flawless." Glenn's fruitless search for his idealized mate bore the message: "I am terrified of being allied with anyone, for fear that their deficiencies will reflect on me! I must keep my image spotless, and I have yet to meet the woman who would not blemish it!"

Clinging Attachment

The power of the tie to the object is also the underlying dynamic in patients whose feeling of defectiveness is manifested in anxiety-driven, clinging attachments. Such patients are motivated by terror of object loss, not by a need to inflate the value of the other. The bond is motivated not by the value of the other but by the fear that, without the other, the sense of defectiveness would be unbearable. Such patients cling desperately to the person who they believe will be there for them without threat of abandonment and who will provide the approval and admiration they need in order to hide awareness of defect. The object of their most idealized romantic fantasy is often considered either actually or potentially unavailable and, therefore, of uncertain value for "repairing" the defect. The chosen object must have sufficiently positive qualities that his admiration matters, but, beyond that, the most important attributes are perceived availability, the possibility of secure attachment, and the object's willingness to admire the patient.

For example, Robert came to therapy to help him get over an ex-girlfriend who had broken off their relationship. Unable to accept the end of the relationship, Robert found himself out of control in his efforts to win her back. During the course of their relationship, whenever they argued, Robert experienced catastrophic anxiety and was unable to eat, sleep, or function until their disagreement was resolved. When the conflict was over, he felt himself almost magically transformed into his former self: relaxed, outgoing, friendly, and apparently self-confident. However, unable to bear separations, Robert demanded his girlfriend's constant availability. When she finally attempted to end the relationship, his obsession intensified, and he began to call her at all hours of the day and night, on one occasion even pounding on her door and begging to gain entrance. Being a characterologically gentle, mild-mannered, soft-spoken, congenial young man, this behavior shocked him and those around him and led to his entrance into psychotherapy.

Robert could not identify any exceptional qualities he found in his former girlfriend. He did not idealize her; in fact, when asked about her attributes, he was quite realistic in describing her as a person with many flaws who was not especially appealing. Good-looking and highly successful for his age in addition to possessing a naturally congenial personality, Robert had no trouble finding women who were interested in him. The intensity of his tie to the former girlfriend can be explained only by the fact that he saw in her someone he thought would erase his defect. He sought in her a potentially transformational object, a person who had the power to change magically his sense of defectiveness to a feeling of wholeness.

Comparison with Kohut and Kernberg

As just described, there are five major adaptive strategies designed to protect the sense of defectiveness, two of which are grandiosity and idealization, the defenses emphasized by Kohut and Kernberg. With this clinical observation as a starting point, we are now in a position to see more clearly the difference between the view set forth here and the conceptualizations of these two major analytic theorists of narcissistic pathology.

In Kohut's (1971) view, idealization and grandiosity are the two primary childhood needs, the relinquishment of which gives rise to the bipolar self of ideals and ambitions. From this perspective, the symptoms and character structures we have just described are products of arrest in one or both of these areas. Conceptualizing the self as initially grandiose, Kohut believed the early selfobjects must provide sufficient mirroring to cushion the loss of this archaic narcissistic state. When the selfobjects fail to provide this function, archaic grandiosity remains, although typically in a walled-off state to protect it from injury. The resulting narcissistic pathology is organized around this split-off grandiose self, with the patient seeking both to sustain it through mirroring and to protect it from the self that makes contact with the world. Thus, in Kohut's formulation, although grandiosity defends against vulnerability, the adult grandiose self is fundamentally an arrest of the childhood grandiose self that was never allowed to evolve into realistic ambitions.

This view is contradicted by the findings of infant research showing that the normal infant is not grandiose. As seen in chapter 2, the infant has a social self from the first few days of life that learns to act in synchrony with the caretaker. There is no evidence the infant believes, even in fantasy, that he has omnipotent control over others or events in his life. Preprogrammed to respond to the ministrations of the caretaker, the infant's early interactional patterns imply an adaptation to the caretaking figure that contradicts the theory of infantile grandiosity.

In concert with these developmental data, the clinical manifestations of grandiosity inevitably point to a defensive function rather than a developmental arrest. Terrence desperately attempted to maintain exceptional feelings of competence, intelligence, and education in order to avoid painful feelings of inadequacy. By eliciting admiring responses, he could convince himself of his adequacy temporarily, but he lived in a state of precarious and delicate narcissistic balance. When a response was not as admiring as he required, Terrence became despairing and self-attacking or flew into a rage, reactions that betrayed the sense of defectiveness covered over by the grandiose defense. To regard Terrence's grandiosity as a developmental arrest does not do justice to its self-protective function, a function that invariably emerges in all patients organized around the bolstering of grandiosity.

The formulation of adult grandiosity as a defensive function rather than a developmental arrest leads to comparison with Kernberg's view of grandiosity as a pathological construction. The current position stands in agreement with Kernberg's claim that Kohut overlooked critical differences between normal childhood illusions and the adult grandiose defense. However, in Kernberg's view, grandiosity protects against excess aggression and envy lying at the root of narcissistic pathology. From the present viewpoint, grandiosity serves to hide awareness of the feeling of defectiveness, and hostile outbursts are a reaction to the pain of exposing this feeling. With regard to the role of aggression, the current view is allied with Kohut's concept of narcissistic rage as secondary to the injury of self-exposure rather than Kernberg's formulation of aggression as a primary motivator of the grandiose self and the resultant pathology. In short, I agree with Kernberg that grandiosity is a defensive construction, but the clinical evidence indicates that the source of underlying pathology is a core feeling of defectiveness rather than excess aggression. I conclude that rage, envy, and extreme expressions of aggression are symptoms rather than root causes.

Similar considerations apply to idealization. Although Kohut's description of the persistent need to attach to idealized figures fits some cases, arrested idealization is not necessarily part of these patients' early histories. For example, although Glenn did not suffer premature disturbance in the early idealization of his parents, he spent his adult life seeking the ideal woman. In childhood and throughout adolescence, Glenn was oblivious to his parents' inability to form relationships, a realization that occurred only in adulthood. By the time he began psychotherapy, he seemed realistic in his recognition that his parents were limited people who were highly critical of others and had few meaningful attachments. Glenn's single-minded search for the ideal woman against whom real figures never measure up cannot be attributed to a traumatic disturbance in his early parental idealizations. That is, the relationship between parental idealization and the pursuit of idealizing relationships later in life is far more complex than is captured by the notion of early arrest in the idealization process.

Attacking self psychology for not grasping the defensive function of idealization, Kernberg (1976) has conceptualized adult idealization, like adult grandiosity, as a pathological defense against aggression and envy rather than as a developmental arrest. The same critique applies to idealization as grandiosity: Excess aggression and envy are not givens but reactions to the feeling of defectiveness and the shame of its exposure. Unable to account for idealization that relieves the feeling of inadequacy, Kernberg's formulation has difficulty explaining the relationship between Glenn's search for the ideal woman and his need for acceptability.

The current object relational theory is proposed as an alternative to Kohut's developmental-arrest theory, which does not seem to be supported fully by either the research or clinical evidence, and Kernberg's neo-Kleinian theory, which is too steeped in aggressive drive theory to fit clinical observations and recent research findings. The narcissistic defenses, in protecting against the feeling of defectiveness, motivate a personality organized around the ever-present threat of exposure.

Maintenance of the Narcissistic Defect

The persistence of the feeling of defectiveness indicates that the narcissistic patient does not simply feel defective, he recruits negative experiences to sustain this feeling while remaining oblivious to positive experience. Such sense of self as the patient has is provided by the feeling of defectiveness. For example, Dick's positive experiences threatened his sense of inadequacy, causing him to feel lost, disorganized, and, most important, subject to annihilation anxiety. As the experience of inadequacy provided him with a sense of self-continuity, recruitment of negative experiences had become necessary to maintain a cohesive self state. Whenever Dick was confronted with one of his many experiences of success, his sense of self was threatened, and he felt compelled to diminish the achievement.

The sense of defectiveness also provides a major source of motivation for the narcissistic patient. Experiencing himself as damaged, Dick felt that he had to prove his value to his father and himself. Given that Dick's ambitions were rooted in his need to overcome his sense of defectiveness, he had no sense of purpose apart from the goal of demonstrating his value to his father. The disproof of defectiveness provided a life plan and primary mode of engagement with the world. Similarly, whenever Zelda considered ending an other-directed relationship in order to live in accord with her authentic feelings, she feared losing her motivation to be healthy and look good. Her immediate response was, "I don't want to be fat!"

The patient's betrayal of authentic experience in order to achieve needed contact is a sin not easily forgiven by the patient himself. The indomitable desire of the true self to gain expression makes the false-self adaptation inherently unsatisfying. Each attack on the self, no matter how painful, affirms the patient's unwillingness to accept his unauthentic life and reflects the hope that, by continually assaulting himself, he can keep open the possibility of a different way of living. Self-hatred is not simply a negative self state but a loathing of the unauthentic life into which the patient is locked. From this viewpoint, attacks on the self are a plea for a more genuine life, a cry for the true self to be heard. Obsessive self-flagellation, being the only way the patient knows to battle his false self, becomes established as a major component of the self organization. The need for repetitious self-attack to gain access to more genuine affects is a primary explanation of the tenacious and refractory nature of the sense of defectiveness.

The recruitment of negative experience is designed to fuel the motivational engine while preventing awareness of affects and the questioning of defensive motivations. Each time a negative experience is added to the store of inadequate feelings, the patient has successfully avoided confrontation with his affects. The feeling of defect and the need to prove otherwise substitute for awareness of authentic experience and motivation. These patients often have a litany of self-flagellating verbalizations easily evoked by negative experiences. For example, Elliot, a patient with a compliant form of narcissistic personality organization, repeated a store of self-attacking statements each time he confronted a limitation in himself or suffered a setback of any sort. When he made an error, he would customarily ridicule himself by thinking, "You stupid, incompetent, miserable, mindless, thoughtless idiot!" Negative memories and thoughts stimulated the mantra. Such obsessive self-attacks are ways of avoiding the uncovering of motivations that would emerge if the obstacle of self-devaluation were not there.

We have seen that a lack of trust in one's affects lies at the root of the narcissistic patient's feeling of defect, and the maintenance of this feeling is crucial to the sense of self, modes of engagement with the world, and motivation. This formulation of narcissistic pathology clarifies the task of therapy: to help the patient achieve the authentic affective expression that will free him from a life of safeguarding and defending against the feeling of defectiveness. How this can be achieved is the topic now before us.

The Therapeutic Process

Some form of symptomatic manifestation of the narcissistic defense brings the patient to psychotherapy. For example, Zelda came for help with her failing marriage, binge-eating, and depression. As mentioned, Zelda had never been attracted to her husband and found him too practical and boring. Nonetheless, she felt the relationship was a necessity. With her husband assuming the role of caretaker, the marriage afforded Zelda a way to avoid all responsibility and stay safely hidden from the world, so that her feeling of inadequacy did not have to be confronted. Facing a life with someone she found uninteresting and unconnected to, she withdrew by sleeping and staying in bed for hours and even days. Her binge-eating, to be discussed in more detail, was a desperate attempt to relieve her feeling of defectiveness without depending on another and, as mentioned previously, was a desperate plea for recognition of more than her looks. Thus, each presenting symptom reflected Zelda's feeling of inadequacy.

Threat of the Interpretive Process

Because the symptoms express indirectly the feeling of inadequacy, inquiry into their origin evokes the anxiety of exposure. When I asked Zelda about marrying someone she was not attracted to and felt so little connection with, she became visibly anxious and appealed to his good qualities, such as reliability and trustworthiness. There being a direct path from inquiry into the state of her marriage to her sense of helplessness and inadequacy, Zelda understandably felt threatened by such questioning as much as she welcomed the opportunity to understand why her life made so little sense. Her response is typical of patients who are attempting to protect a feeling of defectiveness: Probing into motivation elicits shame anxiety, the defense of which is manifested interpersonally as narcissistic sensitivity.

The patient's primary modes of defense employed in opposition to this awareness become the initial presentation of the transference, a phenomenon that has been called the defense transference (Schlessinger and Robbins, 1983). The transference coalesces around (a) one or more of the kinds of object relationships already described that wall off the defective feeling or (b) those that attempt to use the therapist as a nonhuman means of soothing narcissistic tension. For example, Zelda was initially compliant, agreeable, and charming on the surface and appeared to be benefiting from the therapeutic process. Unconsciously at first, and later consciously, she fully expected the therapist to be as manipulable as everyone else in her life, including her two previous therapists. Her superficial agreeableness was the way she tried to keep me from seeing her emptiness and intention to continue her pattern of searching for a man to take care of her while bingeing in the evenings.

Anxiety in response to interpretation is, of course, not unique to the narcissistic patient. Every analytic patient, to some degree, opposes the insights he consciously seeks, a phenomenon recognized by the time-honored analytic concept of resistance. But, the narcissistic patient reacts to this awareness with a special form of anxiety: the dread of having his defect uncovered, the threat of a shame experience (Morrison, 1989). When I suggested to Zelda that her agreeableness was a way to render me ineffective and unable to see her more deeply, she agreed and felt relieved at being seen, but her humiliation led to intense anger and even a feeling of persecution by the therapeutic process. As her desire to find a man to protect her from the world intensified, Zelda began to fantasize returning to her ex-husband, and she even resumed contact with him, only to find herself disappointed and unable to return to her former life.

Elliot, the patient beset with obsessive self-attacks (discussed earlier), entered analysis out of fear of losing his girlfriend, who felt that he was too passive and dependent on her. Hungrily seeking out her company, he was constantly anxious to gain her approval and needed continual reassurance of her feelings for him. He associated from these feelings to his father's alcoholism, neglect, and verbal abuse. When we recognized that he accepted his father's negative judgments in hopes of gaining acceptance, Elliot unleashed a tirade of self-abuse, accusing himself mercilessly of being a wimp. His mixture of rage and shame were so intense that at times he felt like jumping off the couch and running from the consulting room.

It was undoubtedly this type of traumatic anxiety reaction to interpretation that led Kohut (1984) to recommend a sustained period of understanding, during which the patient uses the therapist as a selfobject experience, before explanation can begin. Indeed, Kohut argued that patients are often better served by empathic resonance than by the imposition of truths they are not ready to hear, even if for prolonged periods the patient can only be listened to, without any new information being provided by the therapist. The responses of both Zelda and Elliot are two examples of the kind of anxiety-driven reactions that led Kohut to this formulation for narcissistically sensitive people.

Despite the threat of depth interpretation, the patient often reacts to surface-level responses with impatience and a sense of stagnation. When I was careful not to go beneath the surface of Zelda's material, she complained that she was "not getting anywhere" and left to flounder when she desperately "needed answers." Thus, Kohut's strategy of not pushing the material beneath the patient's level does not necessarily satisfy the patient or contain the anxiety. Indeed, in Zelda's case, it seemed to exacerbate her sense of threat. This is not to say that depth interpretation will always relieve anxiety, whereas empathic sensitivity will not; it is only to suggest that there is no perfectly optimal, easy solution to interpretive tact with the narcissistic patient because both interpretation and its absence can be unsatisfying. The result is a conundrum. When the therapist is sensitive to the patient's vulnerability to injury and careful not to expose sore areas, the patient tends to feel that the process is not going anywhere; when the therapist illuminates the patient's vulnerability and sense of defectiveness, the patient tends to feel injured and regards the therapist as insensitive, perhaps even sadistic, and the process too painful.

These two patient reactions define the horns of the therapeutic dilemma, a conflict reflected in the two major theories of narcissistic pathology. The self-psychological clinical strategy has the merit of staying within the limits of what the patient can tolerate, but this stance is responsive to only one side of the dilemma. It encourages sensitivity to the patient and a sustained period of attuned understanding before explanation is attempted (Kohut, 1984) but risks increasing anxiety and patient frustration at a stagnant process. By way of contrast, Kernberg's (1975, 1984) neo-Kleinian approach attempts to reduce anxiety by interpreting its meaning and is therefore much more aggressive in addressing narcissistic defenses to arrive at underlying affects. Whereas Kohut was concerned about the possibility of doing injury with premature interpretation, Kernberg is more troubled by the potential danger of supporting defenses at the expense of resolving the issues hidden beneath them. Each theory has a legitimate concern. With narcissistically defended patients, the therapist must be vigilant regarding the danger of exposing the sense of defectiveness in a way that humiliates the patient and disrupts or arrests the process, on the one hand, and of being so careful not to do injury that the treatment never gets past the patient's defenses and becomes unproductive, on the other.

Interpretation of the Buried Self

How can the therapist navigate between the Scylla of superficiality and the Charybdis of shameful exposure by interpretation? If we carry through consistently our concept that the purpose of interpretation is to uncover the buried potential hidden beneath the patient's defensive constellation, a way out of the dilemma begins to emerge. Exposure is feared by the patient as a revelation of defect, but the therapist sees possibilities of self realization that the patient cannot consciously perceive. In this model, interpretation is the vehicle through which the therapist conveys recognition of who the patient is, but the self revealed under the defense has a dual aspect. Hidden beneath the narcissistic defense is not simply a feeling of defect but also a potential self that has not been allowed direct expression in the object world (Loewald, 1960). This dual recognition means that being seen is not simply shameful but includes a sense of attunement to new, undiscovered possibilities.

To continue with the example of Zelda, her need to hide behind a presumably agreeable persona was interpreted as a product of her conviction that she had no merit other than her comely appearance. I pointed out (a) that this belief was rooted not only in her parentally instilled identity as the pretty one but also in her belief that she could sustain relationships only by complying with others at the expense of her potential and (b) that, having buried all other potential ways of attracting others' interest, she had developed very little of her intellectual and emotional potential. These interpretations in terms of arrested development imply greater potential for ways of being and relating than suggested by her own one-dimensional picture.

Early in therapy, Zelda remarked that there had to be some meaning in having binged almost in front of her parents' eyes as an adolescent. When she later defined herself as the pretty one who had been socially popular while feeling empty inside, I suggested that her bingeing was a protest against being imprisoned in an identity she found devaluing and false. Unable to contain tears at being recognized, Zelda felt that her plea had finally been heard. Most meaningful to her was the realization that I saw her bingeing as a reflection of her buried desire to be more than her looks, a meaning she had not been able to articulate to herself. For a period of time thereafter, Zelda felt like crying almost every time she entered my waiting room for appointments. Tears provided the emotional outlet for the feeling that another person saw unrealized potential within her.

My conviction that the actualization of untapped potential was not only possible but potentially gratifying to her came not from a preformed Pollyannish optimism but from indications in her behavior. First, her symptoms were an index of her dissatisfaction with her life of helpless dependency. Second, in sessions she evinced virulent self-hatred, attacking herself mercilessly for being weak and ineffective. Finally, with even the slightest prompting, she showed abundant intellectual and emotional curiosity regarding herself and others. I was convinced I was in the presence of a woman with untapped intellect and starved for mental stimulation while also convinced of her inability to achieve goals. From these elements of her behavior, I constructed an image of her as capable and desirous of exercising intellect and ambition.

Zelda's response to this interpretive theme was that she had construed her identity as "the pretty one" to mean she possessed minimal intellectual capacity and, as a consequence, she had always assumed she was "stupid." Only when we understood her lack of intellectual confidence to be rooted in her parents' need to dismiss her as "the pretty one" whose only value lay in her physical attractiveness to men could she recognize that therapy "supported my intelligence." That is, the interpretation conveyed that I saw intellectual capacity in her, and, if I believed it was there, she might also be able to believe in it. In this way, the interpretation of her socially agreeable veneer as a defense provided holding—a positive, hopeful environment within which she was able to sustain new awareness of her vulnerability and motivations. She felt held not because I gave empty reassurance but because, in seeing who she was beneath her limiting self-definition, my vision of her embraced unrealized potential. Thus, when we saw beyond her defenses, I did not find a defect, as Zelda expected, but new possibilities, and this vision allowed her to achieve a new level of self-understanding that was relieving rather than traumatizing.

During this phase, Zelda's dissatisfaction at never having used her intellect or pursued ambitions began to emerge. She complained bitterly that her brother had been expected to go to medical school, whereas she had assumed the world of academia was beyond her. Despite her considerable curiosity about the body, health, the mind, and their relation to emotions, she had never considered the possibility that she was capable of pursuing any of these interests. In discussing this frustration, Zelda often exploded with rage at feeling cheated out of opportunities. She connected her chronic depression and bulimia with what she now referred to as "the starvation of my intellect."

This need for recognition, as I am using it here, is not the same as the mirror hunger conceptualized by self psychologists (Kohut and Wolf, 1978). From the latter viewpoint, a mirror-hungry personality is focused on receiving continually confirming or approving responses in order to bolster self-esteem. The need for recognition, on the other hand, is a reflection of the indomitable striving for self realization, the longing for recognition of possibilities that the patient cannot articulate to himself (Loewald, 1960). Interpretation that satisfies this "recognition hunger" points to the possibility of transcending the existing self rather than echoing it. A significant difference in interpretive emphasis between the self-psychological and current view lies in the object relations emphasis on the "not yet," the unrealized possibility. Whereas self psychology tends to limit empathy to the patient's actual affective experience, the current view emphasizes both actual and possible affective experience—that is, unrealized possibilities for who the patient may become.

This function of interpretation in the treatment of narcissistic defects can be differentiated from the views of both Kernberg and Kohut. Interpretive focus on aggression and envy, such as advocated by Kernberg and Kleinian theorists, emphasizes negatives and is unlikely to sustain the patient through periods of shame and anxiety. On the other hand, the caution about interpreting advocated by Kohut is unnecessary if one holds a view of interpretation as the uncovering of buried potential. Both Kohut and Kernberg see interpretation as the conveyance of unpleasant truths, a one-dimensional view that either risks iatrogenic reactions, on the one hand, or leads to constriction of the therapeutic process to avoid doing injury to the patient, on the other. In contradistinction to Kohut and Kernberg, the current view emphasizes the creation of new possibilities inherent in the interpretive process.

Oscillation: Development and Regression

That interpretation provides a holding experience for the narcissistic patient does not eliminate the tendency to regressive avoidance. During this phase of the process, patients frequently wonder why they want to change and even question whether they need to relinquish their ways of relating. Confronted with the shame and vulnerability of exposure, the most direct route for immediate relief is return to the old patterns. At the very time Zelda was able to be direct with people and relinquish her coquettish exterior, she seriously considered returning to her ex-husband and her former life of hiding. The promise of a more authentic life does battle with the pain and anxiety of exposure, but the therapist's vision helps the patient see that the old patterns resulted in the symptoms and need for help. For example, despite the temptation to return to her husband, Zelda could see that an existence without expectation, a life of hiding from the world, only made her feel depressed and deepened her sense of worthlessness.

Oscillation between the old, protective object relationships and new, more authentic ways of relating to others becomes the crux of the process during this phase. Realizing that reliance on her looks fostered self-hatred, Zelda quit her job (because she felt it relied on a false presentation) and secured temporary employment in an industry that paid less but that evaluated her strictly on performance. She found this vocational arena to be a welcome relief that freed her from concern for appearance in the workplace. Nonetheless, when she started her new job, she felt she could not "make it"—she almost quit the first day. With little money to support herself, she again considered calling her ex-husband and fantasized returning to her former life of dependence on him. This ambivalence reflected her conflict between the anxiety of trying to engage the world in a new way, a pattern in which her old sense of self was lost, and returning to the known patterns that provide a sense of self but that would consign her to the very symptoms for which she sought help.

Transitional Space and the Development of Authenticity

At this juncture in the treatment, the creation of transitional space assumes a central role. When the interpretive process proceeds far enough for the loosening of the defense transference, transitional space emerges, and possibilities open up for more authentic modes of engagement than were previously possible.

The therapist may try different probing to access underlying affects, but his criterion of successful inquiry is the patient's affective reaction. When the therapist's comments stimulate new affective responses in the patient in a way that fits the mystery of the patient's symptoms, the true self begins to emerge. This is not simply a case of "getting in touch with feelings" but of finding access to potential that had been unrecognized in the patient's life, elaborating these nascent ways of being, and using them for guidance in the conduct of life. Because the narcissistically injured patient believes that the articulation of his genuine affects will cost him relationships, it is imperative that the therapist provide room for the elaboration of the patient's authentic affective expressions. The formation of this new object relationship issues in the growing belief that affects can be used to engage the world without loss of connections with others.

Elliot acknowledged that, despite his intellectual understanding of the analytic process, his assumption had been that he would do what I told him to do. He often asked me for advice on how to behave, and, when he did convey feelings, his purpose was to fulfill what he regarded as my implicit request for affective expression. As we struggled with the conundrum of his efforts to comply with me by accessing his affective states, Elliot became aware of anger at what he felt was my demand for compliance. This interaction marked the beginning of a major analytic theme, which Elliot captured with the pithy remark, "I'll do what you say but hate you for it." As his long-suppressed anger rose to the surface, Elliot became increasingly aware of his rage at his father for demanding compliance as the price of the father–son relationship.

In response to this material, Elliot associated to a seemingly endless series of injuries suffered in response to "female rejection." For example, when a woman wished to end a phone call before he was ready, or when a woman showed interest in focusing her attention on almost anything other than him, he felt wounded and often became depressed. As this sensitivity emerged, he realized that he needed to be the sole focus of the woman in his life, and he could not tolerate her providing room for anything else. Awareness of the unrealistic nature of this narcissistic need, which he referred to as King Elliot, evoked the realization that the enormity of this need had made him fearful of exposure. His sense of shame was intimately connected to his excessive demands on others and fostered the burial of his affective life.

In the analysis, he became obsessed with my movements and habits, constantly trying to read them for my feelings about him. When he heard me move in my chair, he feared that I was bored with him. Preoccupied with my punctuality, he often felt that I was a minute or two late even when I was not, and he felt hurt by the perceived injury. When he heard me laugh as I said "goodbye" to another patient, he assumed I had a much better relationship with that person than with him, and he felt chagrined and depressed in response. Demanding my total attention and concern for him, he feared that I preferred other patients. As real as these experiences felt to him, he recognized that his reactions were precisely the same as occurred consistently in his romantic relationships.

My interpretive focus was dual. First, we understood the creation of King Elliot as his anxiety of abandonment: So fearful was he of losing relationships that he required constant devotion and reassurance. Second and most important, I pointed out that, because his alleged "royal" behavior was anxiety-driven, it could not be part of his genuine affective life. Although he felt ashamed of his entitled expectations, they were a defense against his feeling of inadequacy and terror of abandonment, an anxiety-driven defense that protected the expression of more genuine affects.

In response to these interpretive themes, Elliot began to use the therapeutic space to embrace his aggression. When he felt that my interpretation of his compliance was excessive, he told me he was angry with my "continual badgering." Rather than feeling threatened that negative affects would damage our connection, Elliot was beginning to use them as indicators of how he wanted to relate. When I pointed out that his anger, before it became self-directed, expressed a feeling of being "cheated out" of controlling his destiny and burying his desires in order to form relationships, he exploded with rage over feeling deprived and empty.

Spontaneously, Elliot expressed a very simple feeling: All that really mattered to him was having an intimate relationship in which he loved and was loved for who he was. His career, he said, although successful, was not important to him beyond earning a living. The problem, he went on, was that he wanted a relationship so much that he buried his desires for contact and thereby defeated his goal. When I suggested that he wanted to have a relationship with me in which he could express what he felt without fear of reprisal, he said that he felt close to me and that this closeness scared him because he was now vulnerable to my controlling, injuring, and abandoning him. Elliot had always sensed that he had this "poetic side" but had never articulated it to himself. The elaboration of this aspect of himself in our relationship became the object of years of analytic work, as he struggled to accept that what made him happy was simple activities of close relatedness that his father would disdain and even find shameful, such as taking walks and sharing feelings with someone with whom he feels close. The decisive therapeutic experience for Elliot was his inclusion of these feelings and interests in relating to me without damage to our connection. His "poetic" affects of tenderness, intimacy, and appreciation of natural beauty, long buried under the complex layering of his defenses, were the basis of this new object relationship and the most authentic expression of his newly developing self.

Zelda also made use of the therapeutic space to gain access to her aggression. In the midst of the recognition that her charming, socially acceptable veneer was a defense against her feelings of inadequacy and emptiness, Zelda came into session one day and unexpectedly exploded with rage. Angry at me for attacking her social adaptation, she felt that my interpretation of her compliance had been assaultive and hurtful. I responded by commenting that her reaction was surprising given that she had appeared to agree with my interpreta-tion. Although not disputing that her veneer hid shameful feelings, she insisted that my persistence in pointing this out reflected an insensitive disregard for her. Zelda was convinced that this aggressive outburst would disrupt our bond. Having no belief in a transitional space within which the aggressive feelings could become a meaning-ful part of the therapeutic dialogue, Zelda was surprised to find that our relationship was not damaged by her newly discovered aggres-sion. I replied that this expression of anger toward me created a new dimension in our relationship: use of aggression to assert some control and influence in how I related to her. This response of accepting her aggression and welcoming it as part of our relationship, a process referred to by Bollas (1987) as "celebrating the analysand," facilitated the inclusion of aggression within the previously constricted therapeutic relationship.

Gradually, Zelda became more fluid in expressing her anger toward me. When she felt that my interpretations were too aggressive and hurtful, she expressed anger at my insensitivity. On other occasions, she decried my passivity, believing that I was leaving her alone to change herself without doing enough to help her. At times, she was angry at me for putting her through the painful process of redefining herself. Zelda did not like being what she called a negative person, but she acknowledged that the anger felt like an outpouring of the frustration from so many years of feeling imprisoned. Consciously entertaining homicidal fantasies toward almost everyone she knew, the intensity of Zelda's anger surprised her. What seemed important to both of us was not the content of this anger but that she included it in her relationship with me and, later, with anyone to whom she felt connected. No longer buried beneath an agreeable veneer, her anger was in synchrony with her way of engaging me. This congruence between affect and relating facilitated the trust that her affective states could direct her relationships—that is, it helped her develop self-confidence.

At the point of being freer from compliance than she had ever imagined possible, as aggressive feelings came to be deployed to achieve greater satisfaction in relationships, Zelda became much less impulsive. Loosening her defenses, she was able to communicate her affects, especially negative emotions, in a direct manner. This synchrony did not mean, of course, that Zelda openly communicated all her angry feelings; it meant that she was capable of negative affective expressions. When she judged that a situation did not behoove an angry expression, she was fully capable of holding the tension until the time was more propitious. That is, aggression was utilized now for self realization. The anger at me and aggression she utilized in her new graduate career were expressions of her personal idiom and therefore fundamentally different from both her former burial of aggression and her occasional explosions. Zelda had achieved ownership over her negative states.

Zelda's more authentic way of relating to me, now including expressions of her dissatisfaction and ambitions and recognition that I valued her intellect, initiated a shift in the nature of our relationship. She began to have explicit sexual dreams of me. Although this development embarrassed her, it signaled a closeness with me she had never before experienced. Feeling understood and valued for who she was, she could manage the emotional intensity of her attachment to me only by erotizing the relationship. All past relationships having been sexual, Zelda had the new experience of being in a relationship that was close but not physical. In the sexual relationships that composed her history, the immediacy of sexual contact had never resulted in knowing the other person. This concretization of relationships defended against her abandonment anxiety, sense of inadequacy, and an authentic relationship in which she and her partner would know each other.

We understood her erotic dreams of me as her way of experiencing being valued and the feeling of gratitude. When she verbalized these feelings, Zelda felt a powerful emotional connection to me, the first nonsexual intimacy she had ever experienced, and the resulting bond became her first genuinely close relationship. She wept frequently as she told me of the importance to her of feeling valued for who she was, but she continued to be angry with me whenever she felt I was not understanding her. The experience of this nonphysical authenticity of both positive and negative feelings was her use of the transitional space to form a new object relationship. She now expressed gratitude directly, indicating her appreciation for my faith in her and willingness to absorb her anger. This gratitude signified a new level of interpersonal sensitivity, the ability to see that I had a subjectivity on which she had an influence. My having survived her aggression shifted me, in her view, from a source of gratification or frustration to a person with a separate mind (Benjamin, 1995).

At this point in the treatment, Zelda began to consider new career paths and intellectual pursuits. Eventually she began graduate school in a field that had always interested her but that she had never pursued, believing that the considerable discipline and study it demanded were beyond her. In her first week of classes, she was absolutely certain that she could not understand the text and lacked the capabilities to do the work. I suggested that she was having difficulty incorporating serious academic interests into her self-concept because such a view implies a more risky way of being with others than her "flighty," coquettish behavior. In response to this interpretation, Zelda realized that the fear of losing control of others' regard for her was the price of taking herself seriously. That night she studied for five hours, and her work has progressed smoothly ever since.

The graduate school experience was one of the first clear indications that Zelda was beginning to have confidence in her intellect, ambition, and judgment. This woman who had always regarded herself as an empty-headed adornment eventually completed a demanding graduate program. In a variety of other ways, Zelda began to trust that her affective states would lead to the formation of meaningful relationships and the pursuit of satisfying ambitions. At times, she disagreed with me and questioned my interpretations of her behavior, a posture that required reliance on her own responses. Especially striking was the dramatic reversal in her way of relating to people, especially men. Having believed all her life that she had no opinions, she now found that she had strong political and social convictions. For example, she believed in holistic medicine, natural healing, and vegetarianism. Most important, she did not hide these views and was willing to engage others in debate.

As she became more and more candid about her feelings and thoughts, Zelda tolerated few deceptions in herself or others. On dates, she no longer felt driven to make the man feel good at any cost. Surprising herself with her honesty, when she found herself in conflict, angry, or possessing any negative or unpleasant feelings, she was open about her responses. More than all other changes, her candor with others and willingness to utilize her aggression demonstrated her trust that she could have relationships based on authentic ways of being and relating. By this point, her grandiose defense, bingeing, and depression had all vanished. Zelda's socially

agreeable false self had been transcended and replaced by the realization of her more authentic self, a self who used intellect, aggression,
and ambition.

That Zelda was able to sustain both positive and negative feelings
toward me would be viewed by Kernberg (1975, 1984) and the
Kleinians as evidence that her narcissistic defect was ameliorated by
the integration of her good object relationships, represented by her
social veneer, and bad object relationships, split off into her binge-
eating. Such a view misses the very nature of those traits: Zelda's
social veneer was not a genuinely positive affective expression but a
defensive posture, and her previously buried rage appeared only in
explosions. When Zelda gained ownership over her aggression, it was
utilized for communication of dissatisfaction and ambitious pursuits.
Integration of a defensive social veneer and explosive outbursts
cannot produce the capacity for intersubjective intimacy and the
exercise of ambition. In her pretherapy state, both her aggression and
her social charm were anxiety motivated. By contrast, her positive
and negative states were now both expressions of her personal idiom,
her true self. Zelda's narcissistic defect was healed not by the
supposed integration of two pathological states but by the shift from
anxiety-dominated self-protectiveness to the realization of her
authentic self potential.

Zelda's exhilarating sense of pride in her academic achievements
was due not only to her academic success but also to the perhaps
most important fact that she chose this path because of her conviction that it was what she wanted and that she was willing to overcome
obstacles in order to achieve it. All clinicians have had patients who
remain unhappy and even depressed despite great, even spectacular,
life success. Zelda's self-esteem was built not so much on her success
per se as on the authenticity of her choice and her willingness to
overcome barriers to pursue what felt most right to her. In this regard,
it is instructive to compare Zelda with Dick.

Dick, it may be recalled, was a highly successful attorney, but his
success, being driven by the anxiety of failure and loss of his father's
approval, meant little to him and provided minimal positive self-
regard. When he was eventually able to free himself from his

anxiety-dominated life, he chose a career that was much less success oriented in conventional terms but that freed him from anxiety about failure and gave him much more time for leisure and family, a lifestyle that fit his value system. Most important, he made a free choice: The new career brought greater satisfaction because his lifestyle fit his affective life. His new life provided an enhanced feeling of self-worth that he had never experienced in his high-level business position.

When Dick turned away from the value system in which he had been raised, it was a nearly traumatic disappointment to his father and set Dick apart from his family of origin. When he took the risk of incurring his father's displeasure, his aggression was in the service of making authentic choices for the first time in his life. Belief in his ability to manage conflict and negative affects issued in this newly aggressive way of relating. Thus, Dick's therapeutic journey, the successful transcendence of his compliant self, was made possible largely via the competence he developed in coping with negative affects.

From the viewpoint of psychological meaning, Dick's spectacular business success was comparable not to Zelda's chosen professional career but to her flirtatiousness and social charm. The latter traits were a surrender of Zelda's true self, just as Dick's business career constituted an act of superficial compliance. Despite their marked behavioral differences, these two paths were both motivated by the anxiety that authentic expression would lead to abandonment by others and a consequent need to relate by compliance. Conversely, Dick's choice of a less pressured, less success-oriented vocation was as authentic as Zelda's decision to pursue a challenging professional career for the first time in her life. That is, the realization of the self, created first in the therapeutic relationship, overcame the feeling of inadequacy for both patients.

Conclusion: Theories of Narcissistic Repair

The classical or ego-psychological perspective traditionally gave little importance to narcissistic problems, tending to view them as secondary to anatomically derived concerns, such as penis envy and castration anxiety. To counteract this reductionistic theorizing, found by many clinicians to have limited value, Kohut developed an alternative theory emphasizing the importance of the child's early, potentially self-esteem-enhancing experiences. Kohut's emphasis on the selfobject experiences of idealization and mirroring had the virtue of addressing narcissism without reducing it to the biological sphere, but his theory relied on unfounded developmental speculations, a fact acknowledged by some of his adherents (Basch, 1985). Basing his concept of therapeutic action on relinquishment of the infantile narcissistic states of idealization and grandiosity, Kohut (1984) believed the healing of narcissistic defects lay in the selfobject functions provided by the therapist after the patient's archaic narcissistic needs had been mobilized in the transference. This view of therapeutic action makes the patient a passive recipient of the therapist's activity and thereby misses the importance of self realization.

The sense of defectiveness, I believe, is repaired not so much by the patient's internalization of the therapist's activity as by new meanings and possibilities created by the patient on the basis of the therapist's interpretations and attitude. Although patients tend to interpret experience negatively in accordance with their sense of defectiveness, this feeling of inadequacy is healed not by internalization but by reliance on affects that enable the patient to actualize his potential in a new relationship. Supporting evidence for this viewpoint is provided by studies of self-actualizing people—studies that demonstrate that self-acceptance is characteristic of individuals who utilize their capacities most fully (Maslow, 1954).

From an ego-psychological perspective, Zelda developed a new ego function, the management of impulses, that provided her with a greater degree of control over her affects and eliminated her former impulsivity. From a self-psychological viewpoint, I performed the selfobject function of identifying and organizing her affects, a function that she eventually became capable of performing for herself. Although both viewpoints offer plausible ways of conceptualizing the shift in Zelda's affect organization, they both assume, however implicitly, the existence of untamed, directionless impulses or affects that had to be organized into a psychological structure, whether conceived as ego or self. But, I neither taught nor even helped Zelda control her impulses. Rather, I provided the conditions under which her aggression, intellect, and ambitions could become actualized in our relationship.

If it is possible to characterize Zelda's relationship with me as a selfobject experience, then my role as selfobject was to help her gain access to and realize latent potential. The therapeutic development of affect organization, emphasized by recent theorists within the self-psychological tradition (Stolorow et al., 1987; Bacal and Newman, 1990), signifies the engagement of the world with genuinely felt affective experience. Similarly, the lack of impulse control conceptualized by ego psychology is a symptomatic manifestation of derailed self development and desperate, defensive efforts to soothe the resulting anxiety. Zelda's binge-eating and chaotic interpersonal life were not symptoms of repressed impulses but desperate, indirect efforts to communicate her distress, emptiness, and frustrated potential. What appeared to be a new ability to control impulses was the emergence of a reservoir of genuine affective experience, her buried self potential. Having acquired the ability to use this experience in the conduct of her life, she no longer needed the symptoms that had brought her to treatment. This conceptualization provides an object relational understanding of why chaos and apparent impulsiveness pervade the lives of narcissistically damaged patients and provides the basis for a clinical strategy for the repair of damaged self-esteem.

Although Zelda, Dick, and Elliot had very different therapeutic experiences, each developed the capacity to articulate previously buried affects and desires, including the utilization of aggression in the service of desired goals. We have seen that the productive use of aggression is essential to the healing of narcissistic defects because the capacity to cope with negative affects and conflict is necessary for the feeling of competence. Kernberg, Klein, and the Kleinians tend to regard the burial of aggression as a root cause of narcissistic defect, but we have seen that aggressive inhibition is symptomatic of the denial of authenticity required by early relationships.

Although contemporary theories of narcissistic pathology see defectiveness in the self-experience as more fundamental than was true of classical psychoanalytic thought, both self-psychological and Kleinian-influenced theories place insufficient emphasis on the patient's creation of the self. Only if the therapist views the patient as a potentially authentic creator, a designer of himself, can he help the patient use the therapeutic space to overcome the feeling of inadequacy that lies at the root of narcissistic pathology.

Chapter 7

Unworthy Self, Bad Object

Dexter, it may be recalled from chapter 1, entered analysis to resolve destructive battles with his wife, a history of chronic underachievement, and grossly exaggerated emotional reactions to routine events. As discussed, Dexter maintained an unconscious conviction that he was unworthy of success and had arranged his life to confirm this belief. After a desultory college career (10 years to obtain a B.A.), he allowed his professional career to languish due to his seemingly inexplicable tendency to make careless and costly errors. Unlike the patients discussed in chapter 6, patients who felt inadequate or incapable of success, Dexter believed himself to possess reasonably good capacities and intelligence, but he sabotaged himself out of an unconscious feeling of unworthiness. As seen in chapter 1, he consciously attempted to succeed but could not control his self-defeating behavior. In this sense, Dexter represents a pattern among a group of patients who appear to have all the necessary tools for success and enjoyment, often including positive self-esteem, but flounder in their efforts at concrete achievement. Different in this regard from patients with a sense of inadequacy, these guilt-ridden patients feel undeserving despite their frequently realistic sense of adequacy about their capabilities.

Patients dominated by a sense of unworthiness are often confused with patients (e.g., those discussed in chapter 6) who suffer from a defective self. As both types of patients are self-devaluing in the broadest sense, they have frequently been assumed to suffer from the same narcissistic defect. Such reductionistic thinking tends to obscure the difference between Dexter's sense of unworthiness and the feeling of defectiveness suffered by patients such as Elliot and Zelda. Whereas the latter two felt invisible and were shamed by exposure, Dexter felt no sense of shame and was not conflicted about his visibility. Believing in his capacities but feeling unworthy of using them, he was arrested by guilt, not shame.

Many clinicians who find object relations theories helpful in the treatment of more difficult patients (e.g., those discussed in chapters 5 and 6) reserve the conflict model for the domain of neurosis, a conceptual move referred to by Mitchell (1988) as the developmental tilt. In this clinical strategy, object relations theories are applied to patients with deficit disorders, whereas patients like Dexter, who are burdened by guilt, are thought to suffer from unresolved unconscious conflict between guilt and unacceptable wishes (e.g., Kernberg, 1984). The assumption of this clinical thinking is that neurotic patients require a more interpretive-based treatment to resolve their conflicts, whereas disorders of the self need a more relationship-based approach to strengthen their self structure. In contrast to this bifurcation of therapeutic models, this chapter tries to demonstrate that the object relations model of interpretation and use of transitional space applies to guilt-based disorders as much as to patients with fragile or inadequate selves.

The Conviction of Unworthiness

Nora, who entered treatment for help with work and a long-standing relationship, is prototypical of this class of patients. The career problem involved recent major changes in her company that made it a less-appealing place to work. Under new management, the company was insidiously shifting toward giving less autonomy to their employees and emphasizing paperwork and procedural detail, as opposed to provision of service, the aspect Nora found most gratifying. Having 15 years of job experience as an office administrator, Nora was quite capable of and accustomed to operating independently. After spending the major part of her professional career working for this organization, however, Nora was unable to conceive of life without it and was despairing over the choice between remaining in the current stultifying atmosphere and leaving.

Nora impressed me immediately as a charming, cheerful, attractive, friendly, healthy-looking, highly agreeable woman who was extremely likable and positive in her outlook and spirit. She seemed to have an active, full life that provided her with a great deal of satisfaction. She loved sailing and yoga, had many friends, and physical health and activity were clearly important to her. In her presence, I could easily imagine that people were drawn to her and would want to befriend her. Despite her statement that her relationship and work presented significant problems, it seemed almost ironic that this apparently happy, satisfied person, who had such a quick smile and positive disposition and who had no visible signs of depression or anxiety, would seek psychotherapy. As she related her history, her need for therapeutic help became clearer, but there remained a sense throughout the treatment that I was in the presence of an uncommonly empathic and positive spirit.

She had been through two unsuccessful marriages, her first husband being a powerful business executive who had financial dealings with the firm of her employment. Although she met him at work, after the marriage, her 10-year-older husband insisted that she not work while he controlled the household finances and made all major decisions. Married at 20 and a mother at 22, Nora spent the early years of her marriage feeling increasingly isolated, stifled, and unfulfilled. The couple had two children, and, while they were young, Nora tolerated her lack of freedom and tried to make the best of it. Although she longed for a house with a backyard for the children, her financially successful husband repeatedly denied this request without explanation, and the family was consigned to apartment life in an urban setting.

Nora was not fully aware of her deep sense of imprisonment until her younger child was school age, at which point she began to feel bored, restricted, and resentful. Her husband opposed her desire to return to work and added that he would not "let her" pursue an alternative plan of graduate school. Nora initially accepted his decision as final, but, as her resentment and anger about her lack of freedom mounted, she found herself unable to tolerate the situation and returned to work over her husband's objections. This act was perhaps her first autonomous step in their now eight-year marriage. Eventually, she began a graduate program against her husband's wishes, although she eventually dropped out, purportedly because she found the curriculum unsatisfying. Even after returning to work, she could not tolerate her isolation, lack of freedom, and the distance between her husband and herself. He made major decisions without considering her views and left the childrearing to her, refusing to participate in the lives of his children. When this sense of imprisonment and isolation became unbearable, Nora filed for divorce.

Although the second husband, Nate, did not have the aura of stature and power possessed by the first, life with him also took place in a suffocating atmosphere. Deeply resentful of Nora's children, he refused to pay for his share of the living expenses, and, when Nora was unable to assume the burden of home maintenance by herself, their apartment deteriorated to an alarming extent. Willing to live with plaster peeling from the ceiling, unpainted walls, and leaking faucets rather than pay his share of the household expenses, Nate increasingly withdrew from Nora and became consumed with his career and graduate education. Again, Nora found herself trapped: Living in a small, deteriorating apartment with no help, companionship, support, or communication with Nate, she felt as isolated as she had with her first husband. The marriage lasted only two years.

In the eight years since her divorce from her second husband, Nora enjoyed the first taste of independence in her life. While continuing to work for the same company, she completed a master's degree that allowed her to advance to a higher administrative level with significantly increased pay and benefits. With this more solid financial footing, she managed to save and invest her money wisely enough to provide herself with the first independent financial security of her life, giving her a precious sense of autonomy. With her children both grown and living on their own, Nora was enjoying a sense of freedom.

Pursuing activities that she enjoyed and supporting herself, Nora had little desire to change her life, and yet she was tempted to do just that for the sake of her current relationship. Alex wanted her to leave the Midwest and join him on the West Coast, an area that he never intended to leave. Despite her lack of interest in living in that part of the country, Nora was considering moving there to join Alex. He made many assumptions about their relationship: They would be married, she would join him in his preferred area of the country, and her hard-won life savings would belong to both of them. Although he had little to offer financially and had not yet divorced his wife, from whom he had long been separated, Nora seemed drawn into acquiescing to his plans. She openly acknowledged that, although Alex was energetic and fun, he was a user. A bright, perceptive woman, she saw in him a history of taking from others. Living in separate towns, the couple saw each other only for weekends at regular intervals. Nora was distressed about the fact that Alex paid very little of the expenses when they were together and insisted on meetings and activities that fit his schedule, predilections, and financial means with little regard for her preferences. In short, she could see with no prompting from me that the relationship went according to his convenience. Despite making this observation on her own, Nora did not seem to draw conclusions from it. She mentioned his tendency to exploit others as an unpleasant but far from alarming fact.

It was an odd experience, indeed, to hear Nora say that Alex was a user in a neutral tone, as though she were discussing an acquaintance whose malfeasance had no implications for her life. She seemed to regard her future with him as a fait accompli even though she was reluctant to live away from her daughter, move so far from her son (who lived in the East), confront an uncertain employment situation, and begin a new life without her network of friends. Given her reservations about Alex and their relationship, Nora's sense of inevitability was both striking and puzzling.

In the three most significant relationships of her life, Nora was treated as the less important of the pair, a role she had unquestionably accepted without articulating it to herself. Her job had positioned her in a subservient role throughout most of her working life and, even at her current supervisory level, had put her beneath a group of executives who were frequently arrogant, condescending, and devaluing of her. But Nora remained unswervingly loyal to this company that even now seemed to be exploiting her.

What struck me most about Nora's work and love life was her willingness to assume a second-class position without apparent conflict. When I pointed out this pattern, Nora seemed unsure that it was a problem. Her awareness was limited to dissatisfaction with all the relationships and the way her company's policy was now directed, but she had not previously thought about her assumption of second-class status. When I brought this attitude to her attention, she questioned whether any other type of relationship was possible and thereby revealed a deep, overriding sense of unworthiness: She did not feel deserving of more than subordinate status and consequently did not recognize such treatment as a problem.

Nora, like Dexter, possessed a strong conviction of unworthiness that drew her to experiences that would likely confirm this belief, a process referred to by Bollas (1987) as psychic gravity. Whenever Dexter seemed to be making progress, he made errors that had the effect of arresting his movement toward success and keeping him in a secondary position. In a similar way, Nora attempted to achieve but was persistently drawn to experiences that sabotaged her hard-won success. During her first marriage, she had entered a Ph.D. program over the objections of her controlling husband, but she withdrew and returned to a subordinate job in which powerful executives treated her as an underling. When, after two divorces, she finally received her master's degree and advanced to a supervisory level, the company changed management styles, and once again she was thrust into a subservient position. Rather than seek another position in which she would be accorded the respect she had earned, she was accepting of the lower status into which the company had placed her. Furthermore, she had assumed a secondary position in all of her major relationships. Both Dexter and Nora, by recruiting experiences in which they were undeserving, created and sustained their conviction of unworthiness.

Patients such as Nora and Dexter present surprising difficulties for the therapist. They are not severely disturbed, rarely engage in addictive or other flagrantly self-destructive behavior, and appear to have great potential, but their feelings of unworthiness impede their functioning and enjoyment. Often intelligent, motivated, introspective, and easy to engage, these people possess strengths so apparent that they seem to be desirable, even ideal, candidates for successful psychotherapy. Both therapist and patient are frequently frustrated, disappointed, and at times even shocked when the self-defeating sense of unworthiness turns out to be stubbornly resistant to therapeutic intervention.

An Object Relations Concept of Guilt

As seen in chapter 1, patients like Dexter and Nora are conceptualized from the ego-psychological viewpoint as neurotic patients whose symptoms are a product of intrapsychic conflict between wish and guilt (e.g., Brenner, 1979). But, as discussed in chapter 2, reliance on conflict alone to explain neurosis encounters two major problems: The very ubiquity of intrapsychic conflict mitigates its ability to explain why conflict results in symptoms on some occasions but not others, and the conflict view has difficulty accounting for the recalcitrance of symptoms to interpretation. As clinicians, we frequently find that patients gain insight into unconscious conflicts only to be frustrated at their lack of progress. We have all too often heard from our neurotic patients, "I understand that, but it doesn't change!"

The shift to a relational-conflict view does not, in my view, ameliorate these problems. Any conceptualization of persistent emotional distress relying primarily on conflict, whether construed as intrapsychic or relational, encounters difficulties differentiating between everyday and symptom-producing conflict and explaining the persistence of symptoms after interpretation. To account for the adhesiveness of symptoms, the clinician must conceptualize pathological states as arrested self development.

This reconceptualization of psychopathology does not diminish the role of guilt. As shown in chapter 2, guilt is a way of maintaining an object tie. We must now show how this concept of guilt helps explain the sense of unworthiness in patients like Nora and Dexter.

Let us return to Dexter. We recall that he was excited by the possibility of becoming the success for his mother that she felt her husband was not; he felt he possessed a very special relationship with his mother but feared losing his father if he outshone him. When Dexter began to master math that his father could not do, his mother was pleased, but his father withdrew from him. It was after this experience that Dexter's grades began to slip and his academic performance fell: He could not tolerate the loss of his father and the feeling that he was hurting him. He loved his father and respected how hard the older man worked to support the family: to wound him was unforgivable.

Dexter made the unconscious choice to martyr his life and wallow in failure rather than risk damaging his father and their relationship. Analogously, believing that only success would win his mother's approval, he strove for achievement in the hope of securing their relationship and earning a special place in her life. Dexter's motivation on both sides of his ambivalence was the anxiety of losing a parent: if he succeeded, his father was threatened; if he failed, he would lose his special relationship with his mother. His guilt was rooted in the anxiety of losing critically important parental figures.

This conceptualization of guilt bears a similarity to the Kleinian (1937, 1940) depressive position, according to which guilt is the anxiety of damaging the loved object. However, in the Kleinian conceptualization, the origins of the potential loss lie in an inborn aggressive drive. If one eschews this assumption of an endogenous aggressive drive and Klein's (1957) unrealistic developmental timetable, the Kleinian view of guilt as fear of injuring the loved object is a useful way to approach Dexter's guilt. However, the anxiety of object loss may be rooted in many types of experiences, only one of which is destructive desires. The threat Dexter felt in losing his father, for example, was not from his aggression but from his success. One may argue in the Kleinian manner that Dexter's success required the deployment of aggression, but the threat of object loss did not derive from a fear of doing injury with his aggressive strivings but from his belief that his father would be deflated by his achievements. That is, Dexter's guilt was not a response to a wish or desire but to the fact that his own development, his success in life, posed a grave threat to a relationship he could ill afford to lose.

Dexter was confronted with having to navigate his life with only a minimal degree of success if he was to maintain his relationship with his father and please his mother. To this end, he constructed a self-concept that appeared to value accomplishment but in fact realized very little of it. That is, to avoid the loss of the paternal object relationship, Dexter formed a sense of self based on sabotage and defeat. Because his aggression per se did not pose a threat to the object, sustaining the object relationship was not a simple matter of repressing aggression but of forming an unworthy self whose relative lack of success would not threaten the father. The Kleinian concept of the depressive position, limited by its reliance on aggression as the threat to the object, misses the fact that the self is formed as unworthy to protect the object tie. Guilt then becomes the vehicle through which self-realization is sacrificed for the maintenance of early object relationships.

But, the dominance of guilt in Dexter's life was still deeper and more complex. Compliance with either parent obliged him to subjugate his own desires. Dexter maintained the paternal relationship by submitting to his father's competitiveness but felt fraudulent in this very submission. His tie to his mother, by contrast, was best secured by success, a fact that motivated him to achieve. However, because this success motivation was in compliance with his mother's use of him, it constituted yet another form of betrayal. Consequently, when Dexter did take steps to achieve goals, he felt fraudulent and ultimately too guilty to sustain his initiative. Whether impelling success or failure, Dexter's modes of engaging the world constituted self-betrayal and evoked a deep sense of existential guilt (Summers, 1996), a feeling of having violated his integrity by denying the needs of his self. We thus see how the self-betrayal involved in Dexter's compliant solutions, whether leading to failure or spurring movement toward success, added a second layer of guilt to his feeling of unworthiness.

Berliner (1947, 1958) developed a similar object relations understanding of moral masochism as a "bid for affection," the dynamic being not the enjoyment of self-injury but submission to an abusing parent in the hope of maintaining a needed object relationship. Guilt, in this view, is a product of the need for the abusive object. By providing the first object relations formulation of moral masochism, Berliner presaged in some respects the view advanced here. However, Berliner did not broaden his theory to encompass other guilt-based pathology; to wit, he failed to conceptualize guilt as woven into the very fabric of the self and did not recognize that development of the self per se may threaten the object relationship. Nonetheless, Berliner's formulation may be taken as a step in the development of a more complete object relations formulation of guilt-based pathology.

The current object relations view differs in three fundamental respects from the conflict model of guilt: Its root lies in the anxiety of object loss, it addresses how the very development of the self threatens the object tie, and it construes guilt as a way of experiencing the self. By including these three components, this object relations model conceptualizes guilt as a major pathological factor without resorting to the drive model or presupposing the pathogenicity of conflict. Most psychoanalytic schools, including self psychology, Kleinian theories, and the object relations theories of Fairbairn and Guntrip, have assumed the conflict model of guilt. The classical view has difficulty accounting for pathological outcomes, whereas self psychology and these object relations views have tended to dispute the importance of guilt altogether. However, one can see from cases like Dexter that the formation of an unworthy self has crippling pathological effects that cannot be reduced to a feeling of badness for unacceptable wishes. The limited explanatory power of the drive model of guilt lies not in the nature of guilt per se but in the conceptualization of guilt as a reaction to unacceptable wishes. I submit, to the contrary, that guilt over a specific wish or desire cannot account for persistent interference with self-development. Dexter's guilt was debilitating because, as a fundamental component of his self designed to maintain object ties, it impeded positive life experiences.

Nora's crippling sense of guilt was also rooted in anxiety at the prospect of loss. Her mother was a strict, harsh, humorless, overbearing, emotionally constricted religious fundamentalist who did not appreciate children's play, received very little satisfaction from life, and expected none for herself or her two daughters. Valuing obedience above all other virtues, Nora's mother expected total compliance with her industrious, rule-following attitude, and Nora's high energy and spontaneity were regarded as disobedient, spiteful, and even sinful. Nora, a fun-loving, playful child, was subjected to continual attack for her cheerfulness, spontaneity, and easy disposition. Her sister was considered the good child, the child who obeyed. Although Nora attempted to conform to her mother's strictures and rarely opposed her openly, she was told that she was a spoiled, mean, willful, and evil child. Distressed by these abusive attacks on her character, Nora sought and found refuge in isolation and in her grandmother and father, the two most significant figures of her early life. Her father was a gentle man who quietly disagreed with his wife's verbal abuse of his daughter but was unable to end it. He provided Nora with such refuge as he could, but his influence was restricted by his limited time at home and passive disposition. Nora's grandmother, who lived nearby, was a greater source of support, and Nora often went to her for comfort. Eventually, she spent most of her after-school time at her grandmother's house, where she felt respected and cared for.

The small religious community in which Nora grew up was close-knit and insular. In an almost clanlike atmosphere, its members were expected to marry within the community. Nora fortified her reputation as a renegade by leaving after high school to live in a large city. Her mother was shamed by this separation from the community and never forgave her for it. By contrast, Nora's sister continued to reside within a block of her mother. Although she managed to establish her own life in the city away from the family, Nora was burdened with a sense of guilt for this separation, as though her independence were a sin for which she could not forgive herself. Her intellectual knowledge that she had made the right choice by escaping an untenable home atmosphere had not shaken what she regarded as an irrational belief that she was wrong for leaving home and for opposing her mother's wishes.

As Nora had not succumbed to her mother's harsh attacks (i.e., refused to live under her mother's direct influence), she believed that physical escape had freed her from maternal influence. Yet, she was unable to develop mutually respectful relationships and to function at a job commensurate with her talents. In the course of psychotherapy, as she associated these problems to her mother's attacks, she realized that her mother was, in this sense, always present, ready to tell her that she was undeserving of the goods of the world and to pounce on any movement toward freedom with harsh judgments about Nora's unworthiness. As this harsh, negative maternal influence was preferable to abandonment, the price of the maternal connection was a life lived in second-class status. In effect, Nora had made an unconscious bargain with herself: She could have some degree of physical independence from her mother at the cost of psychological submission and an agreement not to violate her mother's strictures about happiness. In this way, she maintained a sense of maternal connection and avoided abandonment without the life of suffocating compliance accepted by her sister. Guilt was the price she paid for her escape.

Strikingly, Nora's compliance with her mother by sabotaging herself and burying her potential only exacerbated her guilt. As we uncovered her unconscious compliance with her mother and its repetition through two marriages, Nora felt a sense of self-betrayal, a compromise of her integrity in favor of retaining a maternal connection. Feeling that she had committed a crime by burying her desires through slavish compliance to her mother and two husbands, Nora's became increasingly convinced of her unworthiness.

Although Nora's harsh judgment about herself would undoubtedly be conceptualized as shame by some theorists (e.g., Morrison, 1989), shame cannot account for the powerful sense of unworthiness and criminality experienced by Nora. Having violated her own integrity, Nora felt unworthy of success and equal treatment. Thus, in a very real sense, Nora could not win, as she felt guilty both for effecting such separation as she could from her mother and for failing to separate psychologically. In brief, she felt guilty over separation in order to secure the tie to her mother, and she felt guilty over compliance in order to warn herself against losing integrity.

The bonds with her father and grandmother provided Nora with an environment in which she could develop a positive spirit, a sense of hope and self-respect, but these bonds could not erase the influence of her mother, who was, after all, her primary caretaker. As Fairbairn (1943) pointed out long ago, early object relationships are so necessary that unsatisfying early relationships tend to be more adhesive than positive bonds. Nora's relationship with her mother is a good example of an object tie that, because of its traumatic nature, could not be relinquished. Without the confidence-inspiring relationships with her father and grandmother, Nora would likely have suffered a fate similar to that of her sister. These other influences facilitated movement toward the fulfillment of her destiny, but the shadow of the maternal object darkened and even arrested this journey (Bollas, 1987).

The persistence of Nora's maternal presence can be thought of as an internalization or a bad maternal object as long as it is understood that such an internalized object is an aspect of the self that maintains the maternal tie. As discussed in chapter 2, adaptations used to sustain early object connections form the very structure of the self. Nora's sense of unworthiness provided her with a major component of her self-definition. She had left her physical mother behind at age 17, but to relinquish the maternal presence would have evoked annihilation anxiety, a gap in her sense of self. That is, despite the harshness of her mother's voice, Nora would have been lost without it. To avoid the loneliness and abandonment of life without a mother, she created a maternal presence in a manner that would sustain the connection: a constant message that she was unworthy of the good parts of the world. The function of guilt in the maintenance of object ties and of the sense of self helps to explain its persistence.

Nora's significant relationships with men were a manifestation of her unworthy self. She expected to be in a diminished role with her partner, and she found mates who fulfilled this expectation. Both husbands and her current boyfriend had stifled her desire to utilize her intellectual and emotional capacities and to that extent repeated her maternal bond. None of these men had verbally abused her as her mother had, but they all had acted to control the relationship and treated her as an unequal partner, a form of denigration that confirmed her sense of undeservingness.

Nonetheless, Nora also felt guilty for these acts of compliance, and this existential guilt represented the voice of genuine integrity refusing to accept total submission. These relationships, which left her feeling suffocated to the point of intolerableness, represented the dilemma of her life: she strove for happiness but felt unworthy of it, and she put up with misery until her sense of destiny screamed, "No more!" However, her freedom and relief lasted only until she formed a new relationship. The nature of her relationships thus embodied her conflicting desires to realize her destiny in freedom and happiness and to remain subjugated to a maternal presence that deemed her unworthy of achieving goals that mattered to her.

The importance and persistence of guilt in certain pathological states directs clinicians to be careful not to reduce all experiences of self-rejection to shame—an affect that does not fit the sense of undeservingness afflicting patients such as Nora and Dexter, whose sense of unworthiness was woven into their very sense of self and whose guilt was powerfully crippling and frustratingly persistent. The unworthy self in such situations becomes the "unthought known" (Bollas, 1987), an assumed aspect of existence that guides ways of being and relating to others. The question now becomes: How does the therapist ameliorate this stubborn, debilitating unworthy self?

The Unworthy Self and Therapeutic Action

The conceptualization of debilitating guilt as an unworthy self implies that the model of self-transcendence is applicable to the guilt-crippled patient. Applying the model of interpretation and the use of transitional space to patients whose self structure is organized around the conviction of unworthiness, the therapist must first interpret the origins and function of the unworthy self in order to open a therapeutic space within which the sense of a deserving self may be created. As this process is seen best in the concrete clinical encounter, we return to Nora to illustrate this dual approach with the guilt-dominated patient.

Nora

The Therapeutic Action of Interpretation

Nora sought therapy partly for help in deciding whether she should marry Alex and relocate. Responding to my inquiries about the two divorces, Nora tended to emphasize her feeling of suffocation in both marriages and to relate concrete problems such as her second husband's unwillingness to repair their apartment. When I pointed out that she had assumed a secondary importance in both relationships, she initially attributed this status to her unequal financial role. After I remarked that in her second marriage she contributed more financially than her husband did without viewing herself as an equal partner, Nora reflected on her assumption of secondary status and began to see its power over her life, poignantly emphasized in her current job. As an underling to powerful business executives, Nora repeated her lifelong relationship pattern by ensuring that others played a more significant role. Whenever I asked for associations to her undeserving feeling, her mother's harsh, critical voice inevitably came to mind. At this juncture in the process, we discussed at length her maintenance of an unworthy self to sustain the maternal bond. We then connected her assumption of a subservient stance vocationally and interpersonally to her need to maintain a sense of connection with her mother. Indeed, when we arrived at this point in the process, it became clear that Nora knew how to achieve trust in relationships only via her sense of unworthiness; she could not imagine having a relationship on any other basis.

In the therapeutic relationship, Nora was always agreeable and conciliatory, neither disagreeing with an interpretation nor voicing dissatisfaction with any aspect of the process. The depth of her need to accommodate was poignantly demonstrated during one summer session when the air conditioning was not turned up, and Nora, who had just finished a taxing workout, was clearly uncomfortably warm. When I asked if she was too warm, she claimed to be fine. After fidgeting in her chair, she pulled out a drink from her purse, and I could see perspiration forming on her forehead. A few minutes into the session, I was distracted at what appeared to be her extreme discomfort, and I suggested that I could turn up the air conditioning. Nora was firm in her insistence that I not do so, reasoning that, if I were uncomfortable, I would have changed it already. In fact, I was also beginning to feel too warm. I told her that lowering the temperature was fine with me and that she was clearly too warm and needed some cooler air. Despite her opposition, I turned up the air conditioner.

Struck by her refusal to ask for cooler air despite obvious discomfort and even more by her unease at my changing the temperature when she needed me to do so, I insisted on pursuing her attitude. Nora told me that, because the consulting room was mine, the room temperature was solely my decision, and any uneasiness on her part was her problem to suffer. Surprised at the stubbornness of Nora's belief that the room was mine to do with as I pleased and that she should tolerate any unpleasant condition, I asked her if she believed she had any rights or claims in our relationship. Surprised and confused by a question she could barely understand, Nora acknowledged that her honest answer was no. She was firm in her belief that she had no right to request changes in the physical environment because, after all, the consulting room was mine and should be for my comfort.

I used the session to make Nora aware that her attitude, which she took for granted, represented her assumption of second-class status, her belief that she was undeserving of equal treatment. I pointed out the obvious connection with all her significant relationships, most concretely her tolerance of the deteriorating apartment in her second marriage, in an attempt to get her to see that her deferential view of herself in the therapeutic relationship was a construction rooted in her sense of undeservingness. Nora associated to her mother's verbal denigration of her, a devaluing attitude that Nora had always assumed to be an accurate reflection of her flaws. She connected her mother's scorn with the close bond between her sister and mother, and Nora realized that she had always hated her sister as a representative of the truth of her mother's accusations. Nora then realized that she had hateful feelings toward both her sister and mother, and her guilt was related to those unacceptable feelings. Able to see the clear thematic thread between her second-class status in significant relationships, her hateful feelings toward her mother and sister, and her self-imposed disenfranchisement in the consulting room, Nora was intrigued by the idea that she had constructed an unworthy self. Nonetheless, the conviction of her subordinate status felt somehow right, as though to believe otherwise would violate some unknown principle of human behavior.

The insight that she felt guilty for her hatred toward her mother and sister felt accurate to Nora but did not appreciably affect her stubborn feeling of undeservingness. The therapeutic issue at this point became the persistence and pervasiveness of Nora's conviction of second-class status. Although she had always in some way known her mother's influence was with her, she now felt her mother's "voice" with an intensity and presence that seemed almost eerie. Seeing and feeling her mother in all that she did, in a routine trip to the grocery store she could "hear" her mother telling her not to buy certain products because they were in some way too good for her. In the midst of this deepening awareness, Nora realized that she used this dominating maternal influence as a guide for action. Asked what would happen if this influence were to evaporate, Nora blurted out unthinkingly, "It would be exciting! I'd be free! But, I wouldn't have a clue what to do! What would control me? It's exciting, but I'd be very confused!" This response, elaborated over many sessions, indicated that, without her mother's voice, Nora feared losing not only her maternal connection but also her very ability to navigate her life and impose limits on herself. Although Nora could theoretically envision that possibilities would open up if she were able to disconnect herself from her mother's influence, she was frighteningly overwhelmed at this thought. Her self structure was based on the maternal presence by which she felt imprisoned.

The unworthy self, construed in object relations terms, encompasses the phenomena addressed by the superego in ego psychology and the internalized bad object in Kleinian thought. Neither concept views guilt as self-definition. Conceptualizing guilt as a structure of the self, as a way of being in the world that defines one's sense of existence, is the essential difference between this object relations concept and other psychoanalytic theories of guilt. The clinical implications of this reconceptualization of guilt can be seen in Nora's treatment.

After understanding that guilt served as a guide, it became clear that Nora had the unconscious conviction that her only protection against selfishness and greed was her sense of unworthiness. This inability to believe in the realization of potential without selfishness is typical of guilt-burdened patients. Dominated by an object relationship of unworthy self and bad object, they believe their only alternative is to reverse roles and become the selfish, dominating subject exploiting an unworthy object. Given the choice, the morality of their guilt-dominated self structures leads them to choose the former. Nora had not conceived of the possibility of pursuing self-interest while maintaining sensitivity to and concern for others. Without a belief in other viable options, Nora stayed attached to her feeling of unworthiness out of fear that her only other attitude would be an unseemly selfishness injurious to others.

Nora thought all of this understanding was profound and even deeply moving, but, to her chagrin, movement toward shifting her relational roles to equal status was slow and erratic. Although never losing faith in the therapeutic endeavor, Nora had great difficulty extricating herself from her unequal status in relationships, although she was able to make some progress with Alex. Increasingly frustrated with his insistence on having the relationship on his own terms, she became more assertive in not complying with his agenda for their meetings and activities. For example, she had been looking forward to a weekend away, but he backed out of the plans for financial reasons, attempted to convince her that their plans had not been certain, and tried to rearrange the weekend for Nora to visit him. In the past, Nora would have acceded, but, in this case, she not only refused to comply but went on the trip without him. This event was one example of a shift in their relationship in which she was beginning to take more control and, to her surprise, found that Alex maintained his interest in her. Nonetheless, her effort to form a more equally balanced relationship was a constant struggle. When they were together, she often found herself acquiescing to plans she did not agree with and easily reverted to accepting second-class status. Although her anger was growing, she found herself unable to either transform the relationship or end it.

I was struck with the sharp contrast between Nora's unwillingness to make simple requests (e.g., for a comfortable room temperature) and the strident, presumptive demands of patients (e.g., Clara, discussed in chapter 5) who become enraged when their requests are not immediately met. I continually pointed out to Nora that she made excuses for me whenever I made an error such as misunderstanding her or starting the session late. Believing expressions of dissatisfaction would be presumptuous, she feared they would threaten the relationship and her sense of self. Equally vexing, her compliance led to a feeling of self-betrayal. Although she could feel the anxiety of loss whenever she conceived of making a demand and guilt when she acquiesced to others, Nora was unable to translate these insights into relationship changes.

Furthermore, Nora desperately wanted to leave her company or, at minimum, change jobs within it in order to work in a more autonomous, less restrictive environment. Despite her discontent, she found herself as trapped by her job as she had been in her two marriages, especially the first, in which she felt financially and emotionally dependent on her husband. Her attachment to the company had the same feeling, as though only in this job with this company could she conceive of making a living. Unable to extricate herself, feeling helpless and yearning for freedom, her experience on the job was all too familiar: she was repeating her suffocating dependence on her mother and both husbands, but seeing these connections had little impact.

Opening the Therapeutic Space

At this point, we understood Nora's sense of unworthiness as her way of maintaining the maternal object tie and sense of self, and we thoroughly discussed the roles of anxiety regarding aggression, especially hatred of her mother and sister, fear of object loss, and her conviction that I would abandon her if she placed even the slightest demands on me. Yet, her progress was insufficient except for some shift in her relationship with Alex. Newly emerging conflict in that relationship led to a pivotal event in the treatment. Nora burst into session one day and, almost before sitting down, told me she was on the brink of doing something, but she wanted to use "good judgment" and requested my help with her decision. She then related the following story.

Sam, a boat owner with whom she had been sailing on several occasions, asked her out. Given the recent friction in her relationship with Alex, she accepted. On the second date, he asked her to accompany him on a yearlong, around-the-world sailing expedition, explaining that he had watched her sail enough to know she was competent and would be a valuable resource. Nora, shocked by the suddenness of this dramatic offer, was surprised to find herself drawn to accepting it. To all of my questions about the trip, she told me what Sam said. I asked her if a yearlong sailing trip was not a major life change and a large commitment to someone she barely knew. Nora replied that Sam, who had been divorced twice, said he was a good judge of character and knew her well enough to know that they were compatible and would get along. When I pointed out that there seemed to be pressure on her to make a quick decision that would have a far-reaching effect on her life, she replied that Sam said that he had been planning this trip for a year and was ready to go. When I asked her how she could be so ready to take such a large risk, giving up her friends, contact with her children, and her job so suddenly, she said that Sam said that she could return at any time and that he would set aside money for her in case she changed her mind and wanted to return home. Finally, I asked Nora what was "drawing her" to go on this trip, and she replied that she felt an urge to "get away" and that she loved sailing. Acknowledging that she did not love Sam and was not attracted to him, Nora saw an almost irresistible opportunity to escape her job and Alex in favor of a more exciting life.

Subsequent sessions were consumed with discussing the appeal of this trip. When I pointed out to Nora that her answers to all my inquiries were Sam's answers, she knew what I meant and realized that she had not been considering how she felt. I wanted to know: Did she think she knew Sam well enough to go? Although acknowledging that she did not, she insisted that the adventure had a great deal of appeal, that she would stay in a separate cabin, and that she could always go home if problems occurred. When I pointed out that, if she needed to escape, there were other ways of making lifestyle changes, Nora, admitting embarrassment, acknowledged that Sam's money and the power that went with it were influential in her attraction to the trip. This admission allowed me to make the connection between Sam and her first husband: She was once again influenced by a powerful man with money and was tempted to put her life under his control. Shocked that she would even consider putting herself under such total influence of a man she barely knew, I suggested that the same motive of sustaining her unworthy self, which had led to suffocation in her first marriage, may be operating in her attraction to the boat trip. I pointed out that the temptation to go on this trip was most likely not an escape but a repetition: She could be entering a new form of imprisonment. It was this statement more than any other that jolted her into reflecting on what she was doing.

I further pointed out the possibility that the suffocation was likely to be much worse than her previous experiences. If she went on the trip, she would be in the middle of the ocean, away from all her supports, friends, family, and activities, and almost totally dependent on a man she barely knew. Perhaps most important, she would have given up the measure of independence she had worked so hard to create. Sam, as owner of the boat and sole support of the trip, would have been in the position of making all the significant decisions, and her influence in directing her own life would be minimal, a position that she had been working assiduously to avoid. Nora's draw to this trip was the reenactment of her lifelong pattern of assuming a second-class status of dependence on the "more deserving" party. These realizations had an impact: Once she saw that the boat trip, under the guise of escape, would have repeated the very pattern she so desperately wanted to change, her temptation to go abated in favor of understanding why she had been so drawn to making a potentially disastrous decision. I pointed out that her defense of the trip with Sam's answers put him in the position of making her decision and relegated her feelings to a peripheral, perhaps even irrelevant, position, and thus once again she would be treating herself as unworthy and dependent on the "more important" other.

The experience with Sam allowed us to gain a deeper understanding of her relationship pattern. She was attracted to these powerful men not so much because she was impressed with their money per se but because, by their power and control over her, they became the personification of the bad maternal object, complementing and satisfying her need to be unworthy. She picked men who appeared on the surface to be decent if not always ideal choices but who ensured her sense of unworthiness by their treatment of her. The masochism of an overtly abusive relationship being offensive to her, Nora found a way to form object relationships to sustain her unworthy feeling in disguised form. Other types of object relationship threatened her very sense of self, but, as an unworthy self, Nora at least knew who she was.

All of this understanding provided Nora with renewed motivation to assume control of her life by exercising her capacities rather than relying on the "more important" male to direct her life voyage. Determined to experiment with treating herself as deserving of equality and autonomy, Nora decided not to go with Sam, a conclusion that created visible relief. By this point, Sam lived elsewhere, but he wrote Nora lengthy letters almost daily and called her incessantly. Refusing to believe her decision was final, he was relentless in his insistence that she change her mind. At first, Nora wrote back, but, as he became more persistent and his unwillingness to accept her decision more evident, she told him decisively that she wanted no contact with him, and she ceased writing entirely in the hope of discouraging him. He kept writing as though she had never asked him not to and, when in town, called expecting to see her, on one occasion even appearing at her apartment. His refusal to respond to Nora's requests and to respect her decision showed her conclusively that he had no interest in her wishes or feelings—that is, he did not treat her as a person with a mind of her own, thus confirming for her the soundness of her decision. The realization that she had been so close to embarking on a yearlong voyage with a man she now called crazy made her shudder. Throughout the course of therapy, she continually referred to this incident as the turning point.

Nora believed that the impact of these insights was due not just to new understanding but also to the fact that my attitude conveyed a sense of her worth. By communicating my conviction that she was repeating a pattern of unworthiness, I treated her as worthy of experiencing herself in a different way. No amount of praise or reassurance had ever affected her feelings about herself because she did not believe such comments reflected an appreciation of why she felt so undeserving. By contrast, my attitude emanated from a recognition of who she was, an appreciation of her need to believe and sustain a feeling of being unsuited for positive life experience. It must be emphasized that this attitude had an effect only after we had gone through a lengthy process to achieve understanding of her need to create and sustain her unworthy self. Within the context of insight into her conviction of unworthiness, my vision of her as deserving of equal treatment opened up the possibility of a new way of treating herself.

By bringing to therapy the temptation to repeat her pattern of submission with Sam along with the desire to "use good judgment," Nora expressed dissatisfaction with her participation in the trip. Here we see the value of her existential guilt. She did not fulfill her fate of unworthiness by simply going with Sam because an unease about coupling with him was surfacing: Something did not feel right, although she could not articulate her doubts. As we discussed her struggling but vague voice of protest, it became clear that Nora, instinctively sensing that she was betraying herself, felt guilty for wanting to submit her life to Sam's control. Asking for help from me in making the decision was the manifestation of her existential guilt warning of the betrayal of her integrity.

This more positive side of the ambivalence had, in the past, spoken through the suffocation she invariably felt when the enslaving relationships became unbearable. That all her major relationships had to become stifling before Nora could end them gave proof to which side of the ambivalence was stronger. However, the longing to experience a greater sense of humanness and to develop her own capacities protested her imprisonment in the disguised form of dissatisfaction with her intolerably suffocating existence. The depression and loneliness for which she sought help from her first therapist were the symptomatic pleas of her buried desire to be recognized as worthy. On the other hand, her draw to the voyage with Sam reflected acquiescence to her sense of unworthiness rooted in the despair of trying to achieve a more equal relationship.

This conflict between her desire for a mutually respectful relationship and her compulsion to confirm her sense of unworthiness by choosing a bad object invites the conclusion that her neurosis was a product of conflict. However, as discussed in chapter 3, the draw to the bad object is pathological per se, with the conflict being a product of this pathological object relationship and the more positive desire for respect. Thus, the tension between these two aspects of Nora's self is an outcome of her pattern of pathological object relationships rather than a cause of it.

My suggestion that she was readying herself for yet another imprisonment opened new dimensions to the therapeutic space. Despite her gratitude, she acknowledged a feeling that I should have been "on top" of this issue before and been more forceful in my efforts to intercede on her behalf. This complaint struck me as important for both the candor of its aggressive expression and its remarkable accuracy. Most immediately, for the first time Nora was willing to communicate a critical feeling to me, risking a potential negative reaction that in the past had always felt too threatening to take.

Nora's remark that I had been too passive with her earlier illuminated an aspect of my experience with her of which I had been previously unaware. I had, indeed, been playing a passive role by watching her accept second-class treatment from Alex—an unconscious repetitive collusion with Nora as a devalued woman who would be left to the mistreating mother. That is, I had been unconsciously reenacting the role of the passive father who was benign but ineffective in protecting her from the abusive mother. It took Nora's dramatic plan to shock me into action. Her draw to this plan was a desperate plea for me to see that she needed more forceful action and to be the active father she never had, the father who would come between her and her mother. Her presentation of this plan was her way of saying, "I am going off to be controlled and abused by another devaluing 'mother.' Are you going to stand by passively like my father did, or will you stop me?" Put another way, placing herself in this dangerous position was her way of telling me that interpretation was not enough, that she needed something more, even if she did not know what.

From a Kleinian viewpoint, Nora was moving from the paranoid position of splitting good and bad objects toward the depressive position, a new mode of psychological organization in which she could integrate her good and bad feelings for me. Although this change was certainly occurring, the movement would not have been effected without the opening of the therapeutic space made possible both by the interpretive work on object loss and her unworthy self and by my response to her symptomatic plea. Splitting is a function of closed transitional space, and shifts toward the depressive position require an opening up of the relational space to include aggression. That is, the movement toward whole-object integration was itself a function of an object relational shift. In turn, Nora's ability to be aggressive with me strengthened her sense of self and opened new possibilities for the realization of previously buried potential. Now that Nora had expanded the dimensions of the therapeutic space, she began to consider steps toward increasing autonomy, such as leaving her company and possibly ending the relationship with Alex.

Nora became freer with her affects in several areas. In a myriad of ways, she took more control of the setting rather than continue her former pattern of presumed helplessness. If she needed to reschedule, she asked for an appointment change rather than continuing her previous pattern of attempting to squeeze the session into an overburdened schedule and arriving late. She sought to have the room temperature to her liking; if she was thirsty, she asked for water. Even more important, Nora asserted herself into her own treatment. When she needed me to intervene more forcefully or, alternatively, to remain quiet while she spoke, she told me so and expected my compliance with her desires. If she thought we were not focusing on germane issues, she spoke up and shifted topics. This active stance reflected an assumption of some ownership of the process, a reversal of her formerly passive stance in which she had unquestioningly assumed that her task was to adjust herself to my behavior and interventions without ever considering other possibilities.

In the past, if Nora did not feel a resonance with my comments, she tried to find a way to concur with my remarks; now, she openly disagreed with me whenever my comments failed to correspond to her experience. She also became much more candid about her demands and expectations of the setting and the therapeutic process itself. What excited her now about therapy, more than the content of insights, was the process of exploring new ways of relating. Although she could not and did not expect all her desires to be met, she tried to find a way to negotiate the meeting of her needs, and this negotiation itself reflected a view of herself as a copartner in the therapeutic dyad. No longer driven to agree with me, there was no self-betrayal, and her existential guilt abated. Her unworthy self was being transcended.

After trying to apply her new way of being to her relationship with Alex, Nora decided that he was incapable of the equal relationship she sought, and she ended their involvement. Her relief was palpable, and, tellingly, Nora felt she won her freedom by the breakup. Although she missed the companionship and was anxious about being without a primary relationship, Nora also felt that a relationship in which she had a secondary role had no value to her. When I pointed out that she experienced the end of the relationship as a "jailbreak," Nora said that she would rather be alone than accept undeserving treatment. As her self was recreated as worthy, her recruitment of complementary objects had to fit a new self-definition: Bad objects were no longer compatible with this self-definition.

For the same reason, Nora resolved to change her employment situation. Continuing in her present position did not complement her growing sense of herself as worthy. For the first time in 20 years, she made a serious effort to obtain a different form of employment. In her position as office manager, she had acquired state-of-the-art computer skills and, after only a brief search, obtained a job doing cutting-edge computer software training. This new position not only allowed her to apply her hard-won competence but also provided the opportunity to continue her professional development in this area. Taking a job that utilized her talents and respected her competence and autonomy was the final step in the transcendence of her unworthy self. She thoroughly enjoyed her new job and, shortly after acquiring it, decided to terminate her therapy. Nora believed that her new sense of herself as deserving had fostered the resolution of the problems for which she had entered treatment.

It is especially important to emphasize the dual nature of the therapeutic action in this type of case because much of traditional psychoanalytic theory has been built around the treatment of guilt by interpretation of intrapsychic conflict. Nora, a guilt-ridden patient, is prototypical of the neurotic patient often regarded as the ideal psychoanalytic case requiring only interpretation for the resolution of intrapsychic conflict. During the interpretive phase, Nora gained a great deal of insight into her feeling of unworthiness, especially the awareness of her hate for her mother and sister, but she was able to relinquish that way of experiencing herself only as she used the therapeutic space to relate in ways that had previously been impossible for her. By assuming rights in the therapeutic relationship and daring to become aggressive, she created a new object relationship with me that resulted in a sense of worth. This therapeutic process

demonstrates the importance of the creation and use of new therapeutic space in addition to the value of interpretation—even with a
guilt-ridden patient such as Nora. Cases commonly labeled neurotic
require the creation of a different form of self, and this shift in self
structure is dependent on the creative use of therapeutic space as
much for these patients as for those with more problematic self
structures.

Dexter

The Therapeutic Action of Interpretation

The analytic process with Dexter also demonstrates the importance of both interpretation and the use of transitional space in the
therapeutic action with the guilt-burdened patient. A prototypical
neurotic patient who appeared to suffer from a guilt-induced success
neurosis, Dexter represents the type of case theoretically most con-
ducive to an interpretation-only clinical strategy, and, in fact, he
found insight helpful in elucidating many aspects of his symptoms.
For example, the interpretive process illuminated his conflict between the need to sustain his "special" relationship with his mother
by succeeding and his anxiety about outdoing his father.

We were able to see the repetition of these early relationships in
the transference. He wanted to be special to me but felt exploited;
he desired to outdo me but feared my envy and retribution. He
compared his life events with what he presumed to be my situation
and usually tended to feel diminished in comparison, although on
occasion he decided that he was "ahead" in one respect or another.
For example, after his second child was born, he presumed that I had
no children and, therefore, concluded that in this area he was further
along, but he then felt guilty and feared I would retaliate for his
"gloating." This persistent, ambivalent competitiveness was understood as his unresolved desire for and anxiety about outperforming
his father. We understood his "forgetting" to do the analytic work as
both his need to fail to ensure my superior position and his anger at

my exploitation of him in my role as the analyst-mother. Although these interpretations made Dexter aware of his primary modes of object relating, he was not able to use them to alter the transference constellation or to create new object relationships.

The recalcitrance of these patterns led to a focus on understanding why guilt had become a major component of his self-experience. As success was equated with subjecting himself to exploitation by his mother and injuring his father, he believed that the fulfillment of his ambitions would be damaging. By burying his desires for success and competence beneath his unworthy self, he ensured self-defeat. Although this self-sabotage entailed the pain of failing his mother, it enabled him to maintain a sense of integrity by not complying with the demands of a woman he regarded as exploitive. By experiencing himself as fundamentally unworthy, Dexter sabotaged the demands of his ice-princess mother and preserved the image of his father. Guilt, which developed into a fundamental structure of his personality, was a compromise solution. It cost him the feeling of satisfying the ice-princess mother but maintained a sense of autonomy by sabotaging her expectations while holding out the hope of eventually fulfilling her wishes; it also appeased the envious father, preserving that relationship. By believing himself to be unworthy but struggling to disprove this very conviction, Dexter was able to maintain connections with both parents and others representing them, thereby maintaining a sense of self.

Expanding the Analytic Space

Dexter's realization that he used his conviction of unworthiness to sustain a sense of self marked a major shift in the analytic process. When I asked what would happen if he did not experience me in either of his typical ways, Dexter was dumbfounded. His inability to even imagine this situation indicated that both his patterns—exploited victim and competition—saved him from isolation, the former maintaining a sense of connection with his mother and the latter with his father. I suggested that the possibility of yielding the only modes of engagement he knew threatened to leave him lost, with no way to navigate the world. Given the choice between such an abyss and his neurotic, self-defeating patterns, he chose the latter. This "preference" is the object-relational understanding of the analytic obstacles. As progress was made, Dexter felt his sense of self threatened; to avoid annihilation anxiety, he returned to his old patterns of victim exploitation or competition, preferring a painful sense of self to none. Thus, Dexter's regressions were not resistance but a desperate effort to escape the annihilation anxiety evoked by the potential loss of his sense of self (Kohut, 1984; Summers, 1993).

Over the course of many analytic sessions, we returned again and again to this experience of nonbeing and, when he was finally able to sustain this feeling, rather than escaping from it with his usual modes of engagement, Dexter admitted a terrifying longing for intimacy with me. "When all is said and done, I want something very simple. I want to be cared about. I want you to care. That's about it." At this point, Dexter realized that his "special" relationship with his mother was not truly intimate. He had misconstrued his mother's ambitions for him as intimacy in order to feel connected with her. His unresolved longing was now appearing in the analytic relationship.

The recognition of his longings to be cared for by me initiated a pattern consisting of close moments in which Dexter conveyed more deeply personal fantasies and desires, a disrupted response to this new experience, and retreat to a safer distance of exploitation–victimization or competition. For example, after the episode of crying, he felt that I was in a "superior" position because I had not cried. I commented that he was made anxious by these moments of intimacy, and, feeling safer at a distance, he returned to his pattern of competitiveness. He could see that conflict protected him by providing distance and the provision of a psychological location, a sense of self. Each time we reached this point, Dexter began to feel lost, but, inevitably, his longing for closeness emerged, as though appearing mysteriously, a striving discovered as it arose. When Dexter was finally able to maintain this sense of closeness, he felt a new depth to the analytic relationship. The experience of simple closeness with me—without anger, competitiveness, exploitation, or victimization—constituted the creation of a new object relationship, the analytic object.

On many occasions, as Dexter repeated that "all he really wanted" was closeness, tears welled up. I pointed out that we now understood his most mysterious presenting symptom, intense emotional reactions to seemingly trivial events. These reactions tended to occur in response to events that were positive, albeit mildly so. For example, a secretary brought him coffee, and, in thanking her, Dexter found himself tearing up while expressing appreciation. His reactions in analysis indicated that such episodes of tearing were the symptomatic appearance of his emotional hunger, a longing so close to the surface that it was triggered by trivial positive incidents. These responses were not symptoms of depression but the expression of buried longings for connections with others.

It was at this point that Dexter erupted in a seemingly endless litany of aggressive and envious fantasies and strivings. His desires to "bite off heads," appearing previously only in dreams, were now directly expressed in his rage at being "held back" by his parents' problems. He fantasized killing all those, including me, whom he regarded as having privileges or successes he believed himself to be lacking. His frustration at being "held back" was so intense in one session that he could not restrain himself from screaming while on the couch, "I hate you all! Assholes!" He felt both relieved and embarrassed at this explosion but recognized a depth of rage that had been held in abeyance for as long as he could remember. His aggression had become so infused with destructive fantasies that he had created a virtual "beast within," an aspect of himself that was now emerging in the analytic space. Although the opening up of his aggression and rage was a significant aspect of his therapeutic movement, it should be noted that it became possible only after the analytic space had expanded to include new object relational possibilities.

The emergence of Dexter's desires for closeness and aggressive feelings marked the most significant aspects of more authentic ways of connecting to me. Previously restricted by feelings of competition and exploitation, the analytic relationship was now broadened to include his deepest longings. Sharing his fondest dreams and convictions with me, Dexter revealed that he had always wanted to be a top executive but had feared telling me out of embarrassment, thinking that I would be envious and attack him as grandiose. As we discussed his dreams of becoming a competent manager, his anxiety visibly abated, although he felt no greater confidence in his ability to achieve his lofty ambitions. The expansion of the analytic space to include these aspirations constituted a new object relationship, the analytic object, within which he could be ambitious and express his desire to achieve goals without the fear of injuring others.

These authentic modes of engagement in the analytic space replaced Dexter's sense of self-betrayal and led to the gradual diminution of his existential guilt. As with Nora, this therapeutic shift may be conceptualized from the Kleinian viewpoint as the integration of previously split good and bad object representations, a resolution that relieves the anxiety of damaging the loved object. However, a pure Kleinian formulation does not account for the fact that Dexter was able to experience the intensity of his destructive desires only after the analytic space had broadened to include feelings of intimacy. The Kleinian formulation assumes that Dexter's destructive fantasies are the source of the conflict, a belief that makes them "psychological rock bottom" and obfuscates the fact that they are a product of frustrating object relationships. Expression of his destructive fantasies required the expansion of the analytic relationship to include intimacy, indicating that the therapeutic movement cannot exclusively be a matter of integrating good and bad feelings toward the same object. Dexter's ability to integrate aggression into the analytic relationship, rather than being a cause of therapeutic movement, depended on the creation of suitable transitional space. When Dexter felt close enough to me to acknowledge the intensity of his ambition, his fear of injuring me abated. That is, the alleviation of depressive anxiety was achieved with Dexter, as with Nora, via the construction of a relationship in which aggression was a component.

After Dexter was able to elaborate the depth of his aggressive desires, the analytic process underwent a noticeable shift. The hesitancies and avoidances that had been so common in his free associations were reduced dramatically as the analytic process flowed more easily, and forgetting to do the analytic work became increasingly rare. An analogous process ensued on the job: As he focused on his work with renewed commitment and sharper concentration, his "careless" errors diminished and eventually disappeared. At this point, he began to take concrete steps toward the fulfillment of his ambitions. Assuming new leadership responsibilities without being asked, Dexter showed an aggressive seizure of authority he had shirked in the past. Acting on the assumption that he was worthy of success and capable of leadership, he actively sought a managerial position. His father's vulnerability to his ambitions no longer dominated his strivings: Dexter's unworthy self had been transcended, and bad objects no longer had to be recruited for its sustenance.

In this new analytic space, Dexter felt close to me without feeling exploited or exploitive; he experienced aggression toward me without feeling guilty or injurious. It then became possible for Dexter to construe the analytic relationship in different ways. He acknowledged his envy of my professional credentials but felt no need to base his own professional development on my record. As mentioned in chapter 1, the analytic relationship was symbolized, from Dexter's viewpoint, by a dream in which he was in a bicycle race with a figure with a better vehicle, and Dexter pushed the figure off a cliff. Dexter saw that this dream included his former belief that his success depended on others' demise, with the consequent inhibition of his aggression. Dexter now believed that the dream not only depicted his father/analyst relationship but also the only way he knew to express his aggression.

The analytic process with Dexter demonstrates once again the critical role of both interpretation and analytic space in the therapeutic action of the guilt-ridden patient. Without the understanding of his inhibition of aggression, guilt, and competitiveness, Dexter would have been unable to see the necessity for creating a new object relationship. His insights provided an explanation of his seeming inability to experience success and thus indicated to him the changes he needed to make to overcome his self-imposed obstacles. Still, as Dexter and I went about the business of interpreting his need to create and maintain his unworthy self, he remained unable to relinquish his old patterns of competition and exploitation. He was able to create a sense of himself as worthy of achievement only as the analytic relationship was expanded to include his longings for intimacy, ambitions, and aggression.

As with Nora, Dexter's guilt was an experience of self, a way of locating himself psychologically in the world and a beacon for navigating interpersonal relationships. Because guilt was embedded in his experience of himself, Dexter could not overcome this guilt through understanding alone; he required a therapeutic space that could facilitate formation of a new sense of self. Once this new experience of the self was consolidated, guilt ceased to be a dominant factor in his personality.

Conclusion

Guilt and intrapsychic conflict have had a special place in the history of psychoanalytic thought. From the origins of psychoanalysis as delineated in *Studies on Hysteria* (Breuer and Freud, 1893–1895) through contemporary ego psychology (e.g., Brenner, 1982; Sugarman, 1995), guilt over wishes has been conceptualized as the central pathological feature of neurosis. From this viewpoint, symptoms are the indirect expression of the wish, circumventing guilt-motivated defenses. Indeed, anxiety-provoking destructive wishes were especially prominent in Dexter, for whom expressing the "beast within" provided an especially helpful use of the analytic space. This articulation of his rage provided clear relief, a result that fits the ego-psychological model of therapeutic action in which the amelioration of guilt over drive-fueled wishes is the crucial ingredient. It cannot be denied that aggressive inhibition was central to the pathology of both Dexter and Nora and that the overcoming of this inhibition in the form of freer aggressive expression had immense therapeutic benefit in each case. Nonetheless, the drive–guilt model omits certain fundamental features that limit its usefulness for understanding and treating guilt-ridden patients.

First, the equation of aggression with destructiveness found in both Nora and Dexter was not psychological rock bottom but a function of their early object relationships. In both cases, aggressive expression was a threat to maintaining the object tie to a parental figure—the mother in Nora's case, the father in Dexter's—resulting in aggressive inhibition to secure a necessary object relationship. In Dexter, the confining paternal relationship, unable to contain any form of aggressive striving such as ambition, led to the buildup of anger and rage to the point of destructive fantasies. The root of the crippling of aggression in both Nora and Dexter was not its connection with destructiveness but the early parental object relationships that required the burial of aggressive strivings.

Second, guilt, like other major pathological factors, buries the development of self-potential. Nora could not permit herself the exercise of her intellectual capacity and ambitious strivings until she could overcome her unworthy self. Dexter was likewise compelled to sabotage himself and inhibit his intellectual potential in surrender to his sense of unworthiness. As the treatment process with both Nora and Dexter indicates, when guilt is overcome, buried potential is able to unfold. Nora sought and secured a far more technical, higher level job than she had ever held; even more important, she expected equal treatment in relationships and jettisoned a current relationship that repeated her former pattern of submission to the other. Similarly, Dexter aggressively sought promotion and a managerial position, a reversal from his pattern of self-sabotage. As a footnote to this pursuit, it is noteworthy that I encountered Dexter by chance two years after termination of analysis, and he informed me that he was operating in a higher level management position than he had aspired to when he ended the analysis.

Finally, there are far-reaching clinical implications to the difference between guilt experienced in response to a morally offensive wish or desire and the guilt-ridden patient, whose life is crippled by the conviction of unworthiness. When guilt is woven into the very fabric of the self, it cannot be ameliorated by interpretation alone; it must be relinquished and transcended by use of the therapeutic space. The emphasis on the creation of a new object relationship as the essence of therapeutic action is the fundamental difference between the object relations model of the treatment of guilt and the ego-psychological viewpoint. In this way, the dual model of interpretation and use of therapeutic space is as applicable to the amelioration of guilt as it is to the resolution of narcissistic pathology or borderline fusion of self and object. For these reasons, the treatment of unworthiness, like the sense of defectiveness and fragility, requires a treatment model that directs itself to the transcendence of the self.

Chapter 8

Conclusion
The Art of Psychoanalytic Therapy

Freud developed the idea of psychoanalysis as a treatment technique for neurosis, a psychological method of symptom removal that used interpretation for its ends. Regarding this procedure as a scientific process, Freud (1933, pp. 158–159) believed the analyst's investigations produced truths about the mind akin to the discoveries of the natural sciences. Subsequent generations of psychoanalytic clinicians have found that exclusive reliance on interpretation is often insufficient to achieve the desired therapeutic result. The transformative limitations of psychoanalytic investigation have raised doubts about modeling the psychoanalytic process on the natural scientific method. Most tellingly, the paradigm of the "scientific observer" neglects the importance of the relationship between the therapist and patient in therapeutic action. A variety of theories has arisen to include, in varying degrees, the influence of the relationship between therapist and patient.

The most extreme of these positions is that the emotional impact of the therapist is the mutative factor and that interpretative content has little significance in the treatment. From the viewpoint of theorists adopting this position, psychoanalysis does not have a definite group of procedures effective for even a class of patients, and, because interpretation has limited impact, psychoanalytic therapy is not a definable technique but a significant relationship (Bacal and Newman, 1990; Mitchell, 1997; Orange, Atwood, and Stolorow, 1997).

The position that psychoanalysis is the provision of a relationship about which no principles can be elucidated virtually eliminates the possibility of articulating a concept of therapeutic process—that is, a theory of technique. There is no opportunity here for psychoanalysis to understand itself. Without a conceptualized process, therapeutic success would depend entirely on the idiosyncrasies of each therapist's unique relationship with each patient. Psychoanalysis would then become a relationship like any other, a blind existential encounter that may well be successful in individual cases, but all such success would be serendipitous.

Such a view would not distinguish the psychoanalytic process from changes people often make outside of the therapeutic arena without understanding its meaning. Whatever factors may catalyze such a shift in any individual case, they are serendipitous. On the other hand, we have seen in our discussion of the therapeutic process with patients like Dexter, Zelda, and Sharon that the factors facilitating therapeutic change can be articulated. In Aristotelian terms, what is done by chance may be done by art. Of course, this is not to deny the importance of the therapeutic relationship; it is to say that to rely on the therapist's indescribable emotional impact is to leave therapeutic action to chance. Rather than eliminating the art of psychoanalytic therapy, the power of the therapeutic relationship may be included in it. As an alternative to the extreme position, I have proposed the dual model of interpretation and transitional space, a model that includes the therapeutic relationship in the art of facilitating self transcendence.

Although Freud's "scientistic" model does not fit the dialogue between therapist and patient, the therapist's impact is not a blind existential encounter. A therapeutic vision of the patient as possessing buried potential makes possible an art of self transcendence. As we have seen in our case discussions, the therapeutic relationship can be constructed in a way that maximizes the possibility of therapeutic movement. Viewing the patient's problems as a reflection of arrested potential ensures that the process becomes a way of discovering the buried aspects of the self through the labyrinth of the patient's defenses and symptoms and finding a way to facilitate their development. The achievement of this goal implies a vision of the therapeutic space as transitional, a space designed not simply for the interpretive process but for the realization of new ways of being and relating. In each case discussed in this book, we have seen a unique pattern addressed and largely resolved through the uncovering and realization of buried-self potential. George, Sharon, and Dexter, for example, all differed markedly in the nature of pathology, defenses, and character structure, but each required understanding of defenses and a relationship within which they he or she was able to realize previously unknown potential.

We have included the strengths of both the classical and relational viewpoints in our model. The ego-psychological approach has the merit of appreciating the importance of understanding and therefore maintains the uniqueness of psychoanalytic therapy as a depth psychology; the relational position recognizes the power of the patient–therapist relationship in therapeutic action. We may describe succinctly the therapeutic process by paraphrasing a famous philosopher: Understanding without a relationship is empty, and a relationship without insight is blind.

The art of psychoanalytic therapy, like any art, requires a vision of the possible: The therapist must have an image not just of who the patient is but of who the patient may be. Loewald (1960) has borrowed Freud's sculptor metaphor to point out that the therapist finds in the patient's material the ingredients out of which he fashions an idea of the patient's potential. This is a vision of the possible, the undeveloped potential of the patient. Classical psychoanalytic thought, and even much contemporary thinking, is a theory of the actual, how patients come to be who they are. If interpretation and therapeutic action are equated, perhaps only the actual need be part of theory. However, once the therapeutic vision includes facilitating the patient's potential to transcend the childhood self, theory shifts to both the actual and the possible.

Winnicott's (1960a) concept of the true self began a trend in psychoanalytic theory toward a theory of possibilities. Bollas (1987) has extended this concept to the articulation of the personal idiom, and other theorists have also seen that psychoanalysis is about seeing the possible. Loewald (1960) from the classical perspective and Spezzano's (1993) work on affects have both seen psychoanalysis as the art of the possible. Most significant, Benjamin's (1997) concept of ownership and the transcendence of opposites has provided psychoanalysis with its most well-articulated vision of the possible. Benjamin points out that the overcoming of opposites, such as active–passive and masculine–feminine, results in ownership over one's states and one's life. The concept of transcending the anxiety-driven self in favor of authentic-self realization is a clinical depiction of Benjamin's concept of ownership. In this book, I have tried to delineate a clinical theory suggesting how psychoanalytic therapy can be the art of realizing self potential—that is, the art of both the actual and the possible.

The technical tools of this art include (a) free association, interpretation, and transference to achieve an understanding of motivation and (b) the design of therapeutic space to create a new relationship in which the self structure can be yielded and a new organization created. The classical model is too limited to become the basis of such an art, and relational analysis does not believe such an art is possible.

We have seen the failure to grasp the importance of therapeutic space in Breuer's treatment of Anna O. Breuer was so taken with the "scientific" method of uncovering Anna's memories that he could not see that the development of her prodigious potential was part of the treatment. He never talked to his patient about her frustrations in not being able to utilize her intellect, literary talent, compassion, and desire for social justice, because he did not see their exercise as part of treatment. Although Breuer helped "Anna O" by responding to her symptoms as meaningful communications, Bertha Pappenheim overcame completely her paralysis and reentered the world only after her relatives, the Goldschmidts, facilitated the exercise of the dormant capacities Breuer had recognized: her intellect, compassion, and desire for social justice.

It is instructive to compare, however briefly, Bertha and Zelda, who in significant respects suffered from parallel problems. Although Zelda did not possess the intellectual gifts with which Bertha was endowed, both women were defined by their families in ways that did not include the realization of their potential, especially the exercise of their intellects. As a result, both had self structures that severely limited their capacity for self realization, a fact that produced symptoms reflecting intellectual and emotional starvation. Both women overcame their symptoms and became productive in the context of relationships that recognized, appreciated, and nurtured their arrested potential. The difference was that Bertha, being the first psychonalaytic case, enjoyed such facilitative relationships only after her psychotherapy ended, a fact that may account for the failure of her capacity to love. By contrast, central to Zelda's psychotherapy was the unearthing and realization of dormant capacities.

It must be emphasized that the realization of buried-self potential does not necessarily mean greater success in conventional terms. Although the exercise of Zelda's intellectual and aggressive potential resulted in a professional career, for Dick the realization of his long-dormant desires for a close family life and more emotionally meaningful existence issued in the abandonment of his highly successful career in favor of a lifestyle that afforded much less achievement and success in societal terms. Dick's therapeutic journey underscores the fact that the aim of psychoanalytic therapy is self realization, not any preset category of success. This concept of therapeutic outcome is tantamount to Benjamin's (1997) concept of ownership: Successful analytic treatment means the authorship of one's states and life lived as a product of subjectivity.

The art of psychotherapy, then, requires the evolution of the therapist's vision of who the patient can be—a vision that, because it includes the realization of previously arrested potential, must in some sense precede the patient's conscious experience. From the patient's material and enactments in the therapeutic relationship, the therapist discerns those aspects of the patient's potential that, although arrested, may issue in self realization. However, the therapeutic space is opened precisely for the creation of ways of being and relating that cannot possibly be foreseen. Crucial to the therapetuic attitude is openness to the new, a not knowing out of which the previously unknown may be realized. The therapist cannot possibly know how the patient's self will evolve, and yet the therapist must have a vision that in some sense precedes the patient's conscious knowledge. As insights are won and new potential found, the analyst forms an increasingly defined image of the patient, but the analyst must be ready for continual shifts in this picture. I submit that the essence of the art of analytic therapy lies precisely in the analyst's ability to hold the tension of knowing and not knowing. Sustaining this tension reflects the analyst's ownership of what he knows and does not know, the analogue of the patient's ownership. The patient decides what capacities he will exercise, but the therapist's vision is key to new possibilities.

Viewed in this way, psychoanalytic therapy is the art of creating new possibilities, the growth that Ruskin defined as human happiness. The ultimate value of conceptualizing the aims of psychoanalytic therapy as self realization is that it overturns Freud's pessimistic view of psychoanalytic outcome. By facilitating the transcendence of the self, psychoanalytic therapy can help the patient achieve perhaps uncommon but very real human happiness.

References

Adler, G. (1985), *Borderline Psychopathology and Its Treatment.* New York: Aronson.

Ainsworth, M., Blehar, M., Waters, E. & Walls, S. (1978), *Patterns of Attachment: Assessed in the Strange Situation and at Home.* Hillsdale, NJ: Lawrence Erlbaum Associates, Inc.

Arlow, J. & Brenner, C. (1964), *Psychoanalytic Constructs and the Structural Theory.* New York: International Universities Press.

Aron, L. (1990), Free association and changing models of mind. *J. Amer. Acad. Psychoanal.,* 18:439–459.

_____ (1992), Interpretation as expression of the analyst's subjectivity. *Psychoanal. Dial.,* 1:29–51.

_____ (1996), *A Meeting of Minds.* Hillsdale, NJ: The Analytic Press.

Bacal, H. (1985), Optimal responsiveness and the therapeutic process. In: *Progress in Self Psychology, Vol. 1,* ed. A. Goldberg. Hillsdale, NJ: The Analytic Press, pp. 202–226.

_____ & Newman, K. (1990), *Theories of Object Relations: Bridges to Self Psychology.* New York: Columbia University.

Bach, S. (1995), *The Language of Perversion and the Language of Love.* Northvale, NJ: Aronson.

Bachant, J., Lynch, A. & Richards, A. (1995), Relational models in psychoanalytic theory. *Psychoanal. Psychol.,* 12:71–88.

Bakan, D. (1966), *The Duality of Human Existence.* Chicago: Rand McNally.

Basch, M. (1985), Interpretation: Toward a developmental model. In: *Progress in Self Psychology, Vol. 1,* ed. A. Goldberg. New York: Guilford Press, pp. 33–42.

Beebe, B. (1986), Mother–infant mutual influence and precursors of self- and object-representations. In: *Empirical Studies of Psychoanalytic Theories, Vol. 2,* ed. J. Masling. Hillsdale, NJ: The Analytic Press, pp. 27–48.

_____ (1995), A dyadic systems theory of the mother–infant relationship. Presented at meeting of Division 39, American Psychological Association, Santa Monica, CA.

_____ Jaffe, J. & Lachmann, F. (1992), The contribution of the mother–infant influence to the origins of self- and object-representations. In: *Relational Perspectives in Psychoanalysis,* ed. N. Skolnick & S. Warshaw. Hillsdale, NJ: The Analytic Press, pp. 83–118.

_____ & Lachmann, F. (1988a), Mother–infant mutual influence and precursors of psychic structure. In: *Frontiers in Self Psychology: Progress in Self Psychology, Vol. 3,* ed. A. Goldberg. Hillsdale, NJ: The Analytic Press, pp. 3–26.

_____ & _____ (1988b), The contribution of mother–infant mutual influence to the origins of self and object representations. *Psychoanal. Psychol.,* 5:307–337.

_____ & _____ (1992), A dyadic systems view of communication. In: *Relational Perspectives in Psychoanalysis,* ed. N. Skolnick & S. Warshaw. Hillsdale, NJ: The Analytic Press, pp. 61–82.

_____ & Stern, D. (1977), Engagement–disengagement and early object experiences. In: *Communicative Structures and Psychic Structures,* ed. N. Freedman & S. Grand. New York: Plenum, pp. 35–55.

Benjamin, J. (1988), *The Bonds of Love.* New York: Pantheon.

_____ (1995), *Like Subjects, Love Objects.* New Haven, CT: Yale University Press.

_____ (1997), *The Shadow of the Other.* New York: Routledge.

Berliner, B. (1947), The psychodynamics of masochism. *Psychoanal. Quart.,* 16:459–471.

_____ (1958), The role of object relations in moral masochism. *Psychoanal. Quart.,* 27:38–56.

Bettelheim, B. (1971), Regression as progress. In: *Tactics and Techniques in Psychoanalytic Therapy,* ed. P. Giovacchini. New York: Science House.

Blatt, S. & Blass, R. B. (1990), Attachment and separateness: A dialectic model of the products and processes of psychological development. *The Psychoanalytic Study of the Child,* 45:107–127. New Haven, CT: Yale University Press.

_____ & _____ (1992), Relatedness and self-definition: Two primary dimensions in personality development, psychopathology, and psychotherapy. In: *Interface of Psychoanalysis and Psychology,* ed. J. Barron, M. Eagle & D. Wolitsky. Washington, DC: American Psychological Association, pp. 399–428.

Bollas, C. (1987), *The Shadow of the Object.* London: Free Association Books.

_____ (1989), *The Forces of Destiny.* London: Free Association Books.

Bower, T. (1977), *The Perceptual World of the Child.* Cambridge, MA: Harvard University Press.

Bowlby, J. (1969), *Attachment and Loss: Vol. 1. Attachment.* New York: Basic Books.

_____ (1988), *A Secure Base.* London: Routledge.

Boyer, L. & Giovacchini, P. (1967), *Psychoanalytic Treatment of Characterological and Schizophrenic Disorders.* New York: Aronson.

Brenner, C. (1979), Working alliance, therapeutic alliance, and transference. *J. Amer. Psychoanal. Assn.,* 27S:137–158.

———— (1982), *The Mind in Conflict.* New York: International Universities Press.

Breuer, J. & Freud, S. (1893–1895), Studies on hysteria. *Standard Edition,* 2. London: Hogarth Press, 1966.

Bromberg, P. (1995), Resistance, object-useage, and human relatedness. *Contemp. Psychoanal.,* 31:173–191.

Burke, W. (1992), Countertransference disclosure and the asymmetry/mutuality dilemma. *Psychoanal. Dial.,* 2:241–271.

Busch, F. (1995), *The Ego at the Center of Clinical Technique.* Northvale, NJ: Aronson.

Butler, J. & Alexander, J. (1955), Daily patterns of visual exploratory behavior in the monkey. *J. Comp. Physiol. Psychol.,* 48:247–249.

Davies, J. & Frawley, G. (1992), *Treating the Adult Survivor of Sexual Abuse.* New York: Basic Books.

DeCasper, A. & Carstens, A. (1981), Contingencies of stimulation: Effects on learning and emotion in neonates. *Infant Behav. & Devel.,* 4:19–35.

Demos, V. (1983), A perspective from infant research on affect and self-esteem. In: *The Development and Sustaining of Self-Esteem in Childhood,* ed. T. Mack & S. Ablon. New York: International Universities Press, pp. 45–76.

———— (1988), Affect and the development of the self: A new frontier. In: *Frontiers in Self Psychology: Progress in Self Psychology, Vol. 3,* ed. A. Goldberg. Hillsdale, NJ: The Analytic Press, pp. 27–53.

———— (1992), The early organization of the psyche. In: *Interface of Psychoanalysis and Psychology,* ed. J. Barron, M. Eagle & D. Wolitzky. Washington, DC: American Psychological Association, pp. 200–233.

———— (1994), Links between mother–infant transactions and the infant's psychic organization. Presented at meeting of Chicago Psychoanalytic Society, Chicago.

Deutsch, H. (1942), Some forms of emotional disturbance and their relationship to schizophrenia. *Psychoanal. Quart.,* 11:301–321.

Edinger, D. (1968), *Bertha Pappenheim.* Highland Park, IL: Congregation Solel.

Fairbairn, W. D. (1940), Schizoid factors in the personality. In: *Psychoanalytic Studies of the Personality.* London: Tavistock, 1952, pp. 3–28.

———— (1943), The repression and the return of bad objects (with special reference to the 'war neuroses'). In: *Psychoanalytic Studies of the Personality.* London: Tavistock, 1952, pp. 59–81.

———— (1944), Endopsychic structure considered in terms of object-relationships. In: Psychoanalytic Studies of the Personality. London: Tavistock, 1952, pp. 82–136.

_____ (1952), *Psychoanalytic Studies of the Personality.* London: Tavistock.

_____ (1954), Observations on the nature of hysterical states. *Brit. J. Med. Psychol.,* 27:116–125.

_____ (1958), On the nature and aims of psycho-analytical treatment. *Internat. J. Psycho-Anal.,* 39:374–385.

Fenichel, O. (1945), *The Psychoanalytic Theory of Neurosis.* New York: Norton.

Fiske, D. & Maddi, S., ed. (1961), *Functions of Varied Experience.* Homewood, IL: Dorsey.

Fosshage, J. (1992), The self and its vicissitudes within a relational matrix. In: *Relational Perspectives in Psychoanalysis,* ed. N. Skolnick & S. Warshaw. Hillsdale, NJ: The Analytic Press, pp. 21–42.

Freud, A. (1936), *The Ego and the Mechanisms of Defense.* New York: International Universities Press.

Freud, S. (1912), The dynamics of transference. *Standard Edition,* 12:97–108. London: Hogarth Press, 1958.

_____ (1915a), Instincts and their vicissitudes. *Standard Edition,* 14:111–140. London: Hogarth Press, 1957.

_____ (1915b), Observations on transference love. *Standard Edition,* 12:159–171. London: Hogarth Press, 1958.

_____ (1923), The ego and the id. *Standard Edition,* 19:3–68. London: Hogarth Press, 1961.

_____ (1930), Civilization and its discontents. *Standard Edition,* 21:59–148. London: Hogarth Press, 1961.

_____ (1933), New introductory lectures on psychoanalysis. *Standard Edition,* 22:1–184. London: Hogarth Press, 1964.

_____ (1937), Analysis terminable and interminable. *Standard Edition,* 23:211–254. London: Hogarth Press, 1964.

Giovacchini, P. (1973), Character disorders: With special reference to the borderline state. *Internat. J. Psychoanal. Psychother.,* 2:7–36.

Goldberg, A., ed. (1978), *Self Psychology: A Casebook.* New York: International Universities Press.

Gray, P. (1982), Developmental lag in the evolution of technique for the psychoanalysis of neurotic conflict. *J. Amer. Psychoanal. Assn.,* 30:621–656.

Green, A. (1975), The analyst, symbolization and absence in the analytic setting. *Internat. J. Psycho-Anal.,* 56:1–19.

Greenberg, J. (1991), *Oedipus and Beyond.* Cambridge, MA: Harvard University Press.

_____ & Mitchell, S. (1983), *Object Relations in Psychoanalytic Theory.* Cambridge, MA: Harvard University Press.

Grinker, R., Werble, B. & Drye, R. (1968), *The Borderline Syndrome.* New York: Basic Books.

Guntrip, H. (1969), *Schizoid Phenomena, Object Relations, and the Self.* New York: International Universities Press.

Harlow, H. & Zimmerman, R. (1959), Affectional responses in the monkey. *Science,* 130:421–432.

Heidegger, M. (1927), *Being and Time.* New York: Harper & Row, 1962.

Hendrick, I. (1942), Instinct and the ego during infancy. *Psychoanal. Quart.,* 11:33–58.

_____ (1943), Work and the pleasure principle. *Psychoanal. Quart.,* 12:311–329.

Hirschmuller, A. (1989), *The Life and Work of Josef Breuer.* New York: New York University Press.

Kernberg, O. (1975), *Borderline Conditions and Pathological Narcissism.* New York: Aronson.

_____ (1976), *Object Relation Theory and Clinical Psychoanalysis.* New York: Aronson.

_____ (1984), *Severe Personality Disorders.* New Haven, CT: Yale University Press.

_____ Selzer, M., Koenigsberg, H., Carr, D. & Appelbaum, A. (1988), *Psychodynamic Psychotherapy of Borderline Patients.* New York: Basic Books.

Klein, M. (1937), Love, guilt and reparation. In: *Love, Guilt and Reparation, 1921–1945.* New York: Free Press, 1975, pp. 306–343.

_____ (1940), Mourning and its relation to manic–depressive states. In: *Love, Guilt and Reparation, 1921–1945.* New York: Free Press, 1975, pp. 344–369.

_____ (1957), Envy and gratitude. In: *Envy and Gratitude, 1946–1963.* New York: Dell, 1975, pp. 176–235.

Kohut, H. (1971), *The Analysis of the Self.* New York: International Universities Press.

_____ (1977), *The Restoration of the Self.* New York: International Universities Press.

_____ (1984), *How Does Analysis Cure?* Chicago: University of Chicago Press.

_____ & Wolf, E. (1978), The disorders of the self and their treatment: An outline. *Internat. J. Psycho-Anal.,* 59:413–425.

Levenson, E. (1991), *The Purloined Self.* New York: William Alanson White Institute.

Lichtenberg, J. (1983), *Psychoanalysis and Infant Research.* Hillsdale, NJ: The Analytic Press.

Loewald, H. (1960), On the therapeutic action of psychoanalysis. In: *Papers on Psychoanalysis.* New Haven, CT: Yale University Press, 1980.

Mahler, M. (1971), A study of the separation-individuation process. *The Psychoanalytic Study of the Child,* 26:403–424. New Haven, CT: Yale University Press.

Maslow, A. (1954), *Motivation and Personality.* New York: Harper & Row.

Miller, A. (1981), *Prisoners of Childhood.* New York: Basic Books.

Miller, S. (1996), *Shame in Context.* Hillsdale, NJ: The Analytic Press.

Mitchell, S. (1988), *Relational Concepts in Psychoanalysis.* Cambridge, MA: Harvard University Press.

_____ (1991), Contemporary perspectives on the self: Toward an integration. *Psychoanal. Dial.,* 1:121–147.

_____ (1993), *Hope and Dread in Psychoanalysis.* New York: Basic Books.

_____ (1997), *Influence and Autonomy in Psychoanalysis*. Hillsdale, NJ: The Analytic Press.

Modell, A. (1990), *Other Times, Other Realities*. Cambridge, MA: Harvard University Press.

_____ (1996), Reflections on metaphor and affects. Presented at meeting of Chicago Psychoanalytic Society, Chicago.

Morrison, A. (1989), *Shame: The Underside of Narcissism*. Hillsdale, NJ: The Analytic Press.

Ogden, T. (1986), *The Matrix of the Mind*. Northvale, NJ: Aronson.

_____ (1989), *The Primitive Edge of Experience*. Northvale, NJ: Aronson.

_____ (1994), The concept of internal object relations. In: *Fairbairn and the Origins of Object Relations Theory*, ed. J. Grotstein & D. Rinsley. London: Free Association Books, pp. 88–111.

Orange, D., Atwood, G. & Stolorow, R. (1997), *Working Intersubjectively: Contextualism in Psychoanalytic Practice*. Hillsdale, NJ: The Analytic Press.

Parens, H. (1979), *The Development of Aggression in Early Childhood*. New York: Aronson.

Person, E. (1980), Sexuality as the mainstay of identity: Psychoanalytic perspectives. *Sigma*, 5:605–630.

Piaget, J. (1952), *The Origins of Intelligence*. New York: International Universities Press.

Rank, O. (1929), *The Trauma of Birth*. New York: Harcourt Brace.

Rayner, E. (1991), *The Independent Mind of British Psychoanalysis*. New York: Aronson.

Rosenfeld, H. (1978), Notes on the psychopathology and psychoanalytic treatment of some borderline patients. *Internat. J. Psycho-Anal.*, 59:215–221.

Rubens, R. (1994), Fairbairn's structural theory. In: *Fairbairn and the Origins of Object Relations Theory*, ed. J. Grotstein & D. Rinsley. London: Free Association Books, pp. 151–173.

Sanville, J. (1991), *The Playground of Psychoanalytic Therapy*. Hillsdale, NJ: The Analytic Press.

Schlessinger, N. & Robbins, F. (1983), *A Developmental View of the Psychoanalytic Process*. New York: International Universities Press.

Simon, J. & Gagnon, W. (1973), *Sexual Conduct*. Chicago: Aldine.

Slochower, J. (1996), *Holding and Psychoanalysis*. Hillsdale, NJ: The Analytic Press.

Spezzano, C. (1993), *Affects in Psychoanalysis: A Clinical Synthesis*. Hillsdale, NJ: The Analytic Press.

Stern, D. (1985), *The Interpersonal World of the Infant*. New York: Basic Books.

Stoller, R. (1985), *Observing the Erotic Imagination*. New Haven, CT: Yale University Press.

Stolorow, R., Brandchaft, B. & Atwood, R. (1987), *Psychoanalytic Treatment: An Intersubjective Approach*. Hillsdale, NJ: The Analytic Press.

Sugarman, A. (1995), Psychoanalysis: Treatment of conflict or deficit? *Psychoanal. Psychol.*, 12:55–70.

Summers, F. (1988), Psychoanalytic therapy of the borderline patient: Treating the fusion–separation contradiction. *Psychoanal. Psychol.*, 5:339–355.

_____ (1993), Implications of object relations theories for the psychoanalytic process. *The Annual of Psychoanalysis*, 21:225–242. Hillsdale, NJ: The Analytic Press.

_____ (1994), *Object Relations Theories and Psychopathology*. Hillsdale, NJ: The Analytic Press.

_____ (1996), Existential guilt: An object relations concept. *Contemp. Psychoanal.*, 32:43–63.

_____ (1997), Transcending the self: An object relations model of psychoanalytic therapy. *Contemp. Psychoanal.*, 33:411–428.

_____ (in press), Transitional space and therapeutic boundaries. *Psychoanal. Psychol.*

Tolpin, M. (1993), The unmirrored self, compensatory structure, and cure: The exemplary case of Anna O. *The Annual of Psychoanalysis*, 21:157–178. Hillsdale, NJ: The Analytic Press.

Tomkins, S. (1962), *Affect, Imagery, and Consciousness: Vol. 1. The Positive Affects*. New York: Springer.

_____ (1963), *Affect, Imagery, and Consciousness: Vol. 2. The Negative Affects*. New York: Springer.

_____ (1978), Script theory: Differential magnification of affects. *Nebraska Symposium on Motivation*, 26:201–263.

White, R. (1963), Ego and reality in psychoanalytic theory. *Psychological Issues*, Monogr. 11. New York: International Universities Press.

Wilson, A. (1995), Mapping the mind in relational psychoanalysis: Some critiques, questions and conjectures. *Psychoanal. Psychol.*, 12:9–29.

Winnicott, D. (1945), Primitive emotional development. In: *Through Paediatrics to Psychoanalysis*. New York: Basic Books, 1975, pp. 145–156.

_____ (1951), Transitional objects and transitional phenomena. In: *Through Paediatrics to Psychoanalysis*. New York: Basic Books, 1975, pp. 229–242.

_____ (1956), The anti-social tendency. In: *Through Paediatrics to Psychoanalysis*. New York: Basic Books, 1975, pp. 306–315.

_____ (1960a), Ego distortion in terms of true and false self. In: *Maturational Processes and the Facilitating Environment*. New York: International Universities Press, 1965, pp. 140–152.

_____ (1960b), The theory of the parent–infant relationship. In: *Maturational Processes and the Facilitating Environment*. New York: International Universities Press, 1965, pp. 37–55.

_____ (1963a), From dependence toward independence in the development of the individual. In: *Maturational Processes and the Facilitating Environment.* New York: International Universities Press, 1965, pp. 83–92.

_____ (1963b), Psychiatric disorder in terms of infantile maturational process. In: *Maturational Processes and the Facilitating Environment.* New York: International Universities Press, 1965, pp. 230–241.

_____ (1969), The use of an object and relating through identifications. In: *Playing and Reality.* London: Routledge, pp. 86–94.

_____ (1971), *Playing and Reality.* London: Routledge.

Index